The Antiracist E̶̶̶ ̶ Arts Classroom

How can you incorporate antiracist practices into specific subject areas? This practical guide answers that question and provides a road map for introducing antiracism into the English language arts (ELA) classroom with teacher-friendly tools and strategies.

Drawing on foundational and cutting-edge knowledge of antiracism, expert Keisha Rembert responds to the following questions: *What* does antiracism look like in the English language arts classroom, given the unique responsibilities of the ELA educator; *why* is it vital to implement antiracist practices that are relevant to your classroom and school; and *how* can you enact antiracist pedagogies that foster critical engagement and stimulate a culture of antiracism?

Aligned with National Council of Teachers of English standards, this accessible resource is replete with hands-on antiracist activities, teacher insights and interviews, questions to spark reflection and action and lesson plans and is essential reading for all ELA teachers. From building an antiracist foundation to evaluating the effect of antiracist practice on students and reflecting on your own lived experience, this book is a truly comprehensive guide for educators who want to empower all students. Rembert demonstrates how to find motivation in progress and joy in the process, pushing past confusion and discomfort in a continued effort to create an equitable, inclusive and antiracist ELA classroom.

Keisha Rembert is a nationally recognized and multi-award-winning educator who spent more than 15 years teaching middle grades ELA and History. Currently, she teaches future educators and leads the education departments' DEI efforts at National Louis University, USA. She is also on the board of the Assembly on Literature for Adolescents and is co-chair of the Committee Against Racism and Bias at the National Council of Teachers of English.

The Antiracist English Language Arts Classroom

Keisha Rembert

Routledge
Taylor & Francis Group

NEW YORK AND LONDON

Designed cover image: © Getty Images

First published 2024
by Routledge
605 Third Avenue, New York, NY 10158

and by Routledge
4 Park Square, Milton Park, Abingdon, Oxon, OX14 4RN

Routledge is an imprint of the Taylor & Francis Group, an informa business

© 2024 Keisha Rembert

The right of Keisha Rembert to be identified as author of this work has been asserted in accordance with sections 77 and 78 of the Copyright, Designs and Patents Act 1988.

ISBN: 978-1-032-28293-0 (hbk)
ISBN: 978-1-032-26733-3 (pbk)
ISBN: 978-1-003-29617-1 (ebk)

DOI: 10.4324/9781003296171

Typeset in Palatino
by SPi Technologies India Pvt Ltd (Straive)

Contents

Author

Keisha Rembert is a nationally recognized and multi-award-winning educator who spent more than 15 years teaching middle grades ELA and History. Currently, she teaches future educators and leads the education departments' DEI efforts at National Louis University. She is passionate about antiracism and equity in schools as evidenced by her work with local and national organizations. She is also on the board of the Assembly on Literature for Adolescents and is co-chair of the Committee Against Racism and Bias at the National Council of Teachers of English.

Acknowledgments

To my husband—

  You have always given me the love, space, encouragement and motivation needed to pursue my goals. Thank you for believing in and pushing me to make this dream a reality.

To my loving family—

  I could not have brought this book to fruition without your unwavering support and sacrifices. Your love, patience and understanding have been an invaluable source of strength, and I could not have done it without you. I am forever grateful.

To the teachers who contributed their voice, time and expertise to this endeavor—

  Your passion, dedication and commitment to educating students and colleagues for an antiracist future is truly inspiring. This book is not possible without your everyday antiracism. I am a better educator because of you. Thank you for your invaluable contributions.

To the students whose words, opinions and honesty are the climax of the story of antiracism—

  You are the pinnacle of this work and this book. I am so encouraged by our future because each of you are world changers. Your words and ideas were and are valuable and necessary. They gave me so much to think about and what you shared could be its own book!

For my mother—

  This book is dedicated to the memory of you, Ma. You are a co-author of this work. In every space that you entered, you held your head high and with your undeniable tenacity challenged racism, sexism and patriarchy. You never wavered in your convictions and instilled in me the importance of being proud of my Blackness and the ancestors who paved the way. This book is the outgrowth of a seed you planted when I was in pigtails.

Preface

My first ELA classroom

As a little girl, I remember my cousins and I sitting on the floor shoulder to shoulder wide-eyed and eager to consume stories that prompted occasional nudges, making it hard to suppress the giggles welling up in our bellies and also the tears clouding our vision and thoughts. Our stories were my family's first texts when a set of encyclopedias (still being paid off) were among the only books on the shelves: stories of our great-grandparents working their land, of our grandparent's southern pride and fear and of our parents coming to Chicago to construct their own skyscrapers—their dreams, an ocean of possibilities, contained in a lake. Those stories, like the tales of Brer Rabbit, which have been passed down for generations in my family, overflowed with lessons and guidance offering hope, love and memory. The living room floor of my grandparent's home was my first English language arts (ELA) classroom. There I learned more about race, racism, justice and our shared humanity than any school classroom I would enter. Those stories, the stories that connect me to the lives of my ancestors including those who first caught a glimpse of the new world from a ship, make this story—and yes, this text is story—necessary and possible.

A Talk to ELA Teachers

What else are our classrooms other than spaces to share our collective humanity? If we acknowledge that our ELA classrooms are storytelling spaces, then we must confront the story of racism that is deeply embedded within them. We must understand how its themes, motifs and symbols are ever present in the lives of our students, especially their educational lives and *our* classrooms, the texts we read, the conversations we have and the writing we produce. Pretending to sidestep the visible and painfully tangible realities of racism all around us sends a damning message to students that such learning is not applicable, relevant and valuable. Nothing is further from the truth; we need to look no further than the nightly news to confirm that the ravages of racism are alive, thriving and consequential to us all.

This book invites ELA educators and leaders to choose a different path: a journey of antiracism for ourselves and for ELA students. On this journey, instead of evading the legacy of racism, we confront it head-on. The goal of this book is to bring the story of racism, radical racial awareness, literacy, solidarity, humility and justice to our ELA classrooms, debunking the societal stratagems of oppression that divide and vilify Indigenous, Black, Latine, Asian, Pacific Islander, Desi and Mixed-race people. It strives to assist us on our quest for an antiracist future in our race-centric world.

Each chapter of this roadmap serves to guide us on our antiracist journey. Storytelling, as the main navigational tool, allows ELA educators and leaders to learn from the antiracist paths and classroom experiences of others. Through this, we gain a better understanding of our own story of race/racism and how to create supportive and courageous environments for students to feel seen, heard and valued, while also critically examining and challenging the legacy of racism permeating our lives, literature and ELA praxis.

On the living room floor, my grandparents did what I hope you and future ELA educators do—present the world as it is. My grandparents, John, Katie, Jesse and Lillie Mae, knew story was more than mere words, and taught us the art of story for shared knowledge and responsibility. They trusted us with their truth and to be agents of change—to use *our* stories to act against a force plaguing our societal structures and killing people. They desired that their stories beget power, freedom, joy and resistance. This is the essence of *The Antiracist English language arts classroom.*

How to use this book

Our journey of antiracism begins by exploring the guideposts provided in this book. The structure of the book follows the plot diagram as outlined below.

- ➤ **Exposition** (*establishes background*) – Provides definitions, facts and details on antiracism and introduces the story's characters: teachers from across the United States, you and me.
  - ○ Chapter 1: Provides a foundational overview of antiracism, its definition, historical roots and distinct features.
  - ○ Chapter 2: Focuses on self-reflection, interrogation and storytelling as the inner work necessary to raise our racial consciousness and humility.

- ➤ **Rising Action** (*decisions that drive the plot*) – How-tos of creating an antiracist classroom culture and design antiracist lessons.
  - ○ Chapter 3: Outlines what it means to build *cariño*, *confianza* and community to achieve a standard of antiracism.
  - ○ Chapter 4: Grounds ELA instruction in history and explicit practices, including the necessary instructional SHIFTs that lead to racial literacy promoting critical thinking, humility and action.
    - ■ The key questions of this chapter are
      - ● What are the daily practices of an antiracist educator?
        - ○ What should antiracist educators be saying and doing in their classrooms?
      - ● What are the expectations in an antiracist classroom?
        - ○ How to ensure the antiracist classroom is a brave, safe and thriving space?
- ➤ **Climax** (*highest point of tension/interest*) – Centers the perspectives, experiences and voices of 7th–12th-grade students

- ○ Chapter 5: Highlights the voices of seven students, their wants and needs relative to antiracism and more.
- ➤ **Falling Action** (*resolves conflicts*) – Handling antiracist objectors and widening the lens
  - ○ Chapter 6: Strategies for dealing with those who disagree or do not understand your antiracist journey and finding your people.
    - ■ The key questions of this chapter are:
      - ● How do I garner support and not backlash for my antiracist praxis?
      - ● How do I gain and connect with allies?
- ➤ **Resolution** (*story ends ... not really*) – Evaluating ourselves, reflecting and thinking ahead
  - ○ Chapter 7: Connects antiracism to other forms of social oppression and how they can strengthen learning in the antiracist ELA classroom.
    - ■ The key question of this chapter are
      - ● What are some of the additional learning benefits of being a part of an antiracist ELA classroom?
  - ○ Chapter 8: Offers suggestions for how to continue this journey and evaluate our progress along the way.
    - ■ The key questions of this chapter are
      - ● What do you do when your mind is blown?
      - ● If antiracism is a verb, what's my next action?

Key features of the text

In each chapter, you will find the following features:

Teacher Lesson in Session	Interview with an ELA educator or leader
Comprehension Checks	Critical points of inquiry to help us process and assess our mindset, heartset and skillset
Waypoint	Brings the chapter into focus by highlighting its main points
Think–Act–Reimagine	Framework for examining, taking action and freedom dreaming the chapter's content
Resources	Additional learning based on the chapter's focus

Section I
Exposition

1

Building Background

How did we get here?

Every fall in my town, cornfields are turned into giant mazes. These mammoth fields with corn stalks standing 6–7 feet tall invite visitors to wander their intricate paths to freedom or nowhere. The first time I took my family to our local maze, I was struck by how analogous the maze was to teaching. There were so many directions and decisions, and everyone had an opinion on what to do and how we should do it. As we braved the maze, we had to listen to one another and learn at every turn on our quest for freedom. Those inevitable wrong turns that led to nowhere cost time but also made it easier to navigate and to trust ourselves in the long run. Teaching is like maneuvering your way through a corn maze. It's a journey of guiding students to freedom, of making many decisions and getting it wrong sometimes, of listening to and learning from others, of being willing to follow another path. Similarly, the journey to becoming an antiracist educator will at times feel a lot like negotiating the multiple paths of a maze. On this journey, I've found myself lost not knowing what to do, where to start, what to say and how to say it and afraid to make a wrong turn. Those feelings resurfaced as I began to write this book. How could I help navigate you, my fellow lovers of books, words and writing, through what it means to be an antiracist English language arts (ELA) educator if I am

DOI: 10.4324/9781003296171-2

still in the labyrinth myself? As you enter this journey with me, don't look for the exit. We will walk the path together, learning what to do when we hit a wall and figuring out the whats, whys and hows so we are constantly moving forward with progress being our journey's destination.

Fellow English educators, whether you are a preservice educator, an educator in your first years of teaching or an educator who has been teaching for 15-plus years, I know you. You have books on books on books. Your best friends are [insert any given characters]. Your journals dating back to childhood are so numerous you are running out of room for them. Your joy is finding a great text and sharing that joy with others. I know you because I am you. I'm also the part of you needing the pages of this book. The part that understands systemic racism and inequity can only be combated with systemic antiracism. The part wanting to be a better educator for students, families and communities. Sometimes this is challenging, considering education tends to throw a lot at us. As learners ourselves, we're tasked with keeping up with the latest initiative, and education has many of them. I cannot count how many times I have rolled my eyes and tallied the use of words like *growth mindset, 21st-century skills, rigor* and *differentiation* in a staff meeting thinking we'll see how long this one lasts. It's the buzzwords and fads that often leave us feeling frustrated and inadequate. It can be exhausting, and yet, here we are seeking to learn more.

There is a Chinese proverb that says the journey of a thousand miles begins with a single step. You've taken an important step toward change. All transformative learning begins with questions, so let me ask you:

◆ *What are your thoughts and feelings as we begin to explore antiracism?*
◆ *What has led you to want to learn about antiracist teaching and learning?*

Are you excited? Are you nervous? Well for me, it's a yes to both and … I, also, feel empowered to be taking steps toward teaching that disrupts the way we have been teaching and learning, we have some learning and unlearning to do, and seeks transformation in students and society. As you read, I want you to have all the thoughts, all the feelings because this is mindset (knowledge and thoughts), heartset (feelings and beliefs) and skillset (praxis) work.

Let us begin our journey of antiracism by exploring the guideposts provided in this book. The structure of the book follows the plot diagram:

◆ Exposition (establishes background)—provides definitions, facts and details on antiracism and introduces the characters: teachers from across the United States, you and me.
◆ Rising Action (decisions that drive the plot)—how-tos of creating an antiracist classroom culture and designing antiracist lessons.
◆ Climax (highest point of tension/interest)—centers the perspectives, experiences and voices of 7–12th-grade students
◆ Falling Action (resolves conflicts)—handling antiracist objectors and widening the lens
◆ Resolution (story ends ... not really)—evaluating ourselves, reflecting and thinking ahead

Additionally, there are points throughout for us to stop and interrogate ourselves. These "comprehension checks" are crucial in providing an opportunity to assess our mindset, heartset and skillset.

My journey

If we are going to be on this journey together, you should know a little about me. I taught middle school ELA and U.S. history for more than 15 years in suburban Chicago. Although I left the middle school classroom a few years ago to become a teacher of future teachers, I am a forever practitioner and middle school teacher since I still read a ton of young adult literature and gravitate toward awkward teens—oh, how I love them.

FIGURE 1.1 My great aunt Ann and her kindergarten students.

I am from a lineage of educators. While I grew up wanting to be Oprah, I was drawn into teaching before I even realized it while visiting my great aunt Ann (Figure 1.1), an early childhood educator who worked her classroom with the precision of a surgeon and the grace of a ballerina. I witnessed her open her own childcare center on the Southside of Chicago and watched caravans of former students who'd kept in contact with "Ms. Ann" trek over to have their children educated by her. I couldn't run from a profession that would feed my love of words and learning and would, hopefully, garner the type of impact I'd seen first-hand from my great aunt—Oprah be darned.

My career is the tale of two educators: the first being the teacher who tried her best but didn't understand the art and science of teaching and learning during her first few years. I often wish I could go back and redo those years. Some of my favorite students deserved so much more than I knew to give. Then, there's the teacher the first teacher birthed. This teacher has worked hard to ensure she and her students' learning is intentional and relevant. This effort to make my instruction thoughtful, meaningful and as impactful as I'd witnessed in Aunt Ann's classroom is what led me on this journey.

As a seasoned educator, I realized that while I was preparing my students for academic success, something was missing. In class, we were analyzing poems and taking argumentative stances and ignoring the barrage of Black death, racialized terror, the rise of hate speech and the xenophobia happening all around us. As a school, we ignored that the day after the 2016 elections, students were being told by their peers to go back to Mexico or they'd soon be deported. We ignored the rise of student anti-Semitism and the anti-Muslim language being spewed in the halls. And yet, in class, we were analyzing quotes like, "The only thing necessary for the triumph of evil is for good men to do nothing" as some abstract concept with no application to our lives. All of the preceding led me to have racial battle fatigue. I'd already spent months trying to convince "friends" that Black Lives Matter and that the 2016 election was consequential to my personhood. It was too much. Something had to change. I started reading and attending professional learning to see how teachers were addressing this in their ELA classrooms. That learning led me to ask myself: *What would happen if I continued to ignore racial reality? What would the future look like? Were my students ready to engage in such learning? Was a school with a 99.2% White racialized staff ready?* After asking the questions and conferring with others who were further along on the journey, I realized that the students were ready and that my response about staff was me privileging their comfort. What we saw happening in the world around us showed students needed to be understanding, dissecting, analyzing and normalizing dialogue about race and racism. It was my responsibility as an educator to meet that need.

Enter antiracist pedagogy. Since the world collectively witnessed George Floyd take his final breath, the word antiracist has permeated our lexicon, and antiracist teaching has been the topic du jour in education. Although it is gaining traction in educational discourse as an important pedagogical practice, **antiracist pedagogy isn't new and shouldn't be lumped in with educational trends and passing phases.** It is not a hastily packaged initiative created outside of students' needs. Unlike many educational initiatives and buzzwords that are not based in reality, antiracist pedagogy recognizes racism as an endemic reality for students, teachers and society at large. Antiracist pedagogy exists because racism exists. Historical and present-day health, wealth and educational outcomes for racially minoritized people bear out this statement. The hierarchy of human value that is racism places Indigenous, Black, Latine, Asian and Mixed-race people on its bottom rungs. Antiracist pedagogy addresses the harm and consequences of an erroneous racial stratification that students of the global majority live, experience and feel and racialized White students are taught is their inheritance. This belief is enmeshed in every system we encounter, especially schools. To think we need not understand, discuss, debate and challenge racism is to bury our heads in the sand in the face of reality—the numbers don't lie. The following statistical data show how this belief affects the lives of racialized people of the global majority.

In the United States,

◆ Indigenous people's life expectancy at birth is the lowest of all racialized people groups at 71.8 years, with a death rate 46% greater than the White population
◆ Black babies die 250% more than White infants
◆ Fatal workplace injuries disproportionately affect Latine workers. Latine workers make up 18% of the labor force and account for 20% of workers who die due to a job-related injury
◆ In 2021, 1 out of 6 Asian American adults reported experiencing a hate crime
◆ White racialized people own 86% of the wealth while accounting for 60% of the population
◆ Indigenous, Black, Latine and Southeast Asian American youth are more likely to be incarcerated than White youth in every state

Educationally,

◆ Indigenous, Black, Latine, Pacific Islander and Mixed-race students receive inadequate instruction and are tracked in lower level classes with larger class sizes, less qualified teachers and poor-quality curricula
◆ Of the 38% of Indigenous, Black and Latine students in schools offering AP courses, only 29% of Black and Latine students are enrolled in an AP course, while only 17% of Indigenous students are enrolled
◆ Indigenous (13%), Black (43%) and Latine (30%) students are underrepresented in gifted and talented programs

- ◆ Only a few states have mandated the inclusion and teaching of Asian, Pacific Islander and Desi American (APIDA) history in curricula
  - ○ Only 42% of Americans can recall one prominent Asian, Pacific Islander and Desi American and 42% cannot think of a historical experience or policy related to Asian, Pacific Islander and Desi Americans
- ◆ Schools are more severely segregated today than in the 1960s
- ◆ Predominantly white school districts receive $23 billion more in educational funding than school districts predominantly composed of students from racially minoritized communities

Race is an idea. Racism is a fact

These statistics are not anomalies. They are the predictable outcomes of a system conceived and actuated by White supremacy. **White supremacy is racism's operating system.** Think of it like the system that manages a computer's hardware and software, ensuring all the components are working together. Its gears move automatically, not requiring individual actions to run. In the same way, White supremacy acts as an elaborate operating system working in predictable patterns, resulting in racism functioning as it was designed and intended. The centuries-old operating system has been fueled by our history of colonization, the continued perpetuation of racism and biases and the use of institutions that privilege access to resources and opportunities for White racialized people, thus maintaining a racial hierarchy that places White racialized people at the top and uses this difference in power to oppress people of the global majority.

Let's rewind a bit to better understand how this operating system was built and enacted in the United States. When the architects of an emerging nation gathered to write truths like, all men are created equal and divinely granted the rights of life, liberty and the pursuit of happiness, their ideals did not match their actions. The theft of Indigenous land and natural resources, coupled with the enslavement of Africans, made those words and ideals of no effect to anyone other than White men. The invisible asterisks in the founding documents (e.g., the Declaration of Independence and U.S. Constitution), and systems of the United States (e.g., education, housing, healthcare, judicial), and in other places around the world affirmed that our laws, principles and values are for White men only and have birthed, nurtured and continue to grow racial inequity through White supremacy. These vestiges of settler colonialism became the blueprint for racism in the United States and continue to be the driving force of its systems. Because the asterisks are invisible and the operating system functions mostly out of view, racially minoritized people, notwithstanding inadequate health care, victimization, failing curricula, disparate funding or any of the other outlined statistics, are often blamed for the failures of a system never meant to benefit or even include them. Yet, they are expected to beat a system designed to beat them. This is the heart of racism. It is not some abstract concept but a very real phenomenon with tangible consequences. **Racism is our collective reality, inextricably woven into our policies and ideals, directly informing our institutions and systems.** Race affects everything for everyone.

Language matters

As a middle school teacher, I often pre-taught vocabulary using methods like the Frayer model to help students understand, connect and analyze the meaning of words. Without a clear understanding of terms and ideas, I knew students would not be able to comprehend the concepts and stories we studied. Similarly, if we don't understand the language of antiracism and its application, then we cannot progress in this work. Knowing these terms gives us the ability to communicate how racism manifests in everyday life, its history and its ongoing effects. Our contextualization of these words and ideas enables us to recognize the power dynamics of race within our own lives, classrooms and society, as well as how racism has embedded itself in institutions, policies and practices. The power of antiracist language is that it allows us to name and address racism in ways that lead to meaningful dialogue and real change.

So before we continue, let's make sure we have a shared understanding of some of the language we'll be using in this book. This is by no means a comprehensive list of all the terms you'll encounter on your antiracist journey, but it's a good starting point. It's worth noting that language is constantly evolving, so the meanings of some of these words may shift over time as we continue to investigate the inner workings of a sophisticated system. Although Table 1.1 looks like a vocabulary study guide, there is no quiz at the end.

While racism is anti-Blackness, xenophobia, anti-immigrant sentiment, imperialist ideology, the bastardization of capitalism, it is also so much more and can take on a number of forms

TABLE 1.1 Some terms common to antiracism

Anti-Black racism	A form of racism experienced by Black people and enacted by all other racialized people that systematically marginalize Black people, devalues and dehumanizes Blackness and disregards Black bodies
Colorblind	The desire to avoid recognizing and acknowledging race, racial inequities and their consequences that reproduce racism
Decolonization	The reclamation of Indigenous land, identities, knowing and ways of being as well as freedom from oppression
Historically oppressed/ racially minoritized	Indigenous, Black, Latine, Asian and Mixed-race people who have been systematically denied power and access; a nonbiological identification of people who have been racialized as non-White
Marginalization	The relegation of a particular group to the edge of society to maintain power by not allowing them an active voice, identity or place
Race	An invented system of human classification created by Europeans for power
Racial equity	The elimination of racial disparities, so race is no longer a predictor of outcomes
Racial hierarchy	The rank and value assigned to people groups based on race, placing White racialized people at the top of the racial hierarchy

(Continued)

TABLE 1.1 (Continued)

Racialized people of the global majority	Racialized denotes the arbitrary nature of race and the ascription of racial identity on groups of people. Global majority accurately describes Indigenous, Black, Latine, Asian and Mixed-race people who outnumber White racialized people worldwide, a replacement for "people of color" or "BIPOC" (Black, Indigenous, People of Color)
Racism	A complex system of power, advantage and disadvantage based on race that sustains racial hierarchy and inequities
Settler colonialism	A dehumanizing form of colonialism in which the imperial power takes over a land, displacing the Indigenous occupants, erasing their culture and imposing a racial hierarchy to subjugate them
Status quo	Maintenance of existing racial power imbalance
Systems of oppression	Forms of discrimination that are deeply entrenched in our social, racial and cultural frameworks, establishing practices and norms that disadvantage certain groups and benefit others
Upstander	A person who speaks or acts in support of an individual or cause
Whiteness	Shifting fictitious construct based on social and political practices that privilege White racialized people, their customs, culture and beliefs as the standard and upholds White supremacy
White privilege	The unearned power and advantages that benefit White racialized people
White supremacy	An institutionally preserved system of exploitation and domination predicated on the faulty belief that a White race exists and is superior to others as a means of hoarding power and resources
Xenophobia	Racial animus and oppression of immigrants manifested in attitudes, behaviors, practices and policies that suggest they are inferior

(as evidenced in Table 1.2). Although many still associate racism with a person's personal behaviors and attitudes, this is an oversimplification. There are multiple forms of racism constantly at play in our society. Racism is not merely a static, one-dimensional concept but rather the entanglement of people, power, beliefs and structures that have over generations perpetuated racial oppression.

TABLE 1.2 Examples and definitions of the different types of racism

Interpersonal racism	The enactment of racial beliefs (stereotypes and biases), behaviors and/or attitudes between individuals that perpetuate racism, intentionally or unintentionally. ◆ Making assumptions about a historically disenfranchised racialized family based on a stereotype or bias
Ideological/internalized racism	Racial stereotypes and biases ingrained in our worldviews, beliefs and society's ways of thinking. These are conscious or unconscious racial beliefs held within ourselves or others. ◆ Xenophobia—Telling a person to go back where they came from ◆ Lower educational standards in schools with majority racially minoritized student populations
Institutional racism	Racial inequity perpetuated by social and political institutions of power to privilege and protect Whiteness. ◆ Disproportionate and excessive discipline practices ◆ Overreliance on standardized testing
Structural racism	The cumulative, society-wide reproduction of racial inequities as a result of racism operating across institutions, thus creating a system of racism that is present and pervasive yet long-standing and historical, replicating with and without intent racial stratification and power inequities. ◆ School-to-prison pipeline
Systemic racism	All the above forms of racism could arguably be systemic. Since systemic means affecting the whole, then all these forms could be applicable. ◆ Interpersonal and ideological racism affect the entirety of one's thoughts and ideas and sometimes whole families (manually operated–people-driven system) but less effectual ◆ Institutional racism and structural racism (commonly referenced as systemic) are the larger, layered and more complicated forms of racism that operate invisibly in the laws, policies, practices and culture of an institution or across institutions to disempower racially minoritized people, effectually restricting freedom and safety (automatically operated–historically and ideologically driven)

The why

With racism functioning in so many ways in our society, anti-racist pedagogy must be an educational requisite since schools are, themselves, not race-neutral spaces. According to antiracist scholar, George Dei (2014), "race powerfully implicates and orients schooling, and any education that sweeps race under the carpet is a miseducation of the learner." Because Whiteness is the operational baseline of education, racism in schools is normalized. Whiteness, not synonymous with White people, situates White identity as the racial referent, the standard-bearer and thus the benefactor of privilege and power. Integrated so seamlessly and subtly into our subconscious, Whiteness rules our academic discourse and curriculum, as well as our policies and attitudes to the detriment of our historically oppressed racialized students and families. If antiracist pedagogy is not viewed as an imperative, educational systems will continue to be places of harm for all students replicating systemic oppression inherent to Whiteness and institutional racism. On our journey to be antiracist educators, we must engage in the intentional practice of working to upend the realities of racism by building our own knowledge of race, racism and its functions, being critically self-aware, constantly checking and challenging our content selections, our teaching methods, building relationships with all educational stakeholders and creating new visions and possibilities for a just world. I can imagine you are reading this thinking: "Yet another thing educators are tasked to fix. *Why is this my responsibility?*"

If the previously outlined statistics were not enough for you to want to disrupt a systemically racially unjust world, just this week as I am writing this book, ten people were murdered while strolling the aisles of their local supermarket on a sunny Saturday afternoon in Buffalo, New York. The massacre livestreamed for viewers on a social media platform was racially motivated and carried out by a violent, racist domestic terrorist. The next day in Southern California as parishioners attended Geneva Presbyterian Church, a church that was hosting a Taiwanese congregation, a racist extremist entered, killing one person and wounding five people citing his political disdain and hatred of Taiwanese people as his motivation for the attack. According to U.S. Homeland Security officials, "White supremacy and far-right extremism are among the greatest domestic security threats facing the United States" (Wray, 2019). By the time you are reading this book, the disheartening, glum reality is that we will surely have other incidents and other statistics to add to the list. Even though racism is complicated and layered, permeating our everyday lives, it is also simple. Simple enough that some of our students live, understand and recognize it and its dehumanization firsthand. As educators, it is not our job to "fix" racism that's society's collective responsibility, but we should want to chisel away at the legacy of racism for present and future generations. Because it is our responsibility to understand the pathology of racism and White supremacy and their effects on students and society so that we can teach our students to understand and act against it if there is ever any hope of its eradication. And as ELA educator Briana M. warns, we must "be aware of white supremacy, and what that looks like in a world that is rapidly changing since our students are now majority nonwhite."

Roots

Three generations removed from my ancestral homelands, my roots run deep. I am a descendant of the American enslaved, the granddaughter of sharecroppers, the daughter of Jim Crow migrants. Both my parents left the South (Mississippi and Alabama) during a time of racialized terror seeking safety and opportunity in the North (Chicago, Illinois). As the children of sharecroppers, they spent summers and early fall working the land and picking cotton, sometimes missing days of school in September to help their parents harvest the last of the season's cotton. The epistemology of the cotton field shaped them. On many occasions, my mother shared that she learned more science, math and social studies in those fields than any classroom could ever teach. It was this education my parents often lauded as their experiences in school failed to recognize who they were and what they knew; school instead showed them through its policies, discipline, curriculum, instruction, and more that the world was unfair, especially to them—Black children.

At a young age, my parents realized racism is more than a person's hate, prejudice and ignorance; it held the power to deem their knowledge, language and bodies inferior. They were keenly aware that the disadvantages they faced were firmly rooted in an invisible power and affirmed in the racial milieu of the United States. My mother's constant refrain to my brother and me was "life isn't fair." She'd lived through enough, crossed the road to avoid conflict enough times, and read enough signs telling her which facilities to use and which doors she could not enter to bear witness to her life's racial injustices. She'd marched and raised her fist in an effort to be seen and treated with dignity and respect. And she needed her children to know, to be constantly reminded, that racism persists. So, I say to you "life isn't fair." This is true, especially for racialized people of the global majority whose murders appear on our screens with unsettling regularity and who sit at desks in schools that are grossly underfunded and believe that the students are the problem. This awakening of racial realism prompted by videos and acquittals is an affirmation that racism is indeed alive and thriving. It's a reality Indigenous, Black, Latine, Asian, Pacific Islander and Mixed-race Americans have always been privy to because it's what our mothers and fathers and grandparents taught and warned us about; it's the roots of racism that support my mother's mantra.

Racially minoritized students, across the globe, yearned as my parents did to have their knowledge esteemed, their innate power recognized and to break free of the White norms ruling their everyday existence and acting as a standard by which they are constantly measured. This idea of all knowledge being measured and filtered through a single lens of Whiteness may be hard to conceptualize if you have not lived it or been proximate to it. Leaning in with an objective view, we see that this is actualized in the way knowledge is taught and disseminated, in the books that are read, in the language that is used, in the images that are seen and in the people who are given platforms to speak. This White lens of knowledge (White-dominant epistemology) reinforces destructive narratives, ideas and values that have been passed down from generation to generation, both through people and systems, thus making it difficult for racialized people of the global majority to access and demonstrate knowledge reflective of their lived experiences and identities. This is imperative to understand if we are to change our mindset and skillset since literacy, identity (specifically, racial identity) and non liberation are interconnected (Harvey-Torres et al., 2021).

Because of this inextricable link, teacher educators, Ullucci and Battey (2011) posit:

> Teachers cannot see racial inequities if they position race as insignificant in schooling and see racism as a historical artifact. Rather, teachers need to be open to the fact that racism still operates in structural and interpersonal ways. Change hinges on our ability to confront potentially negative and/or outdated normative beliefs that determine who is worthy of an education, which students are deemed able, and who is pushed and who is left behind.
>
> (1196)

To be an antiracist educator is to first be willing to recognize the role race plays in education and to understand that the educational racism my parents experienced is not a product of the American South but a long-standing global phenomenon that continues to be prevalent today.

My parents' grasp of the power dynamics of racism in society and schools is why my brother and I spent every day from 1st grade to 8th grade trekking past several local public elementary schools before arriving at Saint Bride's, a Catholic school a stone's throw away from Lake Michigan on Chicago's far southeast side. They made this conscious choice fearful we would "get lost" in the public school system. As a young child, I wondered why they worried so much about us getting lost. Even as young children, we could by ourselves draw a map of the Southside; we knew it so well. And while Chicago Public Schools seemed cavernous compared to our little Catholic school smaller than the church bearing the same name and its rectory, I could not fathom my brother and I not finding our way in a school no matter its size. Listening to my parents talk about their school experience, I later realized "lost" was them not fully trusting the educational system to *find* us—to find value in our knowledge and to cultivate it—not the other way around. My parents understood that our first exposure to institutional racism would be in school, and they wanted to limit the inevitable damage caused by it. They particularly worried that our talents, joy and the essence of who we were would not be esteemed in any school system, but they took a chance, paying more than a quarter of their salaries each week to the Archdiocese of Chicago hoping we didn't fully "lose ourselves." After working long days and fighting to be seen and valued themselves, they spent time doing what they knew school would not, listening to us and sharing the stories of their past and of the greatness that existed in us and had existed throughout our lineage (Figure 1.2). They wanted us to know that we did not bear the excessive burden of proof school placed on us: of intellect, of creativity, of compliance, and so on. My parents taught my brother and I to follow the path of our own choosing that they knew led to greatness. Ultimately, even if they did not express it as such, my parents were ensuring my brother and me would not become like Lewis Latimer, a brilliant man who was the brains behind the invention of the lightbulb and yet a historical footnote. They wanted us to evade the trappings of racism and Whiteness to have a chance at being wholly who they knew we could be and who they had fought to become.

FIGURE 1.2 Homework time with my parents, John and Beverly, and my brother TeJay.

There are surely some racialized students of the global majority in your classroom who are trying to avoid getting lost. They've entered a school that expects less of them, so getting lost and erased is not difficult. This is also not the only system some racialized students of the global majority are trying to survive. Conceivably before their butts hit the classroom seat on the first day of school, they are already combating messages of inferiority, incapability and unworthiness. And they learn quickly that they are expected to persist in an educational system operating in constant pursuit of Whiteness that rejects those who do not conform. While we have heralded schooling as the great equalizer, it often simply reproduces inequity, so parents like mine do all they can to stymie the gears of the operating systems of oppression to give their children a fighting chance. As a result, some racially minoritized students come to school feeling both powerful and powerless at the same time (Jalen, an 8th-grade student, featured in Chapter 5 is a prime example of this dichotomy).

No me quieten mi idioma

This desire to exist as self has historical roots. In the late 1950s, a group of students huddled around their school's flagpole watching a cigar box that served as a makeshift coffin be lowered into the ground as they buried a part of themselves. A mere 60 miles from the Mexican border in Marfa Texas, there was only one school Mexican and Mexican American students could attend in the area. The children of Marfa were used to being treated differently, treated as if they deserved less. It was no secret to them; they could read the signs around town stating "No dogs, No Mexicans." They were accustomed to their parents being denied services or publicly humiliated. Their small, adobe school building was no different. De facto segregation, rigid rules and strict disciplinary measures were a hallmark of the school (Figure 1.3). Even though most of the students, at the one school they could attend, spoke Spanish and were just beginning to learn English, they were instructed to never speak in their native language at risk of getting paddled. To illustrate this point, a teacher gathered students around the school's flagpole for a "ceremonial" burying of slips of paper written by 4th graders. The slips read,

FIGURE 1.3 Blackwell School students and teachers circa 1910. Courtesy of the Blackwell School Alliance.

"I will not speak Spanish in school or on the playground." Like my parents, those families, too, desired for their children to not lose themselves, to "que no me quieten mi idioma."

Koj yuav tsis lwv kuv

The operation of oppression and Whiteness is past and present in schools. The Hmong are another racialized people group who have experienced erasure and fought to be valued and seen. It was after spending a decade fighting on behalf of the United States in the "Secret War" in Laos and, subsequently, joining the fight in Vietnam, that Hmong families began to arrive in states like Minnesota, Wisconsin, California and Colorado in the mid-1970s seeking refuge. By the mid-2000s, the Hmong population in Wisconsin had increased by 106% (Behnke, 2022). In Wisconsin dairy country, the Wausau community, grateful for the Hmong's dedication to United States' interests at a risk to their safety, welcomed their newest residents. In this small, close-knit community, residents were not used to newcomers. According to Census data, Wausau was the least ethnically diverse city in the country before its 4,399 new residents arrived. This population and cultural shift presented challenges, especially for the Wausau school system. Less than a decade after the Hmong's arrival, school board meetings had turned tense. Discussions around bussing and over-crowded schools polarized the small town. There were whispers in the teacher's lounge and chatter about "those people" at bus stops, where huddled masses of adults talked about "how nice things used to be." The talk of guns in schools and gang violence having not been a problem until *they* came to town circulated. "Those people" were the reason English was a second language in several schools and a once highly regarded school system was struggling to educate all its pupils. Gratitude had given rise to contempt, and Hmong students were the target of adult and peer bullies, as well as school policies aimed at preserving Whiteness. Although they fought the erasure of their identities, *koj yuav tsis lwv kuv*, Hmong students assimilated and learned in school that in order to survive their new environment, they had to adapt to the "American" way of life and its oppressive attitudes, actions and racist ideology. This is the historical pattern of racism in United States schools.

Pulling weeds up by the root

Clearly, our educational system is rooted in inequity precipitated by racism. It is evidenced in the experience of my parents in the American South; Mexican and Hmong American students and families in Marfa, Texas, and Wausau, Wisconsin; and that of my brother and I on the Southside of Chicago. The seeds of inequity sown, historically and presently, have produced weeds. They hamper the growth of racialized students of the global majority, determining the opportunities and resources to which they have access, the acceptable ways for them to learn and behave, as well as their treatment by their peers, teachers and school leaders. To ignore race and its resulting power, privilege and freedoms is to not provide students with an accurate representation of their world and the experiences they will likely encounter as adults. Instead, it creates a false narrative about the function of race and racism and its effects. Antiracist educators must take a proactive approach to addressing racial oppression and its implications in our classrooms by pulling these weeds up by the root. This means unearthing and examining the intricacies of systemic racism to understand the historical and contemporary experiences of racially minoritized students and the impact oppressive systems have had and continue to have on them. It means cultivating classroom cultures and instructional practices that understand, validate and honor racially minoritized students, providing them with the tools necessary to pull up the weeds, aka fruits of oppression, and plant themselves in their place.

Antiracism is a verb

Many Indigenous languages are verb-based to represent the communal nature of our lives and experiences, rather than noun-based indicating an independent, self-reliant view of life. Being an antiracist means shifting our perspective from an individualistic focus, common to Western ideology, to a community-focused orientation. This paradigm shift is imperative because racism operates in the collective. Envisioning and enacting antiracism for a racist-free society is a collaborative effort. My grandmother used to say "many hands make light work." I think about history's successful rebellions and revolutions, and a primary feature has been to organize a coalition of like-minded people. If we are to rebel against the rule of racial inequity and marginalization, it requires all hands working. While writing this book, I adopted a communal approach by interviewing more than 30 educators and students from across the United States to include their perspectives on antiracism in the classroom. Listening to them, I learned our definition of antiracist teaching is varied and contextual. Additionally, I learned there are many hands already at work.

While what it means to be an antiracist educator can differ based on our racial identity, the racial identities of students, our positionality, context and other factors, there is value in a unifying definition. Simply stated, antiracist teaching equips teachers and students to be racially conscious, racism disruptors. This means applying a critical race lens to every facet of learning and the educational systems we inhabit **and** includes learning and sharing how to challenge racism and engage in meaningful activism. These actions are personally and professionally applicable. Yolanda, a Boston area educator, asserts, "You have to first be an antiracist person to be an antiracist educator." Being an antiracist educator is applying the pedagogical principles of antiracism while also seeking to restructure societal power dynamics, starting with schools, and transform all systems that marginalize non-White racialized people.

WHAT DOES BEING AN ANTIRACIST EDUCATOR MEAN TO YOU?

➤ Sarah R.-W., a librarian, said it means including counternarratives and racially diverse representation, visually and textually, in curricula, giving students the language and space to have challenging conversations around race and crafting lessons that give students entry points into real-world activism.

➤ Mark L., a recently retired educator, said being an antiracist educator is twofold. It is being active, teaching students to examine and interrogate their beliefs, biases and racial stereotypes and being an activist who helps students recognize what they can do to be heard and make a difference.

➤ Felicia H., a high school English teacher, said to be antiracist is to oppose racism, so antiracist educators must look at how racism shows up in their school and in their classroom, and seek to disrupt that … whatever that is.

➤ Shannon B., an instructional leader, said an antiracist educator means pushing against systemic racism inherent to the educational system and working on revamping this broken system.

➤ Ugochi E., a middle grades educator, believes an antiracist teacher's instruction is historically grounded and empathy-led.

➤ Rachel B., a high school literacy and language educator, said it means listening to your students and their needs and paying attention to how they respond. It is thinking about how White supremacy has impacted every corner of our globe and bringing that into the classroom.

➤ Barbara P., a high school History teacher and adjunct professor, said it is telling historical truths and providing a classroom environment focused on teaching with wholeness and humanization.

➤ Lisa T., a high school English teacher, said to be an antiracist educator one must confront their identity, space and privilege, understanding how these play out in your classroom in both obvious and complex nuanced ways.

I love the varied and personal meanings shared by each of these educators. In conversation with them, it was evident the work necessary to espouse such beliefs confidently. It required that they assess themselves, taking stock of their own principles, attitudes and behaviors and fortifying their racial consciousness and literacy, and that they make purposeful and shared decisions (with students) about how to apply this knowledge to the classroom. They also had to be willing to be uncomfortable, stepping outside of their comfort zones to challenge themselves and others. To make tangible progress in eliminating racism, they knew they needed to be open to learning, evolving and unlearning to confront their biases, be vulnerable and be willing to ask hard questions. In talking to these and other thoughtful and amazing educators, I was able to glean some key understandings imperative for this antiracist journey.

Antiracist teachers understand...

◆ The historic legacy of race and racism (including bias, oppression, power and privilege) and its operation in society presently

◆ A classroom culture of community, safety and care engendered learning

◆ The role of the educational system in perpetuating White supremacy and their responsibility to challenge it

◆ Being an antiracist educator is not confined to the classroom (includes school, community, society)

◆ Curricular choices must provide opportunities for students to develop racial literacy, challenge assumptions; examine and discuss power, positionality and the intersections thereof; and practice being upstanders and change agents

◆ Centering history and counternarratives is every teacher's responsibility

◆ Culturally responsive, multicultural, social justice and anti-oppressive pedagogies are critical pedagogies that are similar to and different than antiracist pedagogy

◆ Antiracist pedagogy is distinct in its focus on race, racism and action to disrupt White supremacy

- Racism affects all people, so all students need to understand it
- There is joy and freedom inherent in its praxis and resistance

These understandings are not meant to be used as a checklist toward earning your antiracist merit badge. They are fundamental principles to guide us as we embark on this journey, providing us with a chance to consider what we already know and what we need to discover.

Pitstop

Let's pause now to consider these questions:

- What are my values and beliefs about teaching?
- How do antiracism and the necessary understandings of an antiracist educator impact those values and beliefs?
- Are any of my principles circumscribing antiracism?
- What antiracist understandings from earlier do I need to work on/learn more about?

Some of the understandings outlined may be familiar to you because antiracist teaching and learning are situated in critical pedagogy. Table 1.3 provides an overview of several pedagogies that are often confused for one another, in order to clarify their distinct characteristics.

Ashley M., an elementary literacy educator, shares her thoughts about the distinctions and commonalities among various pedagogies and antiracist teaching and learning:

We need to do both and thinking. Those other umbrellas [pedagogies] allow us as practitioners to do "good" without undoing bad. Let's just for the sake of argument say, I have a child with a disability, and I believe that their learning experience needs to be responsive to their lived experience. Most people, I would say, could get on board with that. Multiculturalism, you have people who would say yes. Globalization, yes. People would say that we need to be exposing students to XY and Z in our classrooms since

TABLE 1.3 Distinguishing characteristics of various critical pedagogies

Culturally Responsive/Relevant	Social Justice Pedagogy	Multicultural Education	Anti-Oppression Pedagogy	Antiracist Pedagogy
Culture is viewed as capital and focal to learning	Students are seen as empowered learners who are also advocates	The idea that centering culture and heritage in all facets of education for all students promotes equality	Students analyze systems of oppression and myriad -isms	Race and racism are focal to learning with an aim of disrupting White supremacy
Utilizes the cultural knowledge of students as foundational to plan, instruct, assess and build relationships with students, families and the community	Issue-based learning	Utilizes the histories, texts, values, beliefs and perspectives of people from various cultural backgrounds	Focus on self-awareness and developing critical consciousness	Historically grounded instruction that includes the voices, texts, values, beliefs and perspectives of racialized people of the global majority
Includes culturally and linguistically rich histories, texts, values, beliefs and perspectives	Liberatory, humanistic, democracy-framed learning		Utilizes histories, texts, values, beliefs and perspectives of oppressed people groups	Seeks to upend power and privilege in the classroom and beyond
Raises sociopolitical consciousness and sociocultural power dynamics	Students are taught to recognize, challenge and counteract instances of inequity and injustice		Includes elements of social justice pedagogy (advocacy)	Includes elements of culturally responsive pedagogy (sociopolitical consciousness), social justice pedagogy (liberatory, advocacy and action-oriented) and anti-oppression pedagogy (systems of oppressions and -isms)

*the world is more diverse, so yes, we want that for students. Even social justice, which I get a lot of pushback on, I think we can pick particular issues we care about like the environment, and say let's go pick up trash or let's read these books about the history of our relationship to water in this country. What requires more work is to do that **and** at the same time acknowledge that doing that alone does not address the underlying blood in the water–the blood in the water and the soil. We can keep building and planting and adding on this new stuff, but if we don't clear out the wrath, then ultimately, we're still building on a poor foundation.*

Racism is the blood in the water and soil, corrupting our systems. While the outlined pedagogies are equity-focused and share some similar attributes and goals, antiracist pedagogy differs in that it seeks to problematize and contest inherent racist structures through curricula, policies and taking action. It should ultimately bring teachers and students to an awareness of the educational promise gap, the gap between the equality that education promises and the inequity it produces through schooling and other structures. An understanding of this gap leads us to proactively resist and question the power of White supremacy in our every action instead of reifying and replicating it (Dei, 1993).

TEACHER LESSON IN SESSION

Shayla E., Pekin Illinois

Shayla teaches 12th-grade writing and AP Language. She is a policy advocate and the English department chair at her school.

TELL ME ABOUT WHERE YOU TEACH:

I teach in central Illinois at a mostly White high school, but our demographics have been changing in the last few years. It has been interesting to see the community react to this change. It's not technically a rural setting, but we have a lot of rural communities that feed into our high school. We're technically urban fringe, but most of our students live in a rural setting and their junior high and elementary schools are coded by the state as rural.

Pekin is a historic sundown town. There's a river that separates Pekin and Peoria, Illinois, and there used to be signs on the bridge when you would enter Pekin, derogatory signage, telling people of color to turn around before entering. I've never found a record of this, and I've tried so hard, but apparently, Jay Leno, back in the day, had a segment on the top racist towns in America, a national segment, and we [Pekin] were number one. I know people in my life who still won't cross the river and come here; it's a thing, but there are a lot of people now who are progressive and working to make change. A couple of years ago, we had a really peaceful and well-attended Black Lives Matter protest at our courthouse, which was a big deal for us. It was great. Still, you have people who have lived here for generations upon generations upon generations and they don't have a lot of outside perspectives because they don't leave the community a lot, so there's this battle and there's always tension.

Our area was also actually part of the Underground Railroad. We have homes in our town that were actual stops because Pekin is on the river. A lot of the people who were trying to capture enslaved people came and stayed in Pekin because we were on the river and close to St. Louis. If you could get an enslaved person to St. Louis, which had different laws at the time, then you could get a bounty. Also the first enslaved person that was emancipated by Abraham Lincoln was a resident of Pekin, Illinois, and her name was Nance Costley.

I incorporate that history and our community a lot into the classroom, but a lot of parents have fears. The things I hear from them is that they don't want their son or daughter to feel, and remember we're talking about a mostly low-income White context here, feel ashamed of who they are. In conversations with parents, I'm telling them we're not teaching kids that they should be ashamed of themselves because they're White or that they're evil, that's not the goal. I want them to understand what's happening in the world, the dynamics of the world and how that came to be are important. That's something for them to understand. There's also a student buy-in piece, and I know if I can connect what I'm teaching to the place we live, then I can talk about our long history and engage them in what is happening today.

WHAT DOES BEING AN ANTIRACIST EDUCATOR MEAN TO YOU?

I consider myself in pursuit of being an antiracist educator. I will speak from the context of the community that I serve, and I would say that it is providing opportunities for students and families, the community as a whole—not just the students in the seat, to change their perspectives or open/widen their perspectives to the viewpoints of marginalized people and other communities. Essentially, it's taking our community experience and saying, okay, this is where our viewpoints are, but what are the experiences of other people? Let's acknowledge that, and then act from that [perspective] in our literacy education: the stories we read, the things we write about, how we share our stories, all of that kind of culminates in, we're not going to do this from our own perspective– we're going to incorporate the perspectives that have been silenced.

I teach White kids in a White context. I teach an AP class, and while I did have some students of color this year, most of the time, there's gatekeeping that happens, so I mostly teach White students. I do my best to bring in other perspectives and have connections to educators and young people who have perspectives that I don't have, but I will always be limited and I don't know if people talk about that as much as they should.

WHAT QUESTION WOULD YOU ASK ANOTHER EDUCATOR ABOUT BEING AN ANTIRACIST IF GIVEN THE OPPORTUNITY?

I think it'd be twofold. *What is the thing that made them want to change?* I feel like everyone has an experience or this moment where your things need to change. I want to know that thing because I'm also a stories person. And then maybe, *what has been the wind or the thing that has kept you going?*

WHAT IS YOUR ANSWER TO THESE QUESTIONS?

The thing that made me change was having a student whose father was a part of a hate group. The student had been inducted into the skinheads at a young age, like 6th grade or something, and he didn't want to join his father's chapter because it was the adult version. Who knew there are youth [skinhead] groups and adult groups? The student was realizing he didn't want to do that, so I had to coach him through that conversation, and also this conversation within himself about who he wanted to be in the world and how to make that decision because he hadn't fully decided whether he was going to join the adult group or not since [he] was already a part of the youth group. This all came up as we were reading *To Kill a Mockingbird* (which we do not read anymore; we have better selections, but this was a while ago). I'd pulled up some newspaper clippings for students and that's how I introduced *To Kill a Mockingbird*. Our town was the Illinois headquarters for the KKK in the early 1920s, and our newspaper, the *Pekin Daily Times*, was owned by one of the KKK members. The newspaper clippings talked about the group that generationally this student's family has been a part of and that's what spurred the whole conversation. After class, I was freaking out in my head, thinking, oh my gosh, what do I do with this kid? I was ill equipped to have a conversation to help him navigate this huge thing. I thought, wow, what I'm doing might change not only the students' life but be a generational change. That's something I'm really interested in for my community—generational change. But also, I knew I needed to go educate myself. Because if that happens again, I wanted to be ready to deal with it and support my students in a way that they deserve.

COMPREHENSION CHECK

◆ What are your thoughts and reactions to what Shayla shared?

◆ What did you learn from her?

◆ How does Shayla's experience demonstrate the need for antiracist pedagogy for all students?

WAYPOINT

Remember, this journey is about progress. Antiracism takes practice; it is a skill we are constantly refining because, ultimately, we want students to be catalysts for change. This will take courage on the part of teachers and students, especially during this time of racial polarization and policy changes, seeking to direct how we discuss race in school. These are challenges, but I know you, fellow ELA educators, we are not easily deterred from doing what is in the best interest of our students.

Whew, that was a lot. Here's what we know:

◆ Racism is woven into the fabric of our nation and its systems and thus affects us all.

◆ Education is a system impacted by racism.

◆ Antiracist pedagogy can and will differ based on your school and community, but its core is to normalize discourse on race and for teachers and students to be the catalyst for challenging and repairing oppressive systems.

◆ Being an antiracist educator takes courage.

THINK–ACT–REIMAGINE

The following frame (Figure 1.4) encourages us to engage in this work on multiple levels. Dismantling a flawed system and creating a new one will require us to **think** and probe ourselves in new ways, to **act** for justice and to **reimagine** our world for an antiracist future.

Think – Act – Reimagine

Think	Act	Reimagine
How did we get here? What history can you add that contributes to where we are today? In what ways I am, presently, an antiracist person? (Remember what Yolanda said)	Write out your own definition of an antiracist ELA educator. What will you need to change to become one?	Your classroom and school environment as you and your students become racially conscious, racism disrupters.

FIGURE 1.4

DO NOW

◆ Check in with yourself.

◆ How are you feeling? What resonates with you? What are you still grappling with?

◆ Answer Shayla's questions about your antiracist journey:

What is the thing that made them want to change? What has been the wind or the thing that has kept you going?

Resources

CARE Framework from Antiracist Future at https://antiracist
    future.org/wp-content/uploads/2022/01/care_2021_
    framework_COMBO_v1.pdf?utm_source=pocket_mylist
Confronting White Nationalism in Schools Tool Kit at https://
    www.westernstatescenter.org/schools
History is a weapon at http://www.historyisaweapon.com/
Transformative Equity Resource from Building Equitable Learning
    Environments Network at https://library.belenetwork.org/
    resources/transformative-equity-organizational-condition-
    guide/

2

Introspection

Where should I start my antiracist journey?

When I first became a parent, my mother used to always tell me, "Keisha, you've got to first take care of yourself." It seemed like such an absurd statement to me. I'd just become a parent and my entire focus, I'd thought, should be devoted to tending to the needs and desires of this child who depended on me for everything. How could I possibly carve out time to care for or even think about myself? The enormity of parenting and the weight of doing it right loomed large, and failure meant imminent peril. Bearing that in mind, I was willing to sacrifice myself for the greater good. "Honey, *you are the greater good*. Your child needs you healthy and strong if they are ever to be those things. Any role, any task in life starts, not at the expense of self, but by considering yourself first." My mother's sage advice rings true as we aspire to antiracism in ourselves and our classrooms. We must consider ourselves first. In order to be educators who value the existence, voice and innate power of racially oppressed people, understand historical ideas of supremacy and its present-day manifestations and take action to disrupt and dismantle racialized power structures in our classrooms, schools and beyond, we must start with self.

DOI: 10.4324/9781003296171-3

Much like the enormity of parenting and the pending doom of failure weighed heavy on me, there is similar perceived pressure as one aspires to be an antiracist person and educator. It is not a small task nor can it be. As outlined in Chapter 1, the legacy of race and racism is so entrenched in our national and global institutions and ethos that it continues to determine life's pathways for many racially oppressed people. At the heart of being an antiracist person and educator is a desire to oppose and change these pathways. Confronting, challenging and healing ourselves require self-knowledge stemming from critical self-reflection and introspection; in tandem, these are the first steps toward self-awareness and self-transformation. Conversely, not engaging in these critical practices has consequences for our students and our larger society. To be an antiracist is to walk with the fire.

Walking with the fire

The mere fact you are reading this book means you are committed to learning about what antiracism looks like in the classroom. You've decided it is not enough to be a good teacher; you want to be transformative. You want your students to live fully and freely using their power to change world systems. This reminds me of an Indigenous story about the origin of fire. In the story, a great thunderbird casts a bolt of lightning onto an old oak tree, leaving hot embers in the devastation. A young boy finds the smoldering embers, and they whisper to him to feed them. The boy soon begins to feed the insatiable desire of the embers, and a large fire develops. Frightened, the young boy hides, watching the fire from afar ignoring its calls to be fed. Eventually, the fire subsides. The brave boy decides to carry the embers back to his community. The fire would keep them warm in the cold, help them smoke their meats and keep them safe from danger. He teaches his community the ways of the fire. The young boy becomes known as a fire walker because he bravely brought something vital back to his community. You are a fire walker. You are meeting a need and helping to create a new future by bravely carrying the embers of antiracism forward.

Priscilla, this chapter's featured educator, is a perfect example of a fire walker. She is a kindergarten teacher who is sharing her anti-bias and antiracist learning with colleagues and students. Being one of two racially minoritized educators in her building, she understands the gravity of providing her students, who represent a number of racially and ethnically oppressed people groups, with the language and skills to be upstanders. She admits it's hard work and sometimes it's scary being the one carrying the embers, but she also believes doing so makes teaching feel like "something of worth."

In my conversation with Priscilla, a kindergarten educator and antiracist and bias curriculum writer, she shared what she believes keeps educators from engaging in antiracist praxis.

There is so much fear, there's so much fear, and I can't even describe how impatient I've been with my co-workers. We're doing it, we're doing it. We're the only two staff members of color, and we're in kindergarten, and we're doing it and you're telling us that you're too scared or you don't feel like you have enough protection. We are lucky to be in Chicago; this is part of the curriculum. These topics [racism and identity] are part of the district standards that we are all supposed to be teaching.

Systemic racism breeds fear and resentment. This fear has been actualized recently in places in the United States where gaslighting and racelighting are being used as divisive and diversionary tactics in schools through policies restricting teaching and discussions around race and gender identity. These attempts are themselves measures to maintain the status quo by negating history and changing the language and learning in our classrooms and are meant to hinder progress toward equity and societal freedom. Our fear is a natural response. However, fear should not deter us, even if our fight, flight, freeze or fawn impulses are triggered when we experience the level of stress this type of fear induces.

> *Retreating to the illusion of safety and comfort is entering into a space that doesn't exist, especially in schools that are wellsprings of inequity.*

This is a fear I understand all too well. A few years ago, I came across the poem "Take a Knee" by Kwame Alexander. The visual poem fit perfectly into the unit the students and I were studying in class providing a counternarrative to some of the unit's other texts. I debated with myself about whether adding the poem would cause backlash from adults at home since the content and title referenced racial injustice and Black activism which were, at the time, topics considered to be controversial in the affluent and majority White racialized school I taught. I shared the poem with my White ELA teaching partner. After asking a few questions, she, too, was genuinely excited about the critical literacy the poem could inspire. She crafted a lesson and used the poem in her class shortly thereafter. I did not. I second-guessed myself. My fawn response kicked in to avoid potential friction from adults with whom I reasoned *I didn't have time to argue*. My teaching partner did field a call from an adult who took issue with the use of the poem; she was ready to justify the inclusion of the poem by highlighting its connection to the unit's objectives. Eavesdropping on her phone call, I realized it was a relatively easy conversation. She shared the goals of the lesson, the depth of dialogue around the poem and the assessment that offered students an opportunity to respond to the poem in whatever way they chose. My teaching partner did not succumb to what I perceived as impending conflict and stress; she knew including the poem had value and bravely taught her students and myself a valuable lesson. I wish I had been courageous enough to share "Take a Knee" with students. Retreating to the illusion of safety and comfort is entering into a space that doesn't exist, especially in schools that are wellsprings of inequity. It was a learning experience and a starting point.

Doing your work

Because I often found myself staring at a blank page while setting out to write this book and many other times along the way, I understand the challenge of starting. Over the years, I have seen students also struggle to know where and how to start. I've created checklists, check-ins at the onset of independent activities and asked them to repeat the steps of assignments while I made visuals to help them process how and where to begin. Starting can be hard sometimes for all of us, especially if the endeavor itself carries weight. The same is true on this journey. This is not a passive process; antiracism is a verb. It requires our active participation, and we cannot progress by standing still. And so we begin. It's time to do our work. Our first antiracist action is critical self-awareness (Figure 2.1).

> *It is through story that we attribute meaning to our lives revealing who we are, how we got to today and what we are in search of tomorrow.*

The work of critical self-awareness focuses inwardly to unearth the truths of ourselves and our mindsets. Dr. Yolanda Sealey-Ruiz, a poet, educator and author, refers to this self-work as self-excavation. We are digging through the layers of our lives and beliefs to ground ourselves in the knowledge of who we are and what we think we know and believe that has shaped how we

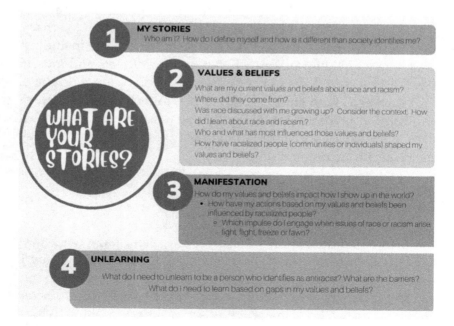

FIGURE 2.1 Guided questions to help reflect and unpack our stories and their impact.

experience, engage and perceive the world. What better place for a literacy educator to start this journey than with story.

What's your story? Starting this journey with our story grounds us in our human experience. To know our story is to know ourselves. Because you are an ELA educator, you know, more than most, the importance of stories. They shape us. It is through story that we attribute meaning to our lives revealing who we are, how we got to today and what we are in search of tomorrow. As ELA educators, we understand the power of story to build understanding, inspiration, trust and community. In the process of unearthing and studying our narrative, holding it up to the light of truth and sharing it, we open ourselves up for growth and transformation. As we recount our stories, we become more attuned to what we tell ourselves—about ourselves—and by listening to others' stories, we are viewing the world through another person's eyes, walking their path, living their histories, experiencing their culture and understanding their values. Sharing our stories is the ultimate act of community building, respect and shared humanity. And yet, it is not solely an emotional and social experience; storytelling is so powerful, in fact, it triggers a physiological response. As we tell our stories and as people listen, our brain waves are synchronized connecting us not only emotionally but also mentally. It is through our connection and stories that we, also, find, in addition to being 99.9% genetically similar, there are many repeated routes in life—making us more alike than different (Hammond, 2015).

Digging in. I am an '80s kid; it defined me. The era may harken all kinds of images for you: neon colors, pleather, boom boxes, break dancing and more. But for me, the images of the 1980s were of survival. My dad, a man who prides himself on his work ethic and providing for his family, was laid off from his job as a forklift operator at the United States Steel Corporation in the early 1980s. He's always been the hardest working person I know, and even now, he is "retired" while working a full-time job, so this was a blow to my family financially and my father emotionally. Like it was yesterday, I remember hearing my parents talking in hushed tones about what they would have to do when unemployment ran out.

Remembering the worry in their eyes still pains me. This memory is coupled with scenes from the sweltering heat of the summer sun of 1982 and 1983 beating down on throngs of Black men in Jackson Park on Chicago's Southside. The steel mill, a huge employer of Black men, had laid off more than 3,000 employees, their steady income replaced with uncertainty. To my young eyes, it seemed like all those employees were Black men who now inhabited Jackson Park two afternoons a week. The men spent most of their days looking for work or doing odd jobs to make ends meet but carved out two afternoons each week to play basketball with their children in tow. This unofficial basketball league and summer camp for their kids was a sight to behold. There were games for us kids, walks to the lake, barbeque and music to help the men forget their despair. There were also constant conversations about their White colleagues who had "just got hired" while they continued to get overlooked for every position they applied for. There was fear in their voice. And while I remember the heaviness in the air some days, I now know this league of men had also used this time as therapy. Whenever I think of my childhood, I think of these images and of Ronald Reagan invading my living room speaking about double-digit unemployment (21% for Black racialized people in 1983) and knowing even as a young child that his racially coded language and dog whistles suggested Black racialized people were societal siphons. My parents talked with each other and their friends about "no one caring" about the Black men who'd lost their jobs and were struggling to pay their mortgages and rent. Those conversations have reverberated in my head as I have walked through life. At the time, my community seemed to be held together by the threads they'd woven together themselves. *Why do I share this story?* It impacted my view of the world and my place in it. As a young girl, I'd seen and heard enough to know the league of Black men, who played basketball in the park for care and support, were not valued and no one was coming to save them. They would have to save themselves. It has hurt me to think about this through the years, and it did not take long for me to realize I would always have to do the same.

Your turn. Here are some initial questions to begin your inter-rogation of self:

◆ What personal memories have shaped and/or impacted your views and understanding of race and racism?
◆ If you had to pick out a couple of scenes from your life that tell the story of your racial identity and how you have come to value or debase race, what would they be?
   ○ What about these scenes reverberates with you?
   ○ What beliefs, values and/or knowledge does the story surface?
◆ How do these stories connect to your present antiracist journey?

Self-interrogation may sound harsh, like what happens in court-room dramas, but think of it more aligned to inquiry. Inquiry-based learning has become a popular pedagogical approach for educators at all levels of learning and in all content areas. Why is inquiry-based learning effective and widely used by educa-tors? Because starting with questions and curiosity creates new neural pathways expanding what and how we think. These new neural pathways allow us to interrupt our conventional/habit-ual thinking carving new routes into our brain that can give rise to new insights and perspectives, criticality and actions (Brault Foisy et al., 2020). As a result, we move from thinking on auto-pilot to critical reflection and introspection, increasing our self-knowledge and raising our consciousness. I am reminded of the time my friend and colleague, Michele, questioned me about the benefit (for students and myself) of the amount of homework I was assigning nightly. The question stopped me in my tracks as no one had ever broached the subject with me; I couldn't give her an immediate answer. The question and its phrasing disrupted my brain's patterned response, leading me to deeply contem-plate her question, examine my own beliefs and ask additional questions of myself: *What was the purpose and goal of homework? Were students demonstrating progress toward mastery through these homework assignments? What compelled me to continue assigning homework when 25% of students weren't completing it and when those who had completed it showed they needed the guided and personalized practice I extended in the classroom?* Reflecting on these questions led me to check my perceptions against reality. I'd believed an exuberant amount of homework was a high school requisite for 8th graders preparing them for the "rigor" of high school when, in reality, it was not rigor at all—it was an unnecessary cognitive load. Additionally, I believed this kind of preparation was customary of good teaching. If that were true, homework, for me, was not about what students needed to know to meet the current objectives and excel, it was to some extent a test of endurance. I, also, came to realize I was using homework as a personal evaluative measure by tying it to good teaching believing if I did not assign enough homework I was not excelling. As I further interrogated myself and attempted to explain my rationale, it became clear the amount of homework I assigned conflicted with my overall beliefs and goals and, most importantly, it was causing undue stress for students because I had not stopped to question myself and disrupt a pattern. I conferred with my teacher friends and students. Those conversations were especially helpful in challenging me to shift my practice and belief. When our perceptions of self and the world evolve, we become more emotionally intelligent, empathetic and better at developing meaningful and collaborative relationships all of which are essential traits of antiracism.

> This continuous self-inquiry is necessary to build awareness of institutionalized racism and one's own racial and social identities (including/especially white race). Awareness of one's social position allows an educator to reflect critically upon that position in relation to course content, teaching methods, and the identities of students in the classroom.
>
> (Harsma et al., 2021)

It makes sense therefore to start with questions.

As Language Arts educators, we are great at questioning. We employ questioning techniques so often it may be tempting to jump right into the deep end asking ourselves the hard *why* questions, however, go easy. Starting with simple *what* questions is more effective and yield positive and lasting results. While excellent for use in the classroom, *why* questions as a means of self-interrogation tend to leave us mired down as we attempt to justify our thoughts and ideologies rather than truly examining them. Although interrogation and self-reflection are critical processes, they are not meant to be critical akin to negativity and judgment. When viewed in this way, interrogation and self-reflection leave us emotionally stuck. Becoming more self-aware should not induce lament, confusion and anxiousness as is the case when we fixate on *why* questions. Let's go back to my homework example. If I had gone down the *why* questions route, I might have asked myself questions like *Why am I not more attuned to the needs of my students? Why do I need to prove I am a good teacher through the amount of homework I assign?* Framed this way, these questions offer more opportunities for me to be problem-oriented and exist in self-blame or pity, possibly leading me to rationalize my behavior rather than being solution-oriented and ready to learn more about myself, my beliefs and values and work toward change. Additionally, these *why* questions limit the depth and breadth of subsequent questions I may ask myself and can if you are not careful instead lead to a recentering of self and Whiteness. It becomes easy to ask and question centering self: *Why did I do that? I am such a bad person.* Exploring the *what* promotes the kind of curiosity and liberatory contemplation that keeps us focused on our potential to be and do better, so as you engage in self-reflection and interrogation stick with what over why questions (Hixon & Swann, 1993).

To thine own self be true

Revolutionist and philosopher Grace Lee Boggs and Kurashige (2012) said, "To make a revolution, people must not only struggle against existing institutions. They must make a philosophical/ spiritual leap and become more 'human' human beings. In order to change/transform the world, they must change/transform themselves." The act of changing oneself is revolutionary. We often want to start by breaking down the doors of the establishment

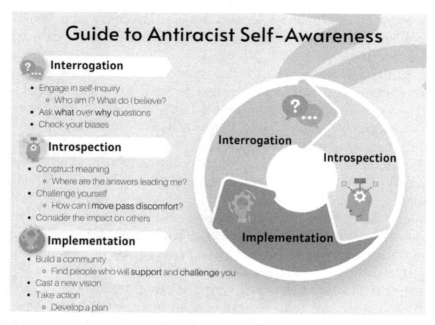

FIGURE 2.2 The 3 I's framework cultivates critical self-awareness to become more attune to our thoughts, feelings and actions.

(i.e., racism, inequity, Whiteness and White supremacy in school) instead of knocking down our own walls. To best access our humanity, we must remove the barriers of self (i.e., Whiteness and White supremacy within self). Transformation begins with a knowledge of self. The additional questions in Figure 2.2 serve as entry points for your self-awareness and transformative anti-racist journey. They provide opportunities for deeper insights into what has informed your principles and ethics and their evolution. The question sets are not meant to be exhaustive; they are a beginning point intended to inspire your own questions. I have asked myself these same questions at different stages of life and gotten different responses. Additionally, where you start is not as important as simply starting. Becoming self-aware like becoming an antiracist is not linear or solitary. You can use the visual and/or ask a friend or colleague to go on this journey with you so that fear, procrastination or apathy don't keep you from starting this important journey. This may sound like a mammoth undertaking. However, critical self-reflection and introspection are lifelong processes, meaning we have plenty of time to practice and get better at them as they are recursive. And we should expect that the routes in this journey have roundabouts, winding roads, bypasses and some dead ends. I mentioned earlier in this chapter that I created checklists for my students who needed help initiating a task, and as much as I wish it were simple enough to check a box and become more self and racially aware, this work—and yes, it is work—is too substantive for the use of a mere checklist. It is messier than that, and if you have witnessed exceptional teaching and learning in action, then you know the messier the learning, the better.

Once we know our stories (from the various narrative perspectives), we can reconcile our past and present and begin interrogating our beliefs and while we may regard them highly they are not facts. This may seem like a simple and obvious statement, but because our principles and values are often instilled from trusted sources (family, friends, culture and society), we do not often subject them to scrutiny. We instead conform and assume the ideologies of those with whom we are in community without checking ourselves. Consider the following long-held beliefs: the earth is flat, women are inferior, lobotomies cure some mental health diseases, smoking is harmless, Indigenous people don't pay taxes, immigrants are taking over jobs. Although these were all widely believed, they are all unequivocally false. The key to upending false beliefs is interruption. The interruption might mean diversifying the perspectives you intake, considering the direct opposite of a long-held belief and outlining its viability or questioning how you came to know this idea as truth and viewing it with skepticism. This is the emancipatory work of critical reflection.

Critical self-reflection is the deliberate process of disrupting our assumptions, contesting the validity of our presuppositions and their meanings and ultimately changing how we think, what we say and what we do. Through critical self-reflection, we hold a mirror up to ourselves revealing our underlying thoughts, emotions and behaviors in an effort to uncover our proclivities and the nature of our biases. Because our biases (conscious or unconscious) can exacerbate racial binaries that contrast self and "other" and use this ideology to inform our behavior, challenging our thoughts and beliefs can feel like unraveling a tangled web—an extremely difficult and daunting task. Yet, this is the metacognitive work necessary to transform ourselves, and if freedom is the ability to make one's own decisions, then deciding what we believe and how to act in an unjust world based on those beliefs is the heart of critical self-reflection.

Pitstop

I am from a family of notoriously fast eaters. We'd finish an entire meal before you were a third of the way through it. The problem with eating too fast is your body takes in more air. Additionally, fast eaters don't chew their food properly, so it isn't broken down sufficiently, making digestion more laborious on the body. The same is true if you race through this text. If you are not breaking ideas down and personalizing them, asking yourself the hard questions and seeking answers, you will get more air than substance and not digest the information.

Figure 2.1 breaks the process of self-awareness into phases. The first phase is the interrogation phase of the process in which we start to question who we are and what we believe in an attempt to shift our racial awareness and ideology. Before moving on to the second phase of the process (introspection), let's stop here to give ourselves time to break down the first steps and ingest what we have learned about ourselves.

Here's what you should be chewing on:

◆ Story is agency and humanity. What are my stories?
◆ Knowing that the world around us shapes our story and identity, who are the second- and third-person narrators of my stories? What do they contribute to who I am?
◆ We are all racial beings who are affected by race. What effect has it had on me? Was race discussed in my household? How was it framed? If not, what did I learn from the silence?
◆ What has fear of race or racism stolen from me?

It may feel uncomfortable to tackle some of these questions. Progress is often not without moments of discomfort. Remember, you are a fire walker and this is bigger than you.

TEACHER LESSON IN SESSION
Priscilla L., Chicago Illinois

Priscilla L. teaches kindergarten in Chicago and is a teacher leader who developed her own antiracist and bias curriculum for students.

TELL ME ABOUT YOUR JOURNEY TO BECOMING AN ANTIRACIST KINDERGARTEN TEACHER

It's been a really great experience. I've learned a lot about myself. I have learned a lot about my co-workers' culture and the culture of our school. I've been here forever, and it has really started to bring to light for me the holes that we have in our practice and as a school community in attending to the needs of our children of color. Some of the silly things that we do with uniform policy and the behavior plans and things like that are because people are so fixated on it. Instead of asking why it needs to be this way.

I'm working with the eighth-grade teacher, and we're trying to figure out how antibias fits in with restorative practice. It all actually goes together. That's what is so great about this, we're bringing all the pieces together. It's not like let's just plop in antiracism but we're practicing being antiracist through everything that we're doing at the school.

We've discovered the *Learning for Justice* Social Justice standards and are starting with that. I'm telling people that they do not have to recreate every single one of those units (identity, diversity, justice and action) but to incorporate these into your units. I think it will be the path of least resistance. Instead of starting all over, it gives the people who are comfortable with their units a lens to look at them.

WHAT LED YOU ON THIS PATH? HAS IT ALWAYS BEEN HOW YOU SAW AND ENTERED THE WORLD OR WHAT PROMPTED YOU?

Pre-pandemic, my son passed away, and he was 17. He died of suicide. We lost him in the most tragic way for a parent. We live in Evanston, and he went to Evanston Township High School. There he developed his passion for equity. He was like, "Mom, we gotta read Bryan Stevenson." I'd be like, "Oh okay." Then there was another "Mom, you gotta read this." And another "Mom, you gotta read that." He was the one who let me know that Ta-Nehisi Coates was coming here, and he said, "We have to go and listen." He honestly was far ahead of me [on this journey]. I grew up in an all-White community. I didn't even recognize the racism that I had experienced or I forgot it or I just didn't think about it. It all sort of started coming to light. I couldn't believe I hadn't identified with that part of who I am, and my son of all people was enlightening me. It was kind of an embarrassing thing.

It is why I chose Evanston to live. For exactly that reason—for the diversity and that kind of education. And here, I am. It's been a crazy journey with my loss and how I honor him, and I just know that this is honoring him. And to be brave enough to do this work. My daughter is also very much the same. She's been like "Mom, that's so cool that you're doing that." And again, she teaches me a lot of things as well.

I lost my mom when I was very young so that part of my culture sort of disappeared. My mom was Filipino, and my dad is from India. My dad was very much the immigrant who was like, "I am going to be as American as I can be. I'm going to change my accent and make sure people can pronounce my last name." My mother would have been the only one to hold my culture for me. My dad was very much on the path of "I don't want you to have anything to do with it." Losing her was losing who we are; that's been really hard on my sister and I. Together, we're sort of doing the same things around equity and antiracism. It does all connect a lot to my son, actually, and so we're learning a lot about ourselves. We're learning a lot about each other and it's been—it's exhausting.

WHAT DO YOU THINK YOU HAVE TO UNLEARN?

There's so much to unlearn. It's keeping my eyes open. I am also an introvert; very much so and it's really easy for me to crawl in my hole and escape, especially in my time of grief. I have to keep reminding myself that hiding is not right. Closing my eyes and turning away, that's no longer an option for me. There are going to be times when I'm going to want to, and it's going to be easier for me than other people, and I recognize that I can't do that.

WHAT HAVE YOU RECOGNIZED AS THE BIGGEST IMPACT ON YOUR STUDENTS?

That they freely talk about race. They freely talk about it and ask questions. There's no shame in it. They're constantly wondering about it. Just today, two White students were having a talk. I overheard them saying something about Black and White, and so I'm like let me listen. I hear one kid say, "Then the White people won, and the Black people, you know, they didn't win and, and so it's not fair." And I asked, "What do you mean winning?" And they said, "Well, a long time ago, people said that lie [Priscilla introduces racism to her students as a big lie that any people are better than another] and so black people lost, and then White people won." And I said, "Yes, but you know, one of the reasons why I teach this to you? It is so you can be upstanders for people of color, even if you're White. That's the most important thing because that is what has made a change is people coming together." And the kids started nodding saying, "Yeah, yeah." For them to use the language shows they are listening and processing. I loved it.

> **COMPREHENSION CHECK**
> ◆ Priscilla talks about her antiracist work connecting nicely to restorative practices. How is the work of anti-racism a bridge to other work?
> ◆ She also uses specific and age-appropriate language and ideas with her students. What language do you have around antiracism? How are you continuing to evolve your language?

Reality check

Our antiracist journey is futile if we cannot first recognize and reconcile ourselves as racialized individuals. If you are White, this is crucial. Oftentimes, being White is perceived as outside the imposed racial spectrum. **It is not**. We have all been racialized, and our racial identity has shaped us whether we realize it or not. A 2019 Pew Research study found that 74% of Black Americans, 59% of Latine Americans and 56% of Asian Americans viewed race as extremely or very important to their identity while only 15% of White Americans said the same. This difference isn't shocking, but it does speak to how Whiteness in the United States has cultivated and fortified the idea of "other," leaving White identity elusive and undefined, thus bolstering our racial caste system. A racial caste system in which White identity is not connected to race but instead akin to privilege, power and hegemony. Because "only white people have the luxury of having no color" (McLaren, 1997), White racialized people must engage through introspection in "unthinking Whiteness" and recognizing their internal White supremacy since the resulting unconscious and unspoken assumptions enter our stories in the form of privilege, entitlement and perceived superiority that form the bases of racism, exclusion and discrimination. It is through the sharing of our lived experiences that we raise our racial consciousness, and hopefully, this leads White racialized people to come to terms with what it means to be White prompting a grappling with and unraveling of both Whiteness and internalized White supremacy.

In my interview with Jennifer, a high school English educator from New Jersey, she explained this unthinking as a reckoning with power—what it looks like and how it behaves and recognizes power imbalances. Jen believes this means giving space to those who have been systematically denied power, ridding ourselves of notions of racial hierarchies and coming to terms with what it means to share power or to give up power. As we develop a more clear sense of our racialized selves, Jen urges us also to consider our positionality and power and how we wield them to amplify those who are systematically disenfranchised and silenced by structures and systems. Her own thinking is illustrated in Figure 2.3. On this journey, we cannot, and must not, avoid examining the cost of racism and our own position and power that comes with or is withheld as a result of it. As we gain self-awareness, we should also be mindful of the role White supremacy has had in shaping our story. We cannot divorce our racial awareness from the system that fosters and feeds racism.

Jessica K., an elementary school educator and instructional coach who is also an antiracist leader, explains why this type of reflection may be difficult for White racialized people.

White educators are afraid to offend, and so that immobilizes them. They themselves aren't connected to their own biases or

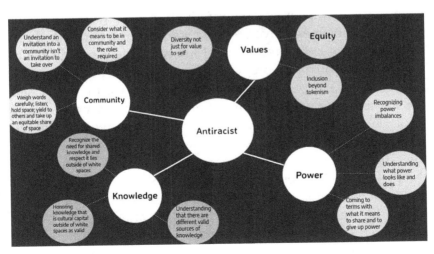

FIGURE 2.3 Jennifer A.'s processing and examination of her own beliefs and their intersection with her understanding of antiracism.

they're not having internal conversations about race. They more than likely don't have friends who are non-White, so those conversations aren't happening in other spaces too. It's fear and self-ignorance. I think a lot about conversations I have had with a friend's mother who for all intents and purposes, is a very kind woman who really wants to do good in the world. But she's said to me, "You know, I don't want to have these conversations because I'm afraid that I'm gonna upset somebody and I don't want to upset anybody." It's that same, do-gooder attitude, that's also the limiting agent. It's that I don't want to hurt anybody's feelings that upholds the status quo. And really, they don't even understand what the status quo is because that's not something that's been taught to them. There is no understanding of the ways in which their complicity perpetuates harmful things in our system. And if they live in mostly White communities where they choose not to leave their community to have conversations or if they don't take on learning on their own, then it does not register. The question really is how do you get people to realize that they have to shift what feels comfortable and they have to accept discomfort.

Mirror, mirror on the wall

With so many impositions on our identity, it is a wonder we can recognize ourselves. Have you ever stared in the mirror and not recognized your own reflection? I know I have. I can glance at myself in the mirror before walking out the door for work and a few minutes later pull down the sun visor mirror in my car and get a whole new vantage point of myself with a new me staring back. Mirrors are said to reveal truth, and yet, as we gain knowledge of self it can be difficult to discern our true selves. Just as my reflection in the mirror is constantly changing depending on the perspective, so too can our self-reflection present us with a reality of the moment. Recognizing our truest selves is a process since who we see staring back at us can be influenced by myriad factors. This is why we must closely and critically examine what we've excavated after interrogating ourselves and digging into our stories.

Phase two of our process is introspection, a vital component of critical self-awareness. Introspection occurs when we examine our stories, reflections and feelings while also considering their meaning. It's an active process of contemplation, self-evaluation and analysis. **Beware, it is not uncommon for this self-work to lead to cognitive dissonance.** It is easy to become overwhelmed as we are caught between what we thought and what we now know. As we are examining the roots of our beliefs, there is a tendency to think: *Why didn't I say, do, think?* To avoid this dissonance, we must be mindful of how we process our behaviors and the subsequent actions we take. Moving through what we've excavated is the goal—not holding ourselves hostage to regret. Through analyzing and building meaning from our stories, we can begin to make sense of our feelings and respond to how they arise in constructive ways. Perhaps, your story involves the summers you've spent with your grandparents and a recollection of the racist remarks that were excused at the time because they were (fill in the blank), and your first feeling is to get defensive because you love them and know they are good people who just did not know any better. Stopping yourself and examining the emotions your stories surface is paramount to true self-awareness and self-knowledge that can lead to self-transformation. Being aware of your defensiveness enables you to consider how to separate your love for your grandparents from the impact of their racist language. When we take time to challenge ourselves, we are not allowing our emotions to fuel racism. Racist language is ultimately grounded in dehumanization and power. To excuse the language of your grandparents would make you a passive participant in the cycle of racism.

> *Structural racism is a silent character in all our stories and the driving force behind other forms of racism.*

It is important to reiterate here that racism takes on many forms. Our stories may be filled with examples of interpersonal racism, but we must remember that structural racism is a silent character in all our stories and the driving force behind other forms of racism. The silent, omnipresent character of structural racism also always has a foil character. If structural racism is ever-present, then the people disadvantaged by this structure are also characters in the story to be considered. Let's go back to the grandparent's example. Even though the grandparents may not be talking directly to someone of a different race as they brandished their remarks, the allusion and othering bring the recipient(s) of such language into the story. Remembering, even in their physical absence, those who are disenfranchised and oppressed based on race in our stories helps us be more critically conscious and emotionally intelligent. We will begin to realize as we flush them out that our stories are not simply our own—just as we are connected, so are our stories.

In our feelings

Some of my White racialized friends have shared with me that surfacing their stories has brought with it guilt, fear and shame. They've expressed feeling bad based on their past actions or the actions of someone else and that guilt coupled with the ravages of White supremacy are hard to move past. I understand our stories induce emotions. I also get emotional recalling my own stories of racism. We have become accustomed to burying what causes pain, especially if it is related to racism. This has been societally normed, and yet **burying the pain of the past does not heal it or reconcile it.** We understand this in other situations but tend to succumb to it when it involves the pain of racism. We have to process and move through the groundswell of emotions our stories elicit. Being laden with guilt and shame is a sure way to sabotage your journey by focusing on yourself and not considering other affected people. Bemoaning that you're a bad person re-centers Whiteness, keeping you stuck in a loop of making the issue of race and racism about you and your need to have your feeling assuaged, and it's antithetical to antiracism. To move beyond these emotions, you might ask yourself the question Sara Ahmed (2005) poses in "The Politics of Bad Feelings": *What does declaring your bad feelings in regards to Whiteness actually do and enact?* or you might consider bell hooks's assertion that guilt is performance embraced and languished in to avoid the real work of antiracism. Our antiracist journey takes fortitude and an emotional commitment, so we must interrogate and not repress the emotions that arise and be willing to grapple with our feelings and findings.

> *While empathy is a good character trait, our antiracist journey does not hinge on our ability to be empaths or have others validate our feelings through simulation.*

Getting out of our feelings means moving through our emotions and beyond empathy. As an educator, I believe empathy is a valuable emotion to cultivate in students and ourselves. Being able to feel and understand the experiences of others is crucial to creating a caring community. For antiracism to thrive, we must nurture our emotional intelligence of which empathy is a part, but we cannot rest here. There is often much talk after events highlighting the need to act against racism, and empathy is frequently touted as the remedy to racial division. However, I want to warn that empathy is not a magic pill. As an empath, I know the power of empathy, don't get me wrong, I find it easy to share in the feelings of others and extend care and support based on this connection. However, I also know this is not the case for everyone. Putting yourself in someone else's shoes is easier said than done. This is especially true if you have been taught and had it repeatedly reinforced throughout your life that the "other's" shoes are different and incomparable to your own—being of less quality and value. Then, of course, it would be difficult to step into those shoes, let alone understand the feelings associated with being in them. Personally, I've spent hours trying to get people I consider close friends to feel the emotions of some of my life's circumstances, and they simply could not. My life and experiences were too foreign for them, and they could not understand the path I'd walked nor the pain I'd endured. And I've actually found I did not need them to stand in my shoes or walk my path. My feelings are my own and trying to convince others of them bordered more on affirmation-seeking than empathy. It took me some time to understand that my White racialized friends had been conditioned to see me and my feelings differently, so those shoes were never going to fit. The problem with an overreliance on empathy is for whom and how we empathize is subject to our biases. Our emotions, like empathy, are themselves racialized. This idea is backed by research. A 2011 study found that White racialized people react more favorably to the pain of other White racialized people and "significantly less than" to the pain Black racialized people experience, and this is directly tied to implicit racial bias (Forgiarini et al., 2011).

Empathy alone is not a means to the type of transformation antiracism necessitates. Our antiracist journey cannot hinge on our ability to be empaths or have others validate our feelings through simulation. This is impractical. Our antiracist journey needs people who can see the injustice in their own stories as well as others' and seek to change it. We don't need to feel injustice the same way another person does to recognize it and act against it; we just need to know injustice occurred. This is the essence of critical racial humility. **Critical racial humility fills in the gaps left by empathy.** It is a lifelong process of introspection and examination of your own racial beliefs and identities while also learning the historical and racial realities of others. Instead of being feeling-based, critical racial humility couples learning and emotion. As we learn about and recognize how oppression and power shape our lives and the lives of others, we gain an understanding of others, accepting that no one is better or more deserving of rights than another. This understanding leads us to hold institutions accountable for injustice and inequity. Critical racial humility is the bridge between introspection and implementation.

COMPREHENSION CHECK

Let's stop to process our thoughts. Go back to Figure 2.2. It's a simple illustration of some complex ideas. Consider the following thinking points:

◆ How have I challenged my emotions (judgment, shame, guilt, defensiveness, etc.)?

- How have White supremacy and structural racism entered my stories?
- What other characters exist in my stories that I was not able to see before?
- How has my perception of other characters changed, having challenged my emotions and noted where White supremacy and structural racism have entered?
- How am I exercising critical racial humility and moving beyond empathy?

Conscientização

In *Pedagogy of the Oppressed*, Paulo Freire posits that as we deepen our awareness, there is a natural progression to activism, and by taking steps to develop and strengthen our understanding of ourselves and the social, political and economic factors within society, the natural outgrowth is conscientization. This is not a microwave process. To be conscious of our stories, our thoughts and behavior are methodical, iterative and lifelong. And while it may seem impossible, incremental theory tells us that we can, with concerted effort, control and evolve our beliefs, abilities and attitudes over time. This is what this process is seeking from you—a commitment to challenge our beliefs and to make behavioral changes aligned with new antiracist ideals and attitudes as fire walkers.

This last phase, implementation, calls for action. **Because silence sustains racism, our first action is to break the silence and begin to share our stories and challenges around race and racism with others.** Self-awareness is not an individual endeavor. Rarely do we accomplish anything alone, and this is no exception. As we change how we think, what we say and what we do, we are going to need thought partners, listeners, people who push us outside of our comfort zones and remind us to persist when we feel like all of this is no longer relevant because enter any excuse (i.e., I don't even teach historically oppressed racialized students of the global majority or my administration does not support it or things are better now).

Nora, a high school English teacher and co-author of *Confronting White Nationalism in Schools,* discussed the importance of the company you keep and the community you build when I asked her what advice she'd give educators about antiracism. Nora believes it is important to be in the company of people who challenge you and what you think you know. This is particularly crucial for White racialized educators who can tend to exercise confirmation bias and seek affirmation rather than being uncomfortable. As Nora suggests, the people you invite to take this journey with you are going to be pivotal to your progress and transformation. They will help you see your willful ignorance and ask you the hard questions that cause you to stop and think like Michele did for me.

We are all products of a system steeped in racism. With new vision, we will be able to see how social, economic and political influences have impacted and informed our racial attitudes and beliefs. And we will also, hopefully, see ourselves differently. We have been birthed and raised within this system, so for some of us, racism is normal. Dr. Beverly Tatum's analogy of racism is one I refer to with my students often. In her book, *Why Are All the Black Kids Sitting Together in the Cafeteria,* she compares racism to smog. She says sometimes we see it and sometimes we don't, but we are always breathing it in. Have you ever bought a car that you rarely saw on the road until you bought it? Then all of a sudden, you saw the car everywhere. Because you are now aware of some of your racialized beliefs and behaviors, you will recognize them more clearly and frequently. Stop and pay attention to them. Interrogate your thoughts and actions.

Once we have interrogated and gained an understanding of our own stories, thoughts and actions, we can shift from personal to institutional inquiry. This broadening of our lens is another layer to deepen our awareness, interrogate and challenge. This is the routine of antiracism. Questioning ourselves, questioning systems, questioning ourselves in relation to systems and making changes to both self and systems.

This journey is both selfish and selfless in that it requires us to heal our own brokenness (we all have shards) before we tackle the relics of White supremacy. This allows us to come to students from a place of vulnerability and wholeness. You will be able to pass the fire to them because you've come through it.

WAYPOINT

It is tempting as an educator to want to skip to praxis, but we must engage in self-work before classwork. Our inner beliefs and histories affect our praxis as much as the texts we choose and the curriculum we use. What we know and believe is the foundation of antiracism, and if that belief sits on a faulty foundation, the entire structure is at risk.

THINK–ACT–REIMAGINE

Think - Act - Reimagine

Think	Act	Reimagine
If you had to narrow it down to three things, what are the three things you learned about yourself through this self excavation?	Invite others to join this journey with you.	Your story.
How is this knowledge of self going to help you on this journey?	Share your stories with them and listen to their stories.	Free from anger, fear, guilt and/or shame.

FIGURE 2.4

Use the following to acknowledge what you've learned about yourself, how you will apply this knowledge and who and what comes as you contemplate a new you (Figure 2.4).

DO NOW

◆ Complete your own mindmap (like Jennifer's).
◆ Forgive yourself for the things you didn't know or realize.
◆ Share your story with a trusted friend.

Resources

Do the Work: An Antiracist Activity Workbook by Kamau Bell and Kate Schatz
Sister Outsider by Audrey Lorde
Yolanda Sealey-Ruiz's 'The Archaeology of Self' at https:// www.yolandasealeyruiz.com/archaeology-of-self

Section II
Rising Action

3

Laying the Foundation

How can I create a standard and culture of antiracism in the classroom?

Petrified, I walked around the building looking for the room number written on the slip of paper furnished by the principal before she walked back into her office shutting the door in a way that I understood meant seek further assistance elsewhere. I was eager to get a sneak peek at my very first classroom. This was real; school was starting in less than a month, and I was going to be a teacher. Room 119, 120, 121, 122, 124, 125, where was this elusive room 123? I circled back around wondering if I'd somehow missed the classroom the first three times around. I looked into empty classrooms with butcher paper covering boards and bookshelves and still could not find room 123. When I came to the end of the hall, to my surprise, I found a teacher head down, deep in thought, who was startled by my presence. "Sorry to scare you, I'm looking for room 123. I am the new 7th-grade ELA teacher." Jacqanai, the 8th-grade ELA teacher, became my first teacher friend and, unbeknownst to her, my mentor. As she walked me to the music room—yes, I was scheduled to teach in the music room—no wonder the principal had closed the door after giving me my room assignment. I remember Jacqanai sharing with me something a principal in the district had shared with her:

DOI: 10.4324/9781003296171-5

"You can't have their mind if you don't have their heart." This became a guidepost for me. And Jacqanai, my first and forever teacher friend and mentor, became a standard-bearer. I watched the way she nurtured and respected her students and affirmed their dignity while other teachers huddled outside their class-rooms or in the teacher's lounge whispering tantalizing "facts" they'd acquired about students and their families. Conversations about students' lack of respect and how the school was chang-ing because "those people" were moving in from Chicago were the talk of most days. Jacqanai was never party to such chatter; her conversations were with students about what their siblings whom she'd taught were doing or their future plans and desires or about their families. She understood her students were more than academic beings, and they existed within structures where their success was an uphill battle. In her classroom, students were intellectually challenged and the discourse was high level even when other teachers in the building wrote students off comment-ing how academically "low" they were. In our staff meetings, Jacqanai often asked the hard questions: Why was the gifted pro-gram almost exclusively White when Black students, now, made up 95% of the school population? Her demonstration of critical care served as an early model for me on this journey. I learned to care for student's present and future, value them and show them their value, understand how systems of oppression impacted them through school policies and how to build a community of hopeful thinkers, learners and leaders. Her valuable instruction and modeling have been priceless to me on this journey.

Setting the standard

What do you think of when you hear the word standard? Do you think of the standards your state has set around ELA, Common Core or Social Emotional Learning? Do you think of professional standards or standardized tests? Standards rule our educational lives. Yet, the word *standard* has many meanings. Think about your favorite pair of shoes. You loved them so much that noth-ing else compares. You try to pair them with everything likely because they are of great quality. They have set the bar for the next pair you will purchase. Standards are synonymous with quality and consistency. Antiracism is a standard. When we uphold an antiracist standard, we are agreeing to provide consistent quality instruction and engagement. We are agreeing to bring our newfound critical self-awareness to bear as we create safe, affirming, thought-driven and action-oriented ELA classrooms. We are agreeing to be, along with our students, a threat to racism. We are agreeing to antiracism as our ethical and moral foundation. As such, this standard directs our every action and decision while also making demands of us. It demands awareness of our racialized world and sets racial equity and justice as benchmarks, guiding everything we do. By agreeing to uphold a standard of antiracism, we are acknowledging it as consequential to the lives of all students. When I talk to future educators, this is a point we spend a lot of time discussing. While examining our beliefs and the standards of the profession, we talk about what it means to position antiracism as a standard, outside of a rigid matrix but as a principle and basis of justice. We discuss how an antiracist standard affects how we think and behave. More than words on a board or a community contract, an antiracist standard is the filter through which we determine how we think about the classroom environment (layout, systems, culture); how we engage students and families; how we plan, instruct and assess students; and the way we conduct ourselves even when no one is watching. Our antiracist standard becomes our normed practice notwithstanding our teaching context (Indigenous lands, rural areas, metropolitan areas) or our race or the race of our students. Like doctors who take the Hippocratic Oath vowing to do no harm, to treat patients to the best of their ability without prejudice and to preserve the privacy of their patients, antiracism as an educational standard establishes our ethical baseline outside of personal and societal biases. By upholding such, we provide our best to students without prejudice and with the compulsory knowledge of race and racism and its societal functioning. We are acknowledging that just as racism has been our modus operandi, an institutionally maintained, economically driven and societally enforced standard; antiracism is a standard to disrupt systems of oppression, racism and the ensuing trauma of the former.

As antiracist ELA standard bearers, we are making the agreements shown in Table 3.1.

Over the course of my career, setting standards and following the model of standard-bearers have helped me grow and evolve. Holding an antiracist standard and the preceding commitments have kept me focused on what it means to create spaces that challenge the destructive forces that tell students they are the problem, and they must conform to White hegemony to be

TABLE 3.1 Antiracist standards of practice and how they are enacted in the classroom

Agreement	In Action
◆ Evaluate ourselves, our role and our position in all systems	Practicing continual critical self-awareness and reflection. Checking our biases and unlearning Whiteness and/or internalized oppression.
◆ Constantly evolve our (self and student) racial awareness and critical consciousness to demystify systems of oppression, privilege, power and racism	Questioning and analyzing social, political and economic forces, environments and events and their relation to racial inequity and injustice (personally as well as with students).
◆ Collectively and authentically, confront racism and other forms of injustice in solidarity and allyship of impacted communities	Examining with students the systems they exist in and real-world contexts of racism. Creating real-world assignments that offer students opportunities to build solidarity with one another and community allies.
◆ Center students in instruction and with intention, select curricular and relational content, craft lessons and experiences that demonstrate authentic care of and for students that lead to agency and power with students and communities	Making space for the ongoing incorporation of student's thoughts, voices and ideas (e.g. student surveys, student co-planning and cogenerative dialogues) in the creation of classroom culture, structure and systems, lessons, assessments and school policy.
◆ Represent history accurately with intentional and thoughtful inclusion of myriad counternarratives	Fortify our historical knowledge (especially of racially marginalized people and communities), and include this learning in all lessons and discussions.

Laying the Foundation ◆ 67

personally and academically successful. I have to tell you—this is heart and head work, and I still wonder if I'm doing it right as if there is one way or a right way. There have been times I've had to speak out when I've wanted to be quiet and be quiet at times I've wanted to speak out (the latter being most difficult for me). I have made plenty of mistakes and missed opportunities to speak as well as failed to take the time to listen on many occasions. As with any learning experience, we grow with every mistake. In these moments, I remind myself I am one of many on this journey and this work precedes me, so it is not all about me. While it is important, imperative work, this is a collective effort and if I start to think it is all about me then I have lost my way. When I am questioning myself or my standard of antiracism, I look to standard-bearers who have shown me the way. I think of the tireless work of my aunt, Ann Martin, who set a standard of building community and engaging across racial lines and showed me care is not control. I consider the sage advice and modeling of Jacqanai who set a standard of mutual respect that affirmed students' dignity. I recall the countless hours of conversations and debates with my best teacher friend, Anne, who shared all her learning about equity with me and challenged my mindset. On this journey, we will sometimes need to exhale and breathe in the words and experience of standard-bearers who precede us and those who are walking the journey with us like the teachers featured in this book for direction and guidance. When the road gets rough, and it will, grab your favorite pair of shoes to traverse this trek and let your antiracist standard and standard bearers lead the way.

Mind the gap

In order to create an antiracist classroom culture of safety, belonging, justice and joy, we must first mind our gap. I first heard the phrase "mind the gap" while taking the train in London. Every time a train arrived at a station, there was an automated audio warning to "mind the gap." The phrase was also written on the platform to draw passengers' attention to the potentially dangerous gap between the train and the platform. I heard those words with such frequency that they played in my head like a jingle even after leaving London. I guess I was not alone. The phrase has become popular, not only on the "Tube" but also as a metaphor for life. As a metaphor, "mind the gap" is a warning to beware of the potential pitfalls of life and, for me, to be mindful of the messages we incessantly repeat to ourselves. As educators, we hear the word gap often as part of the lexicon of education, for example, the opportunity gap and the outcome gap. Our understanding of these gaps can, if we are not careful, fuel a new gap. A lesser known but critical gap that antiracist educators must recognize and confront to have thriving antiracist ELA classrooms is the belief gap. The belief gap is the discrepancy between what parents/caregivers and teachers believe about the academic abilities, and I contend teacher's general proclivities about students, particularly racially minoritzed students. As a parent of Black children, I am all too familiar with this gap. My husband and I felt we were often fighting the school system when it came to our children. We were constantly having to advocate for things that as an educator I knew were normed for White racialized students. We sent our children to school knowing they had immeasurable talents and gifts, and, yet, much like my parents had, we worried their brilliance would not be realized or nurtured in school. Additionally, as an educator, I heard what teachers and administrators said about "those kids" always needing extra help and we can't put "those kids" in the gifted program and "those kids" are a discipline issue. Jai was an example of an educator always minding the gap. She chose her words carefully when she spoke with students or when she talked about them with colleagues. She was constantly working to build students' self-efficacy. She made certain her beliefs and the beliefs of others around her were not deficit minded. The belief gap is ultimately a product of deficit narratives and thinking. Deficit narratives and ways of thinking purport racialized students of the global majority exist as a monolith: unmotivated, unruly and academically unprepared. The truth is this type of thinking is lazy and narrow, and to even peripherally hold such narratives in part or whole is dehumanizing and, itself, a form of oppression.

Since deficit narratives about racially minoritized students pervade all spaces but flourish, especially, in educational spaces, minding our gap cautions us to be cognizant of the dangers of holding such thoughts and beliefs. The danger lies in that our internalized beliefs directly connect to our student's beliefs about themselves as their academic perceptions of self influence their learning. We cannot believe in students and, in turn, have students believe in themselves, and build communities of safety and joy with our perceptions of them entrenched in harmful, negative narratives. Our inability to mind our gap and to hold our beliefs up to the light of truth can impact students' beliefs about themselves, their attitudes about school and their academic success. It can also lead us to engage in motions of antiracism as charity rather than justice (Herbel-Eisenmann et al., 2013). If these are the messages we are repeatedly hearing and speaking, we have to ask ourselves: *How are we minding our beliefs? What do we actually believe about racialized students of the global majority? How do these beliefs shape our behavior and the classroom culture?*

From the teacher's desk

Ashley M., an elementary literacy educator, shares her thoughts about the importance of unpacking our mindsets as antiracist educators.

> *It really starts with mindsets. What is it that we believe about children, about students and really about people? It's a matter of unpacking some of the more explicit things that come to mind but also doing the work to figure out what are some of the implicit biases that are directing my language, my curricular choices, my interactions, my beliefs about families, my beliefs about the community, where I teach, or other communities where I don't teach. Leaning into that work is mandatory as a required and necessary part of developing my own practice and creating as safe and productive a space as possible for students, families and coworkers as well.*

Take a moment to write some belief statements you hold about racialized students of the global majority. No one is going to read your list, grade or judge you, so you can be completely honest. Writing them down is an exercise in realization because we cannot change what we do not acknowledge. Now think about the actions each belief produces and add them.

For example:

I believe *racialized students of the global majority are the source of most discipline issues.*	**My actions based on this belief have been** *to adopt zero-tolerance policies in my classroom because swift discipline mitigates disorder and distractions to the learning environment.*

- ◆ How do you feel having written those beliefs and actions down?
  - ○ Are there any emotions physically showing up in your body (e.g. sweating, headache)?
- ◆ What do you notice looking over the list?
- ◆ How might these beliefs and actions affect students?
  - ○ Their beliefs and actions toward one another?
  - ○ The overall culture of the classroom?

Uprooting the belief gap
Here are some steps to take to uproot the belief gap.

1. **Pull your beliefs up by the roots**
   - ◆ Question where and how these beliefs originated → This allows you to release them.
     - ○ *Where did I first come to believe that racially minoritized students are disciplinary issues? In my teacher preparation program, all the representations in texts and discussions of racialized students of the global majority were negatively framed, especially when it came to discipline. I presumed these examples of historically oppressed racialized students as rowdy and insolent were the truth and did not question them. When I became a teacher, I immediately engaged with them based on this perceived truth.*
2. **Till your thoughts**

- ◆ Replace your beliefs with facts → This helps remove stereotypes, biases and prejudices.
    - ○ *I've believed that racialized students of the global majority distract from the learning environment. Make a list of students who are positive contributors to the class. Ask yourself: How have these students been leaders and sources of joy for their peers and I? Conversely, how have I created an environment of exclusion based on my beliefs and behaviors?*
3. **Plant something new**
    - ◆ Focus on changing your actions → Your repeated action can override your deficit beliefs.
        - ○ *I seek input from students about ways to change the power dynamics in the classroom. I will work in collaboration with students to define language and outline conditions of a safe, inclusive learning ready classroom.*

Cariño y confianza

"Keisha, you know me, I love my students and build relationships with them," a teacher friend repeated more than once while talking about antiracism in her classroom. It's a common refrain. I've used it myself in response to discussions of antiracism. It was understandable for my friend to point to her care for students as an example of her antiracist journey as it is a foundational practice for all critical pedagogies. It's true; care and relationship with and for students are essential in a classroom seeking to repair historical harms, create avenues for liberation and build transformative racial upstanders. I also know love and care isn't enough to redress the racism students will see, experience and be party to in an unjust world. Knowing this, I posed additional questions to my friend: *How do race and racism influence the care you give students? How are you rethinking and reorienting your relationships with students and communities based on race and power?* After contemplating the questions, we discovered through conversation that my friend had always applied a universal, colorblind approach to her care for and relationships with students. **Being an antiracist educator requires us to closely analyze and scrutinize the power dynamics of our relationships with students and families to assess the care we offer and its relation to our own positionality and Whiteness.** As a racialized student of the global majority, I didn't, my parents and my own children didn't need superficial love from educators—we needed justice. Antiracism demands we are justice-oriented and color-conscious, understanding the application of a colorblind ideology creates an environment of harm through its erasure of students' personhood, devaluing of their experiences and silencing of their histories. To feign colorblindness is a lie of comfort, an attempt to distance oneself from the hard truths of racism. When the reality is, the United States is a nation today because it *saw* skin color and *used* White supremacy, a fictitious racial hierarchy, to secure power, control, free land and labor. These were realities of my teachers from kindergarten through graduate school, who purported to be colorblind and just but were quick to suggest I be mindful of how I look, speak and behave so as not to emote too much Blackness without care for or of me. To be educators who lead transformative antiracist classrooms means moving beyond indiscriminate care and passé notions of loving students.

> *This cariño, which is itself critical care, understands students, especially historically oppressed racialized students, need classrooms to be supportive and protective spaces where they can exist as their authentic, whole selves with educators who are intentionally connecting, listening and relating to students' expressed needs.*

Care, while seemingly simple, is really nuanced when we delve beneath the surface to examine what educator and researcher, Rosalie Rolón-Dow (2005), calls the "messy intersections of caring with race and racism." This intersection necessitates that antiracist educators engage in *critical care* that recognizes and orientates care accounting for and centering race. This cariño, which is itself critical care, understands students, especially historically oppressed racialized students, need classrooms to be supportive and protective spaces where they can exist as their authentic, whole selves with educators who are intentionally connecting, listening and relating to students' expressed needs. All too often, teacher care is constricted to academic care, is conditionally applied and does not apprehend the structural barriers historically oppressed racialized students face. Authentic cariño acknowledges the system is rigged; it affirms and nurtures students. As a result, teachers engage with students as individuals existing within complex systems who are attempting to navigate their way through the maze of these structures and life. **Cariño is reciprocal and nonjudgmental, taking the time to see students, whatever the age or context, as having innate power and agency.** Our ability to understand this moves us to provide authentic care. In contrast, aesthetic care is superficial and would "rather than address the enormity of the issues ... take solace in blanket judgments about ethnicity and underachievement or 'deficit' cultures that are allegedly too impoverished to value education" (Valenzuela, 1999). When we see the problems racism creates for students as too big or inappropriate to address in school, it leads us to engage in aesthetic care. At the first school I taught, the community was experiencing White flight, and the school was a revolving door of students entering and leaving. It had a profound impact on the students and families that stayed as they were having to adjust to so much change. While some teachers offered students space to process their grief and discuss what was happening, most teachers' act of care was a smile and pat on the back to students as they walked into class and a second later told them to sharpen their pencils and be in their seats before the bell rang. Aesthetic care maintains the status quo whereas authentic care disrupts systems. The difference between the two kinds of care is realized, understood and felt by racialized students of the global majority.

In my sophomore year of high school, my family moved and I transferred to a new school. I'd spent the summer nervous I'd never make the kinds of connections I'd made during my freshman year. It did not bode well for me that I was a lanky and relatively awkward teenager. Although the new school was less than a 15-minute walk down the street, I tried convincing my parents to allow me to stay at my former school, which would require an hour's long ride on public transportation each way. My parents could see no logic in my request and repeatedly rebuffed my pleas, so I readied myself for a short walk to a foreign place. So scared, I barely looked up when trying to find my homeroom teacher to get my schedule. "What's your name, dear?" she asked, beckoning me forward. "I'm Keisha Flanagan," I muttered, still failing to make eye contact. "Hmm, I expected a cute little red-headed Irish girl," she replied, taking time to fully survey me before handing over my schedule. I carried that introduction with me all day, all my life, honestly. How many people would be disappointed to meet an awkward, shy Black girl instead of a cute little red-haired Irish girl? My homeroom teacher offered me little care the entire school year. She never acknowledged mistaking my identity or talked to me about the history of my family or how a Black girl from the Southside of Chicago ended up with an Irish surname. She failed to recognize I was a transfer student who often sat quiet and alone in an otherwise chatty classroom. She never bothered to get to know me beyond her initial disappointment. My first year at this new school would have been different if this teacher, who I spent time with daily and was supposedly my point of connection, had shown a modicum of personal interest in me. A simple conversation about my previous school or how I was adjusting would have offset her initial greeting. If she had tried to break through the wall I'd built that year to protect myself, there would have been opportunities for me to interact and connect with my peers. Her authentic critical care could have made a difficult year more tolerable.

A student cannot have confianza in an educator who does not see or understand their racial identity. Perhaps my homeroom teacher thought she was treating me like everyone else in the classroom and did not need, in a multiracial classroom, to provide authentic care. I am sure she thought she was caring for students, and I'm also sure any challenge would have been met with "I treat all my students the same." The problem with universal, colorblind care is that "even as we purport to care about all students equally, we also often tolerate policies in our districts and schools that harm students of color.... Racism in these forms involves failing to ensure that institutions care for students" (Pollock & Nieto, 2008). My homeroom teacher proved in her initial interaction with me that she lacked racial literacy. Grounding ourselves in the authentic critical care of cariño y confianza requires that we are racially literate. Dr. Yolanda Sealey-Ruiz, in a policy brief written for the National Council of Teachers of English (NCTE), defines racial literacy as "a skill and practice by which individuals can probe the existence of racism and examine the effects of race and institutionalized systems on their experiences and representation in U.S. society" (2021). For antiracist educators, this means delivering and demonstrating care with an understanding that historically oppressed racialized people are existing in and surviving through myriad systems of oppression and racism. It also means we must be historically and politically informed. In action, this would have looked like the teachers at my first school using their understanding of the history and social implications of White flight, especially in Chicago with its history of racial segregation, to help students and families process their grief and the changes and challenges that lie ahead of them. There would have been community talks and co-created teacher and student lessons/sessions/events to examine the past and future. This is how racial literacy and care work together to create authentic cariño y confianza. It requires that we probe our racialized beliefs seeking to understand how they might affect our ideologies as well as our student's lived realities. And we must use this knowledge to shift our praxis, challenge structural barriers and build meaningful relationships to meet our students' expressed needs (Rolón-Dow, 2005).

From the teacher's desk

Jennifer R. (former high school ELA teacher and current equity and inclusion school leader) shares how racial literacy and care affected her as a student as well as its impact on her as a teacher.

I feel like I was very fortunate and blessed to have very diverse teachers. I went to a school where my principal was Black and the majority of my teachers were actually from Central and South America because I was in a dual-language program. I was also a product of bussing, and it was one of the only schools that offered English as a second language, so a lot of my teachers really looked like me and talked about our identities in school. I bounced around to several different high schools. I ended up in an inner-city school, and people didn't think we were going to be successful, but our teachers really believed in us and it was very evident. The teachers who taught at this majority Black, probably 95% Black, International Baccalaureate school with kids from working-class to low-income families were there because they chose to be. They had high expectations for us, and I'm successful because of them. When I got to college, it was a huge shocker for some that I'd attended an inner-city school. People were like, you went where? You can read? I didn't know you kids could read like that from that school.

I think those teachers who taught in spaces like mine in the inner city realized they were those children once, so whether they were a teacher of color or if they were a White teacher who chose to be there, they weren't pivoting, and I think that makes a difference. I think most of the White teachers who taught there really were in it to win it with their kids and realized that caring about the kids and yourself is really important. I feel like that's the piece we want teachers to have, not that we have to be superhuman or anything but if you don't really know all this information about the community, about the kids—you can't just kind of show up. I think that's why suburban schools are struggling with this so much because they really don't know what that care is or how you learn that and what's important to those cute kids.

My first year of teaching I taught at an all-Black male school. Being able to work with those young men and see them blossom and grow was really foundational for me as an educator. The White teachers in that space were using all avenues to leverage learning. They were inquiring about students and saying things like, "You know that they're the step kids, and so we're going to do this," and they were very much into the culture. We were able to make connections between cultural traditions and how we learn. In the suburban school experience, this doesn't really exist, and so the kids are not really seen. There are no touchstones or anchors, and the teachers don't know how to bring those into the class in a natural way. You have to know your students and know about them and how they exist and why, and I was, actually, just talking to my student equity belonging students about that today. If you aren't steeped in knowing, then it's difficult for you to believe in your students, in equity and justice. And part of our job is to help shine light on inequities and then to dismantle them. That's a part of what education needs to look like versus being stuck in skills. We need the skills but we have to understand how this knowledge or this education [of self and antiracism], whether I'm going to college or not, is going to help me or is going to improve things for me. It has to answer: What does this have to do with who I am? And students have to know that you care about them, understanding who they are, and you wanting them to be who they are.

Our cariño y confianza is not confined to our classrooms. Critical care is personal and institutional, and therefore antiracist educators demonstrate care for and about the conditions their students encounter in their classrooms, in the halls, in the cafeteria, in the next grade, at the next school and so on. Caring extends beyond classrooms to challenge schools, districts, state and national policies and practices that foster educational inequity and injustice. And this is diametrically opposed to deficit thinking. When we are providing authentic cariño, students are entrusting us to be fully committed to caring for and about them and about the structural changes necessary for them to thrive in an educational system that devalues them. Much like my aunt Ann's relationships with students and their families, she demonstrated personal and institutional cariño y confianza as she validated students by getting to know them and their families, opening her classroom up to the community and encouraging and showing interest in students and families in and outside of the classroom. Students and families may get a call from her on the weekend to see how they were doing. By doing so, she was challenging and working to upend the complex power dynamics in schools. She asked questions about students' lives outside of school and shared her own. She celebrated their differences and used it to build community together. Her active engagement and care illustrate probative, racial literacy as necessary to begin to understand how the daily operation of schools can affect racialized students of the global majority and our role in its disruption.

Too often, programming designed for racialized students of the global majority becomes about fixing them rather than caring for and supporting them in ways that do not require them to acquiesce to White norms of thinking and/or being.

Early in my teaching career, I upheld policies that were to the detriment of Black and Brown racialized students. As a middle grades teacher, I was expected to strictly enforce the dress code. Even as I realized the dress code policies were fraught with racial and gender bias and coded language, I sent Black students to the office for wearing durags, aka hair wraps, and baggy pants. Although Black students, in one of the schools I taught, accounted for less than 10% of the school population, their innocuous fashion trends and freedoms of expression were deemed inappropriate and suspect for reasons unable to be articulated in the school handbook, by administrators or teachers enforcing the policy beyond the canned response, "These fashion statements are not acceptable for school." The unspoken subtext of such policies was that these fashions were too proximate to Blackness and thus bred fear. It is this subtext I later questioned in an attempt to get others to see the anti-Black racism demonstrated by the policy. The lack of understanding and the desire to understand showed me how ingrained these biases were and how targeted Black students, especially, are in schools. As a result, I teach future educators to closely examine policies and programming assessing them first through their potential positive or negative impact on historically oppressed racialized students. I teach them to ask themselves: *How does this policy or programming impact racialized students of the global majority? What is the rationale for such a policy or program? How might it be overly punitive for historically oppressed racialized students? Does it attempt to fix them? What are the physical, social and emotional effects of this policy or program on racialized students of the global majority?*

A few years ago a principal asked me to be a mentor for students in an after-school program he'd created. He wanted to provide racialized students of the global majority with a productive space to do their homework and build relationships with a trusted adult. I asked some pointed questions before I agreed. I wanted to better understand if the program was taking a deficit-minded approach to students. I, also, wanted to know if any efforts were being made to provide a supportive, culturally responsive environment during the school day. Too often, programming designed for racialized students of the global majority is about getting them to conform to White normative ways of thinking and/or being. It is about control, not care. As Jennifer R. alluded, there is an overemphasis on skill and students only as academic beings when authentic cariño is all-encompassing. It makes me think back to my mother's desire to send my brother and I to a school that regarded our present and our future. A place that simply saw us—really saw us. The program I ultimately agree to be a part of was performative and aesthetic, at best, and damaging, at worst. Like many school programs designed to help historically oppressed racialized students, it put the onus of change on the students only and made no other systemic changes.

In my interview with Heather D., an award-winning former early childhood educator and current educational leader, she pointed out, cariño y confianza are in direct contrast to "performative wokeness" or self-serving, aesthetic care because color-blind, one-size-fits-all care "gets derailed quickly." We cannot say we love our students and have meaningful relationships with them if our care is bound in an easily broken facade.

Distinguishing care is outlined in Table 3.2.

Priscilla L., the kindergarten educator who was featured in the previous chapter, highlighted that a culture of antiracist care should also extend to our colleagues.

> *The majority of our teaching assistants are women of color. They have been part of our community for a long time. They are strong, have strong relationships with families, strong relationships with students, but have not been given that avenue to lead. And now, they have teachers that they work with, new teachers, who think they [the teaching assistants] are undermining their authority instead of recognizing what assistant teachers know and have to offer. I've never recognized it in the way that I'm recognizing it now. Being more aware, I'm trying to make change around how I incorporate the assistant teachers into these leadership roles and on committees in my school.*

TABLE 3.2 Distinguishing between authentic and aesthetic care

Authentic Critical Care is ...	*Aesthetic Care is ...*
◆ Racially aware and literate	◆ Colorblind
◆ Compassionate & nurturing	◆ Pity
◆ Exhibits critical humility	◆ Sympathy
◆ Relationship-oriented	◆ Superficial
◆ Integrates academic care	◆ Performative
◆ Whole person-oriented	◆ Control-oriented
◆ Exhibits radical hope & support	◆ Judgmental
◆ Reciprocal	◆ Academic only

In the classroom, authentic critical care is ...

◆ Creating a welcoming space
  O Greet students and use their names (correctly pronounced) as much as you can
  O Check in with students and notice when they may need comfort or space (every day is ideal but especially during times of racial trauma in the community or society, e.g., Breonna Taylor; the Buffalo, NY, Grocery Store Massacre)
  O Authentically share stories and vulnerabilities with students
  O Design the classroom with students in consideration of what is comfortable and affirming for them (visually and physically), how the layout communicates power dynamics of the classroom and how it communicates"a pluralism of ideas, people, language and cultures" (Schieble et al., 2020)
  O Create an antiracist classroom policy with students
◆ Ask *every* student about themselves and their lives outside of school
  O Make time and space to chat with students
  O Repeat what you hear and learned about students and their interests in class dialogue, class examples, lessons and assessments (when appropriate)
◆ Ask students for feedback/opinions through surveys, exits slips, first/last question on an assignment, set up a space in the classroom for students to leave notes for you
  O It is not enough to ask questions or solicit feedback. We must **listen** and **respond.**
  O Share survey results with students and analyze results together
◆ Discipline through empathy
  O Taking time to hear a student who may be engaging in misbehavior
  O Seeking first to understand rather than criticize
  O Reengaging students with respect and fairness after a disciplinary issue
◆ Celebrates students and bring joy
  O Regularly celebrates small and large successes of individuals and the class community
  O There is time and space for laughter, social spaces and students taking the lead

Pitstop

Contemplate the following:

◆ What would it look like to care for the racialized people of the global majority in your building (everyone from the secretaries to lunch attendants to the teaching assistants to other teachers to administrators)?
◆ How would caring for the racialized people of the global majority change the culture of your school?

As racially minoritized teachers, we are, ourselves, navigating multiple systems of oppression while also having to show up for students, parents and caregivers and the community in ways that sometimes require more from us than our White racialized colleagues. My Latine teacher friends have shared stories about being asked repeatedly to act as a translator, and my Black male teacher friends talk about being called on regularly to act as deans of discipline and mentors. Their additional, and often invisible labor, warrants more recognition and care.

As Priscilla explains, critical care humanizes both students and teachers. Constant question posing is vital to check if our cariño y confianza is aesthetic or authentic. Here are some questions to think about care in our classrooms and beyond:

◆ How is your care personal and institutional?
◆ How is your care color-conscious (racially aware and literate)?
◆ How does your care demonstrate both cariño y confianza?
◆ How does your care extend to the racialized people of the global majority in your building?

It is important to note this is a process. We should not all go to school tomorrow railing against every policy in our schools or send a "I'm here for you" text to every historically oppressed racialized person you know. Critical care demands our intentionality and "strategic thinking to decide how to act in the best interests of others" (Eaker-Rich & Van Galen, 1996). Since critical care is a benchmark for antiracism, antiracism is a standard of critical care all students and staff need and deserve.

TEACHER LESSON IN SESSION

Jordan L., Chicago Illinois

A self-professed literary nerd, elementary and secondary English educator and instructional leader.

I feel like the movement of antiracist educators has really come forward, especially in light of the uprisings and the Black Liberation Movement. But for me, my career didn't start with that stuff. I've never been able to choose to be an antiracist educator or to be an abolitionist teacher. I had to be. I was teaching kids that look like me or that had experiences similar to me or didn't look like me but were locked in these cycles that I knew would ruin their futures. I had to do everything I could to shift that. And so it's almost like they finally gave a name to what teachers of color have always been doing. And that's great. Because once we quantify something sometimes then we can actually start to understand it, replicate it, but I think what it loses is the sense of urgency for some people. Because you have teachers who are trying to be an antiracist educator, and I don't mean to make light of it—they want to be an antiracist educator, they want to get it, they want to care, but the reason I've never had a choice is because my fate is tied up with theirs [students]. I have to believe that if I can't help make this manageable for those kids, that are like me, that are me, that have been just like me—if I can't get it right for them, then they won't be able to get it right in whatever field they choose. And if education is supposed to be liberatory, then I have to use my platform to liberate.

IF IT'S SO INGRAINED AND TIED TO WHO YOU ARE, WHAT THEN DO YOU SAY TO WHITE EDUCATORS WHO ARE ON THIS JOURNEY? HOW DO THEY ENGAGE IN THIS PROCESS?

I don't want you to teach like a pirate. I don't want you to teach like your hair's on fire. I don't want you to be a book thief. I want you to go to the front of your classroom, and I want you to think about your favorite student. The student who you think could do no wrong, the one that gets your heart, even though we love all of them. It's human nature, we see ourselves in some kids or we see kids and we want to protect them. I want you to think of that kid that makes your heart swell, and I want you to teach like tomorrow that kid could be killed. I want you to try and change that kid's life, whatever you think their life is going to be right now. If you think he/she/they are going to be a doctor, I want you to imagine that their life could be cut short, and they'll never get to be a doctor. What would you tell them? How would you treat them? How would you treat them if you thought that they would go and try and take the MCAT and they might be discounted because of their name? How would you treat them if you thought that other teachers were saying that they weren't good at science even though you saw it? I want you to teach like your favorite students' future is dependent on how you provide access and opportunity to them. Because it does, except it is all your kids.

IS THERE A SPACE FOR ANTIRACISM IN ALL-WHITE SCHOOLS?

Absolutely, that's where a lot of it has to be happening. If there's space for racism in White schools, if there's space for White supremacy in White schools, then there's space for people to have their own ideas and views pushed. If you teach White students, teach like their humanity is on the line. I think that's the thing we don't talk about as much when we do this work when we're talking about White teachers—humanity. I always think about the Stanford Prison Experiment, and it showed that incarceration dehumanizes both of us. Sometimes that's just how I have to posit, as good as a person you think you are, how would you feel if what you were actually doing was reinforcing some of the things that you vehemently disagree with. Some of the people who have all the badges and buy all the pins and buttons and donate to all the causes have never had it broken for them, never had the wool pulled from over their eyes, they're still committing harm.

Teach like their humanity is at stake. For the bulk of them, they'll be fine without antiracist teaching but they won't be okay. They won't be the people you hope for them to be. And for most teachers, we want our kids to be better people. We want our kids to go out and change the world. If we're not talking about this stuff, they are going to go out and they are gonna change the world by shooting Black people in the grocery store.

DO YOU THINK BEING A BLACK MAN IN EDUCATION IMPACTED THAT EXPERIENCE AT ALL?

I think one of the weirdest things about being a Black male educator is when people tell me that I'm a unicorn because unicorns are magical, and you don't have to truly believe that they exist in the space that they are in. I am real, and kids need to see and hear me. Kids need to hear that I have multiple degrees and I'm tatted up. Kids need to hear when I'm in my Socratic seminar that I don't always speak common English. That I love falling back into my African American Vernacular. That I love talking to my colleagues saying, "Boy," "What?!" and "yeah" because it doesn't change my intellect. My circumstances haven't always shown me that is the thing people want. They want what they think a Black educator is, not what we actually are.

DID YOU FEEL LIKE IN THOSE SPACES YOU WERE ABLE TO JUST EXIST AS YOUR AUTHENTIC SELF?

No, no, no. I haven't always been able to exist as my authentic self. I worked at a school on a reservation, and there I was able to exist as my authentic self although as a young teacher I was also still developing my full identity. There was one school that I got to show up just as me, and it was so fun. I'll never forget one of the best days of my life, I won the Black Panther award. They gave me a T-shirt and everything; it was one of those moments that when you think back on it—it's kind of cheesy and you're a bit embarrassed, but you still love it. The award was for being the person who goes above and beyond and protects our schools. Yeah, my kids were vibing and we were all happy, and it was a thing for the rest of the year. We celebrated—like we did every day with dance breaks or as we roasted book characters for doing dumb stuff. Romeo and Juliet would have never withstood the barrage of "y'all dumb" from my students. When I am able to be myself, then so are the students.

COMPREHENSION CHECK
◆ Reflecting on Jordan's words, what do you think needs to change in schools and classrooms for racialized students and educators of the global majority to thrive and experience joy in school?
◆ Jordan focused a lot on humanity and antiracism as a human imperative. How should/does this imperative impact our curriculums, the data stories we share about students, the textbooks we adopt, the people we choose to represent us on school boards and teachers' unions?

Amóípiisaawa

I am willing to bet that within the last few years you have heard, said, seen or wrote "Maslow before Bloom." It was all over my timeline during the pandemic reminding everyone to focus on the essential needs of students. Most educators are familiar with Maslow's pyramid outlining his hierarchy of human needs theory, but many of you may not know the story of the theory's origin and how its origin is essential for establishing a culture of antiracism in the classroom.

Here's the story. After finishing his dissertation, Abraham Maslow packed his belongings and headed to Siksika (the land, language and name of the Blackfoot nation) in 1938 for 6 weeks. Maslow whose research sought to question if people had control of their lives or if systems controlled humans' destinies wanted to observe a culture different than his own to begin to test his theories and ultimately develop new ones. During his time with the Siksika, Maslow was astonished by their levels of overall satisfaction with life, their cooperative nature, their care for one another that led to minimal to no deprivation or inequity and their high self-worth. These attributes were almost in direct contrast to what he'd observed in people in New York. Maslow was further shocked to learn that Siksika people measured wealth not by money and capital but by one's ability to give things to others (Ravilochan, 2021). In disbelief, he tried to find the outlier to no avail. He talked to members of the community to understand what made the Siksika such a peaceful, content place and people. The Siksika shared with Maslow their long-held belief that individuals are born with most of their individual needs met. They believe babies are born with everything they needed to be their best selves since it is the community's responsibility to provide food, warmth, safety and love. Because they exist in gratitude and generosity, they see it as their collective responsibility to meet each other's needs as the earth has already done for them. Also, for the Siksika, self-actualization is innate and not the zenith of human need as Maslow's hierarchy suggests. The Siksika entrust their communal wisdom to the community's youth to preserve and enact for generations to come. Maslow heavily borrowed from the Siksika belief system to build his own hierarchy of needs. In doing so, he inverted the ideology of the Siksika presumably to account for differences in cultural beliefs and Western ideals about individualism, community and wealth. The Siksika as Maslow came to conclude were the ideal, but Americans were not ready to enact the ideal. The Siksika provide a blueprint for establishing equitable, collaborative, caring and content communities that have endured for centuries. Perhaps, we should Siksika before Maslow as a model to establish a culture and standard of antiracism in our classrooms.

Establishing amóípiisaawa. bell hooks (2003) reminds us that "to build community requires vigilant awareness of the work we must continually do to undermine all the socialization that leads us to behave in ways that perpetuate domination." As an exemplification of the words of hooks, the Siksika are a healthy, supportive and safe community because they decenter individualism and Whiteness. For them, true satisfaction comes from their ability to take care of one another. Maslow could not fully understand this concept because while culture is visible in so many other ways, it is also intangible. Belonging is a feeling, and building a culture is a process of creating conditions to realize this feeling. This is why a classroom culture can be difficult to imitate and replicate. When students feel safe and valued, free from threat, judgment and societal narratives, they are able to move from reactive to reflective. They are able to build community and cognitively engage with their teachers and peers without constraint or the need to retreat to protect their thoughts and emotions. This is the power of a culture of belonging; it enables students to be their authentic selves and connect with others without barriers creating a sense of community, comfort and trust.

While there is no one checklist for establishing an antiracist classroom culture, there are conditions like reciprocal authentic cariño y confianza and amóípiisaawa that serve as foundations for thriving antiracist classrooms. Amóípiisaawa is an invitation to gather as community. **An ELA classroom focused on ridding itself of White-dominant ideologies, challenging racism and actively engaging in freedom dreaming means inviting students (e.g., their voice, their ideas, their concerns) into every aspect of the classroom with a focus on the collective good rather than the individual.** This looks like classroom environments in which students operate in the best interest of one another. The classroom community becomes, itself, a model of solidarity. The goal of the classroom is not self-actualization, that is, the realization of one's own potential, but instead like, the Siksika believed, the realization of our potential as a free, equitable society. The Siksika had a common pursuit of peace and community efficacy. In the classroom, this can translate to synergy as students understand that the goal of community is to work together toward a common goal and that it is our collective capacity, wealth of knowledge and emotional intelligence that will create new futures. This means challenging young adult White racialized students to realize their White identity and privilege in a racist society and not hold the class hostage to their racial awareness (Blackwell, 2010). In the classroom, this synergy should be owned and led by students, who as modeled by the Siksika, are the wisdom keepers ensuring the communities commitment to equity and contentment endures.

Consider this:

- What might it mean to believe that the needs of others supersede our own?
- What would it mean to think of students as already self-actualized?
- How do these answers free our students and ourselves?
- What would it look like to build a classroom community aligned to Siksika beliefs?

Anita B., a high school English teacher, really drills down how she views and builds community in her classroom.

This concept of community really explicitly needs to be taught more and more. We [teachers] sit in class and become very granular and task-oriented. Within 140 days, if you don't know these people [the students] in the space, there's something wrong, really wrong. That takes work, that takes effort and takes questions like, Why are these two students so isolated all the time? Why is there no joy in this space? What does joy actually look like in school? Because I've never really experienced it, what does it mean to de-center Whiteness? What does that look like as an Indian woman? What are the privileges I'm bringing into the space? And what is it that my Black counterpart is experiencing that we have to name? We have to be honest with our students; there's this idea that you just have to work hard, and it's not that simple. We must bring our truth into the space and be able to tolerate and hear the voices of those who are most impacted by this institution.

TABLE 3.3 Examples for building classroom community in various grade bands

Early Childhood	Elementary	Secondary
◆ Morning Meetings ◆ Rotating check-ins ◆ All-about-me projects ◆ **Classroom acts of care**	◆ **Walking and talking buddies** ◆ Co-create norms ◆ Lunch bunch with teacher ◆ Weekly conferencing ◆ Identity charts, I am & We are project	◆ Community circles ◆ **Classroom meetups** ◆ Weekly conferencing ◆ Chalk Talk ◆ Head, heart reflections ◆ Gratitude board
For early childhood students, these activities are entry points for teachers to gain valuable insights from students to help teachers create an environment of belonging that meets students' needs. They also serve as opportunities to model care and solidarity. *Classroom acts of care are weekly class discussion and student-led decisions to care for the classroom, school or larger community.*	*For elementary students,* these community builders give students a chance to own who they are and express themselves authentically. They also provide space, freedom and choice for students to connect and share their thoughts and feelings with one another. *For walking and talking buddies, students partnered up for a walk around the school sharing a predetermined prompt with one another or a topic of the student's choice. It gives students time and space to get to know one another and share what is on their minds.*	*For secondary students,* community may seem ancillary but is vital. Young adults are experiencing general and social anxiety at higher rates. Our classrooms may be the only safe space in school for some students to build community and understand who they are and explore their innate power. *Class meetups are a great way to create smaller communities in your classrooms. Students create affinity spaces that meet for short periods of time during class. I hear you— when do you have time to do this? You don't because there is never enough time but because everything we do starts and ends with students, we make time. It can be 10 minutes a week. Trust me, your students will appreciate the time to bond over a common interest.*

How to build amóípiisaawa in the ELA classroom is detailed in Table 3.3.

These community-building activities are about authenticity and wholeness, so students can, like the Siksika, realize satisfaction and peace through caring for and understanding one another.

Shannon B. discusses how community is also about creating space for students to be honest, leaders of their learning.

I really started to push for more student input and not just input because that still puts me as the decision maker, but more of a student-led classroom—although that seems kind of cliché as a phrase because a lot of people use it and they don't mean it. I started out thinking how can I start small. I did a lot of student surveys, I did a lot of "I want your opinion on this, and I want you to actually give me your opinion." Then I realized the students were just giving me the opinion that they thought I wanted. If I said how best to do you learn, check the boxes that apply, they would all pick writing and speaking because they thought those were the easiest and those were the things that I wanted them to do or expect them to do. I was like, "No, no, no. I actually want you to tell me what you how you want to learn." I decided I have to create relationships with these people, and I frequently call them people and not children or students because a lot of the people that I teach are adults who have children of their own. I stepped back from the surveys and started doing more discussions and questioning: Did this work for you? If so, why? If not, why not? In your previous history classes? Did you like them? Why didn't you like them? Was it the teacher? Was it what you learned? Can you pinpoint what was boring? Well, what we learned was I had one girl literally say it was just old White guys. And I was like, there it is. Okay, so we're getting somewhere. Let's dig deeper into that. We don't have to learn about old White guys. In this class, we're gonna learn about so much more than that. And we're gonna learn about the impact of those old White guys on other people. How's that sound? And she was like, "Wait, they did stuff to other people." This is literally her quote. She was like, "Wait, they did stuff to other people." And I was like, "Yes, they did. Let's talk about that."

Real Talk

I wish I could tell you this is going to be easy. It is not. It will be messy and you will want to stop because a student will say or do something requiring more time and energy than you have. It will make you say, "Forget this." I had to spend an hour on the phone with a parent, lose my lunch period talking to administration and my prep time collaborating with others to set up a restorative chat, so it's not worth it. In those moments that are bound to come, I want you to ask yourself why. Why is antiracism important for you and your students? Why did you pick up this book? What would happen if you stopped building an antiracist culture and community in your classroom? Going back to why you are on this journey in the first place will help you gain perspective.

From the teacher's desk

When I asked educators what they believed were indicators of an antiracist classroom culture, they had **a lot** to say. Table 3.4 highlights the responses from Anne P., Jessica K. and Holly S.

TABLE 3.4 Antiracist educators share what they believe are classroom indicators of an antiracist classroom culture

Educator	Antiracist Classroom Culture Indicators

Anne P., IL
Early childhood professor and clinical supervisor
	I would be looking for tangible and intangible things.
	◆ Tangible indicators
	  ○ Racially diverse dolls
	  ○ Pictures of children on the classroom walls, but also throughout the school that show the students and community are valued
	  ○ Two way communication between the teacher and students
	    ■ Who is doing the talking during the morning meeting? What are things students are sharing? How does the teacher respond?
	    ■ During the afternoon wrap-up, who is leading the discussion about the learning that occurred? Is the conversation authoritarian (controlled)?
	  ○ Variety of learning spaces
	    ■ Learning is not prescribed
	    ■ Teaching is happening in multiple spaces and teachers take the learning to the space the students are choosing
	◆ Intangible indicators
	  ○ What are the connections being made with the families and the community?
	  ○ What opportunities for advocacy exist in the classroom?
	    ■ When are students talking about their needs and the needs of their community?
	  ○ Autonomous classrooms
	    ■ Classroom where teachers are not told what to teach; the teachers and students have autonomy
	  ○ If antiracism is working to combat systems that take away autonomy, choice and voice, how is that being challenged?

(Continued)

TABLE 3.4 (Continued)

Educator	Antiracist Classroom Culture Indicators

Jessica K., IL 5th-grade educator	*In an antiracist classroom, I would be looking to see*
	◆ Co-created class agreements
	◆ Student photos and work
	  ○ The embodiment of students' humanity
	◆ Antiracist library and images (or quotes from folk of color)
	  ○ Representation and elevation of the work and ideas of racialized people of the global majority
	◆ BLM and LBGTQ+ flags
	  ○ Accompanied by information for students on the principles of each
	  ○ Actively acknowledges the sociopolitical realities of students' lives
	◆ Flexible seating options with plants that students keep alive
	  ○ Speaks to a space that is alive, thoughtful, nurturing, comfortable and comforting
	  ○ A safe of belonging with agency for it
	◆ Class jobs posted
	  ○ Provides the opportunity for racialized students of the global majority to hold leadership positions in the classroom
	◆ Created spaces for students to talk, process or opt out
	  ○ Active and ongoing acknowledgment of students' and societies' racial realities
	◆ Regular parent communication*
	  ○ Messaged to communicate care and truth
	    ■ After the murder of George Floyd, the 5th-grade team sent a message to parents condemning the act and offered support, love and a commitment to a safe community for children.

Holly S., NY High school English	*Here are the things I would look for and/or notice:*
	◆ Students in the classroom
	  ○ Who is sitting where?
	  ○ What are their body postures saying?
	  ○ Are they seen? Are their voices valued and ideas included?
	◆ Representation
	  ○ Whose work, quotes, photos, textbooks, authors and materials are presented and used?

(Continued)

TABLE 3.4 (Continued)

Educator	Antiracist Classroom Culture Indicators

	◆ Class dynamics
	  ○ Is there a syllabus/community agreement/class expectation list prominent in the class?
	    ■ Whose voices contributed to it?
	    ■ What does it say?
	◆ Educator disposition
	  ○ How does the educator in the room position themselves? Among the students? Lurking over them? Separate from them?
	  ○ Does the educator use the same tone/approach with all students or is it different with different groups and why?
	  ○ Whose work is the educator using as PD/reference material for themselves? Is it visible for others to see? Is it hidden? Present at all?
	◆ Language
	  ○ What language is used in the classroom?
	  ○ Does the educator sound authentic?
	  ○ Does the educator try "correct" language when Black and Brown students speak?
	◆ Resource Material
	  ○ In an ELA classroom, is the NCTE position statement posted or any other antiracist/antibias materials posted or prominent in the room for all to see?
	    ■ Does the teacher reference this material?
	    ■ Do the students see, acknowledge or refer to it?

* Not in the physical classroom but vital to an antiracist classroom culture.

Ashley M., a 5th-grade literacy educator, shared a simple but salient example of an important aspect of an antiracist classroom.

Instead of asking students, "Does anyone have any questions?" which really puts the onus on students, especially my younger students, to think "Do I have a question? I don't want to be the dummy that has a question." There's a lot wrapped up into that versus "What questions do you have?" which puts the responsibility on me and us as a learning community to do work together versus constantly putting responsibility on children to do the heavy lifting.

COMPREHENSION CHECK

◆ Think of your classroom. If Anne, Jessica or Holly, came to visit, what would they see?

◆ What are your thoughts about the indicators they shared?

◆ What surprised you? Why?

◆ What can you commit to add or do to create a culture of antiracism?

WAYPOINT

I am a huge fan of former first lady Michelle Obama. I like to think we're practically sisters since we grow up less than 2 miles away from one another, but I digress. In her book *Becoming* (2018), she shares, "becoming isn't about arriving somewhere or achieving a certain aim. I see it instead as forward motion, a means of evolving, a way to reach continuously toward a better self. The journey doesn't end." Whether you have mastered antiracism as a standard or are still minding the gap, you are on the road to becoming an antiracist educator with antiracist students. Learning is the pursuit of a goal; the desire to accomplish something. **We are in exactly the right place—we are not standing still, we are moving and becoming.** If you are still processing and thinking of the culture of your classroom, think about what you praise and prize and what is punished. This will tell you a lot about the culture of your classroom. Also, ask students! It's their space and they can and will tell you all you need to know about creating a culture that is best for them.

THINK–ACT–REIMAGINE

Think - Act - Reimagine

Think	Act	Reimagine
If racism lives in policies and structures, where does racism reside in your classroom?	Discuss and outline a standard of antiracism for the classroom with students.	An authentic, collaborative, connected, caring classroom community committed to racial equity, justice, freedom and joy.
How are you shifting your beliefs, thoughts and actions?		Your community of friends and family with you on this journey.

FIGURE 3.1

DO NOW

◆ Write out an antiracist standard for yourself.
◆ Make a list of things you can do immediately to create and sustain a culture of antiracism in the classroom.
◆ Brainstorm some ways to connect and care for students every day (check-ins are always a quick, easy and effective option).

Resources

Classroom Community resource from Building Equitable Learning Environments Network at https://library.belenetwork.org/resources/classroom-community-learning-condition-guide/

Cultivating Genuis by Gholdy Muhammad

Design for Belonging Toolkit at https://www.designforbelonging.com/toolkit

National Council for Teachers of English Committee Against Racism and Bias Posters and Bookmarks at https://ncte.org/get-involved/volunteer/groups/committee-against-racism-and-bias-in-the-teaching-of-english/

Teacher Caring from Building Equitable Learning Environments Network at https://library.belenetwork.org/resources/teacher-caring/

4

Shifting Your Instruction

What does instruction in an antiracist ELA classroom look like?

It started with a parent phone call. One of the units of study in my 8th-grade ELA curriculum was titled Two Sides to Every Story. The unit focused on Civil War perspectives and centered Civil War middle grades and young adult literature to explore the theme. I cringe now just thinking about the harm of the unit and of some of the text selections offered to students. It is no wonder this unit was our least favorite. Before students began reading their selected novels, I wanted them to understand the historical context of the Civil War and build background, and I outlined the reasons brother would fight brother and foes would risk fracturing a young nation. The call came this day.

"Mrs. Rembert, my son came home talking about class today and I wanted to talk to you about it." I immediately started tallying the number of novels I had to see if I needed to borrow books from another colleague in order to switch her son to his first choice, certain this was the reason for the call.

"Our son told us you shared with the class some reasons that prompted the Civil War. He told us you said one of the primary

DOI: 10.4324/9781003296171-6

reasons was states' rights. And I am presuming you just did not get a chance to complete that sentence. Is it okay if I send you some research from a family friend about the dangers of not finishing that sentence?" I was stunned. This was not about books at all. I paused a bit, taken aback. I agreed to read the article published in a prominent research journal. I also tried to defend myself. I don't even now recall the basis of my defense. I just remember feeling embarrassed and defensive, thinking "Yet, another parent telling me how to teach."

After the call, I checked my email for the article, printed it and glanced over it quickly before shoving it into a forever-forgotten pile on my desk. At the time, I did not fully appreciate the gift that parent gave me. I labored in lament over the encounter for a while. I had taught the unit this way for years. No one else had ever challenged or corrected me. It was not until the unit's conclusion and I reviewed the learning we'd done that I realized the harm I'd enacted. In a unit primed to explore issues of race, I had failed to adequately engage students in meaningful discussion on the topic or pull in other texts to thoughtfully address the complexities of race and racism in our country. I had given my students nothing of consequence to help them understand the origin of racial oppression or how to combat it. In failing to make space for rich and consequential learning about White supremacy and racism, I upheld it.

It was my inability to tell this historical truth that propelled my antiracist teaching journey: The Civil War was fought over states' rights to preserve the institution of slavery. That's the complete sentence. It was reflecting on that call, putting uninspired and possibly harmful texts in the hands of students year after year and having discussions absent any connection to present realities that I determined I would never again allow my instruction to be a bastion for racism. I had a responsibility to myself and my students to do better. In a majority White, affluent school district, my students needed to understand racism, how to navigate conversations about race and what it meant to be antiracist. The unit and its outcomes were ideally suited for such meaningful discussions and lessons, and yet, I had not included any of them.

I had to ask myself some hard questions:

◆ What stopped me from finishing the sentence?
◆ What compelled me to continue introducing and including potentially harmful novels with a Southern apologist lean with no real literary merit in this unit of study?
◆ How could I as a Black woman have shied away from talking about race and racism? What was I scared of?
◆ What made me comfortable relaying an erroneous master narrative rather than myriad counternarratives that would have rightfully complicated history and enriched students' learning?
◆ What harm had I perpetuated over the years?
◆ What did students need and deserve from me?

I did not realize it at the time, but these questions laid the groundwork for future antiracist planning and lesson implementation. It is my responsibility to always finish the sentence, to always lead with truth and to trust my students.

And since education is a human right, then being literate always means having full participation in one's own humanity. More than most, we know literacy is power.

Ang hindi lumingon sa pinanggalingan, hindi makakarating sa paroroonan

Literacy is a complex system of thinking, communicating and making meaning. According to the United Nations Educational, Scientific and Cultural Organization (UNESCO), what it means to be literate is ever-evolving to meet the demands of a changing world. As a result, literacy can no longer be viewed as a set of conventional reading and writing skills; instead, societal progress demands, at present, that literacy functions as "a means of identification, understanding, interpretation, creation, and communication in an increasingly digital, text-mediated, information-rich and fast-changing world" (UNESCO, 2022). Literacy is a vehicle for people to engage, contribute and challenge society, and thus, it improves conditions for all people, and since education is a human right, being literate means having full participation in one's own humanity. More than most, as ELA educators, we know literacy is power. Presently, this leaves 3 billion people and roughly 250 million children globally unable to exercise this power. These staggering numbers are not disconnected from the privileges of developed societies. The inability to read and write or to do so effectively comes at a cost to us all. In 2019, the National Assessment of Educational Progress (NAEP) reported 4th, 8th and 12th-grade Black, Latine, Native Hawaiian, Pacific Islander and Indigenous American students lagged in literacy proficiency compared to their White, Asian and Multiracial American peers based on standardized measurements. However we feel about standardized tests as a determinant of knowledge and skill, these statistics are correlative to systemic poverty, mass incarceration, poor health and wellness outcomes and increased mortality rates. Educational historian E. Jennifer Monaghan aptly posits that "the continuing disparity between the literacy abilities of different social, racial and ethnic groups poses a danger to American democracy … [since] literacy offers personal liberation [and is] a prerequisite to political freedom" (1998). As ELA educators, our job is to help students actualize the power and inherent humanity of literacy. *No pressure, right?*

Over the course of my career, I have witnessed the changes and challenges of literacy instruction. My teacher friends and I have often engaged in spirited discussions/debates about best practices, the reliability and fairness of standardized tests, what constitutes worthy texts and what are acceptable forms of written expression. I'm sure you have stories about how these age-old debates persist on your team or in your department meetings. I can personally attest that disagreements over the merit of a five-paragraph essay are enough to tear an ELA department apart. While the ultimate resolution to these debates is based on what students are communicating they want and need from us, I am, also, a firm believer the past holds answers to the present. Ibram Kendi, author and director of the Center for Antiracist Research at Boston University, defined antiracism as "locating the roots of the problem in power and policies." To understand the present state of literacy education, let's dig up the power and policy roots of literacy in the United States.

Since humans began uttering sounds, making gestures and drawing symbols and pictures on cave walls, literacy has been a prized skill. It has also been used as a tool of subjugation and liberation. The significance of literacy is evident in the first educational law sanctioned in the "New World." In 1642, the Massachusetts Bay Colony passed a law requiring all caregivers to teach their children to read. Colonial children as young as 3 years old repeated words syllable by syllable to develop their literacy skills. In a budding nation, these skills were used to reinforce piety and civic loyalty. Early schools used the Bible and patriotic essays as the primary texts for reading practice and instruction. The founding fathers believed the success of "the great experiment" depended on White men reading, so they could be properly governed and obey laws. According to Monaghan (1998), literacy has been socially controlled by the elite and the aim of government relative to literacy has not been "with the view of promoting individual freedom ... [but rather] to inculcate their own political or religious agenda and promote social control."

This was especially true for free and enslaved Black people in the new nation, their literacy threatened the institution of slavery and the myths of Black people as unintelligible beings. Several rebellions led by literate enslaved people, including Nat Turner's Rebellion and David Walker's rebellious text *Appeal*, which called for enslaved people to rise up, substantiated literacy as a powerful weapon against oppression. An example of this is the 1733 *cédula*, or edict, issued by Philip V, King of Spain promising freedom to enslaved people who escaped to Spanish Florida. The cédula was an attempt to cause friction and then seize power in the North American colonies, and it successfully achieved its goal. The Stono Rebellion, the largest uprising ever attempted by enslaved people in South Carolina, is thought to be a response to the Spanish cédula being read and circulated among enslaved South Carolinians. Consequently, by 1740, South Carolina's slave codes restricted enslaved people from being taught to read and included a specific suppression of "any manner of writing whatsoever." The power of the pen birthed the nation, so controlling writing equated to controlling freedom. As the crown jewel of the literate, writing was esteemed as an indispensable instrument for business, a construct of government and a means to constrain the citizenry. In fact, all the southern states' slave codes required enslaved people to carry written passes whenever they left the plantation. The specific prohibition of writing in the slave codes across the nation, north and south, connected written expression to White superiority and a mechanism to thwart liberation.

Between the mid-17th century and the early 19th century, literacy was used as a tool of assimilation and coercion for Indigenous people. To subdue a people and take their land, the idea of Indigenous people as unteachable "savages" was constructed. Forced into residential schools, Indigenous children endured violence including physical and spiritual death. In these schools, children were not allowed to speak their native language or engage in any cultural practices. They were forced to read, write and speak according to the "White man's ways" to erase parts of themselves. Zitkála-šá (1921), a young girl who was a member of the Great Sioux Nation and attended a residential school, wrote in her diary:

> They were no more young braves in blankets and eagle plumes, nor Indian maids with prettily painted cheeks. They had gone three years to school in the East, and had become civilized. The young men wore the white man's coat and trousers, with bright neckties. The girls wore tight muslin dresses, with ribbons at neck and waist. At these gatherings they talked English.

Even when Indigenous children returned to their homes, they read their world through Whiteness. Their literacy of self had been rewritten, and being literate equated to changing oneself. Zitkla-Sa wrote:

> My mother was troubled by my unhappiness. Coming to my side, she offered me the only printed matter we had in our

home. It was an Indian Bible, given her some years ago by a missionary. She tried to console me. "Here, my child, are the white man's papers. Read a little from them," she said most piously.

Zitkála-šá's mother assumed her comfort would come from reading not in her native language but from the "white man's papers." Her mother had acceded to a perceived literary deficiency tied to language and race. The fallacy of the uncivilized Indian fueled by the invention of race and carried out via the written word upheld the racist ideology of literacy being something Indigenous people could not attain. For Indigenous people, literacy aided ethnocide. Additionally, erroneous, harmful treaties and coercive acts exploited language and literacy gaps and were used to enact White Supremacist genocide.

As the nation grew more advanced and powerful, the purpose of literacy instruction shifted from morality building to building a productive labor force. This shift linked education to capitalism and classism. During the Industrial Revolution, literacy became the primary goal of education causing literacy rates in the United States to soar. More Americans were reading and writing than at any other point in history. However, texts continued to feature mostly White males, and written language did not account for other styles, voices and patterns of language(s). The landscape of literature and prose continued to disenfranchise racialized people of the global majority. Even as people of different cultures and ethnicities made the United States home, a faulty belief emerged that speaking, listening and comprehending standard English and its text made newcomers Americans. This resulted in legislation like the 1968 Bilingual Education Act and the 1974 Supreme Court case *Lau v. Nichols* that brought attention to bilingual education without going far enough to address its racism and structural inequities. What resulted was an onslaught of English-only policies that made literacy learning more difficult and forced racially minoritized students to separate from parts of their identity.

Rooted in power and policies, we can see that racialized people of the global majority have been historically deprived

of the right to literacy. As an educational bedrock, literacy has been one of the master's primary tools of oppression, as well as, the tool used by the oppressed to chisel their way toward freedom. **The dichotomy of literacy as a mark of power, privilege and freedom for racialized White people and a means of annihilation and assimilation for historically oppressed racialized people complicates classroom instruction, especially since the remnants of harmful literary history remain in our beliefs, curriculum and instruction.** As antiracist ELA educators, it is important to know that literacy has been weaponized, and students' literary experiences are still racialized and steeped in settler colonialism, erasure and oppression. The Filipino proverb that titles this section, *a person who does not remember where he came from will never reach his destination,* reminds us that taking this history and its effects, past and present, into account is necessary to recognize patterns, behaviors and policies that are regressive and not in the best interest of students.

COMPREHENSION CHECK

Let's take some time to reflect on this historical information.
◆ **What** did you learn to help you better understand literacy and its connection to race in the United States?
◆ **Why** is this information important to understand as a present-day antiracist literacy educator?
◆ **How** will you use this knowledge to inform your praxis and antiracist journey?

Our mentor teacher

Pennsylvania Anti-Slavery Society member Benjamin C. Bacon said of educator Susan Paul, "Many are abolitionists from the mere force of circumstances. Not so with Miss Paul. The simple fact that oppression existed was enough to call forth her most self-denying efforts for its overthrow." In 1830, Miss Paul's primary students at the Abiel Smith School, Boston's first school to service Black free students, had certainly experienced (some of her students were formerly enslaved) and been privy to various forms of racism. In Miss Paul's antiracist literacy-centered classroom, she understood her instruction must be responsive to students and the societal realities of the day. This resulted in her students accompanying her to antislavery meetings around New England to hear from local and international abolitionists. Students, as young as 6 years old, listened to antislavery orators' arguments for freedom and their critiques of the institution of slavery. Any educator who regularly attended such happenings with their students would certainly also bring that learning back into the classroom. Surely, Abiel Smith students examined the claims, argumentation and word choice abolitionists made against chattel slavery. Miss Paul's classroom was the world, and she was with intentionality creating an environment of free thought, courage, criticality and activism.

In addition to teaching about the ills of slavery and other forms of racial oppression, Miss Paul also taught her primary students to engage in antiracist action. As a young Black educator, she laid the groundwork for what it means to be an antiracist literacy teacher. She inspired her students to form a youth choir, and their choir performed around New England at antislavery meetings and donated the proceeds of the concerts they held to the abolitionist cause. Miss Paul was so dedicated to both her students and antiracism that she wrote the first biography of a Black person published in the United States. Since texts did not reflect or represent her students, Miss Paul wrote her own. Her book *The Memoir of James Jackson: The Attentive and Obedient Scholar* was published in 1835. Groundbreaking, the book is wholly devoted to memorializing her student James, a 6-year-old boy who died of tuberculosis, and debunking racial stereotypes. Unlike texts of that day, the biography is not a voyeuristic view of the harshities of Black life from an outsider's perspective; instead, it showcases James's innocence, dedication and intelligence from the vantage point of his own community. In her classroom, Paul used the biography to affirm the character of her faithful student. For White readers, Paul desired to illustrate the intellect and morality of Black children and "let, then, this little book do something towards breaking down that unholy prejudice which exists against color." An example of this is Paul's recollection of James's reaction when she first tells his class about enslaved people and how "a great many thousands of their color who were not allowed to read, who had no schools, nor any books" (Paul & Brown, 2000). This news filled James with anguish as he could not fully comprehend such deprivation and was led to tears and fervent prayers for those enduring it.

For her audience, Paul highlighted the rights and liberties denied enslaved people while also demonstrating that her student, James, at an early age understood racial oppression. He not only understood it, but he was also so moved for his brethren that it also prompted action (i.e., his prayer). In sharing this anecdote, Paul supposes that if at 6 years old, James could understand, empathize and act, then anyone should be able to do the same. According to Paul, James died with this burden heavy on his heart and with the question of who would change things. The book, in his honor, is her effort to continue to do the work. Miss Paul's work demonstrated authentic *cariño y confianza* for her students and the community by exposing them to text and thinking that ensured they understood the legacy of race and racism. She offered them opportunities to be change agents, demonstrated her fierce advocacy, and highlighted the need for authentic textual representation through her own writing. In at least one instance, White children at the Union Evangelical Sabbath School, after reading the biography, wrote the students of Abiel Smith empathizing with the plight of Black children and offering their prayers, support and a monetary donation to the school.

Almost 200 years ago, Miss Paul understood life was, itself, a text to be read, decoded, discussed and written about. She knew her students needed to understand the inhumanity and commodification Black people, free and enslaved, faced in the early 1800s. Miss Paul's students, as do all students, needed to be able to comprehend, interpret, evaluate and assess the complexities of race as citizens in a changing world. And she bravely and boldly taught her students history, texts and truth. **Miss Paul's teaching was a political and revelatory act as should be the case for every educator.** She knew schools existed within a political system and, therefore, were politically charged spaces. Whether past or present, opportunity, guidance and space are necessary to exercise free thought, the essence of political action, that informs views of self, society and civic engagement. **Our students cannot be passive or neutral because their lives and the future of the nation depends on their active engagement.** Along with her students, we are also benefactors of Miss Paul's antiracist model. As Bacon noted, Miss Paul's understanding of the existence of oppression was enough for her to know it had to end and she could play a part in that through her teaching. Her legacy acts as a road map for us on our antiracist journey.

> *Without historical knowledge and a plan of disruption, we are, as literacy educators, accomplices in the promulgation of racism.*

Every teacher is a history teacher

Why did I start this chapter with such a heavy emphasis on history? To highlight some of the histories of literacy in the United States is to make visible the people, events, policies and structures that have been erased but vital to the construction of literacy, its injustices and what we do and consider on a daily basis as ELA educators. To force us to wrestle with literacy as White property (see Table 4.1 for a definition of this concept) since historically "literacy has been sustained primarily as a response to perceived threats to White property interests, White privilege, the maintenance of 'White' identity, or the conception of America as a White nation" (Prendergast, 2003). To understand that as we privilege literary knowledge, texts, discourse and the written word, we must do so with knowledge of the enmeshed history of literacy and racial stratification. Without historical knowledge and a plan of disruption, we are, as literacy educators, accomplices in the promulgation of racism. **To acknowledge that literacy has been key to the reproduction of Whiteness and White supremacy in schools, frees us to, therefore, reimagine its instruction moving toward more humanizing, anti-oppressive and antiracist ELA pedagogy.** It is, also, to illustrate the need for ELA educators to

TABLE 4.1 The tenets of critical race theory (CRT)

CRT Tenet	Explanation
Permanence of racism	Racism is endemic, an inescapable part of American life.
Whiteness as property	Whiteness ascribes value, lays claim and ownership to ideas, rights, lands and bodies.
Counter-storytelling	People of the global majority have a right to tell their stories. Their voices, stories and experiences are real and valid.
Interest convergence	Legislation serves White interest, even when it is intended for the advancement of people of the global majority.
Critique of liberalism	Challenges any and all ideologies that refuse to acknowledge race, racial differences and racism.
Intersectionality	There are countless ways people can identify themselves. No one can just be identified one way.

center myriad histories, literacies and counternarratives as we move beyond the White gaze of literacy instruction. Our ELA classrooms are inevitably historically rich spaces. Author and educator Jamila Lyiscott (2020) reminds us that all literacy practices are, "a unique composite of history, culture, memories, and ways of knowing, they each possess a unique capacity to open new worlds for you, your students, and your classroom." Our listening, lesson planning, instruction, assessment, community building and reflection should demonstrate an understanding and positioning of history as indispensable since historical knowledge enables us to bring more critical and nuanced perspectives to the problems and progress of our present and future worlds. All of these ELA educator functions are also necessary as we problematize literacy's role in the construction of White dominance. And if, as we have been taught to believe, literacy is a human and civil right, then we should ask ourselves the question Prendergast (2003) poses in her book *Literacy and Racial Justice: The Politics of Learning after Brown v. Board of Education*: "What kind of literacy instruction will serve the cause of racial justice in the post civil rights era?" Our response to this question requires historical knowledge to repair the damage caused by White literacy dominance. When we consider history as essential to unmask the complexity of racism, we do so with an understanding that history, not only, impacts the present but also the future. If I could go back and reteach that Civil War novel unit, I would definitely teach hard history and its often hidden racism letting students grapple with its present-day implications. I would equip students with the skills to discern, decipher and challenge racialized rhetoric and its structures, especially how those structures affect school. I would be asking students questions like: Why are there so many texts in classrooms with a Southern apologist and sympathetic leaning? How does one recognize subversive racial rhetoric and challenge it? Is the title of the unit (Two Sides to Every Story) itself rooted in racial ignorance? Who has the power to decide what books are included and excluded in the curriculum? Whose voice is missing from curricular decisions? How can other voices be added and valued? There are so many things I would do differently, and the beauty is, now, I have the knowledge to do so and so do you.

Felicia, an 11th-grade English teacher, notes that *"for every text that we explore, there's always this contextuality that students need to understand. We have to ask: What's happening in society that this author may be responding to? It requires us to do a little bit of research to have historical and contextual knowledge of the pieces we assign."*

COMPREHENSION CHECK

The question posed by Prendergast is an important one. Let's pause to reflect on it and other assertions raised.

◆ **Why** is the incorporation of history into your ELA classroom a vital component of antiracist teaching and learning?

◆ **What** is your understanding of literacy as White property?

◆ **What** else do you need to know to better understand this concept?

◆ **How** can you create space for critical discourse and reflection on Prendergast's question?

As a collection of memory, people and language and all the things in between, Heather D., a 10th-grade English teacher, affirms, *"literature is the recording of human history whether it is a book, a document or a love letter. It's all just a written history."* These histories give way to various forms of literacies, some of which have been ignored or deemed unacceptable relative to White normative standards. It is imperative to remember that stories, fictional or actual, are the dialogue of history, and writers are often writing to enter their thoughts and perspective into a conversation around an event, idea, person or viewpoint they find important. These texts (in all forms written or visual) are the products of history that embody myriad literacies for our students to understand, dissect and interrogate. To ignore the personal or historical history of a text is to hold us captive to only the present, and we would be remiss to not engage in the exploration of stories as forms of history and truth.

From the teacher's desk

Jessica K., a 5th-grade literacy educator, instructional coach and antiracist leader, shares the importance of historically framing all texts with students.

When we select a text for ELA, that author has been informed by their own experiences, by their education and by parts of American history. It's our responsibility to engage in that conversation and to support, encourage and push our students to do the same, so they see the things we read and write are in conversation with one another and are able to connect the dots.... There's a lot of room for the framing and the contextualization. There's been a lot of pushback about not teaching To Kill a Mockingbird, *but there's a lot of potential if that text is selected for educators to think: How do I position my students to think through the text with a literary criticism lens and to understand the bigger conversation that this book had within a historical framework and to be critical of it? To be critical of its author, message, the limitations of the book or whatever it is, and to see it within this bigger framework, this bigger historical piece. To think like a historiographer: What are the limitations of this piece? Why is this person saying what they're saying? What are their biases? That's really powerful, and it's really difficult to do, but that's where students can be truly empowered. Because they're no longer passively ingesting information that you're giving them. They're now part of the greater dialogue and meaning-making process where they are, actually, actively critiquing and understanding.*

For years, my classroom instruction revolved around finding the main idea, author's purpose and writing argumentative essays about school uniforms or other nonthreatening topics. Students were engaging in schooling but that learning lacked criticality. Students' ability to question history, people, context, words and stories leads to critical reasoning, reflection and action, and by doing so acknowledges that "the fundamental effort of education is to help with the liberation of people, never their domestication. You must be convinced that when people reflect on their domination they begin a first step in changing their relationship to the world" (Freire, 1971). As a result, to seek historical truths is a bedrock of antiracism in the ELA classroom. **We cannot escape the histories within the texts we read, the pieces we write or the words we speak**. And therefore, every teacher is a history teacher. I am not alone in believing this assertion. When discussing antiracism in the ELA classroom with educators across the United States, I found that ELA teachers agreed, and many stated that historical truth was a compulsory component of being an antiracist educator because historical illiteracy feeds racism.

The following literacy educators share their stories and the role and importance of history in their classrooms.

DILLIN'S HISTORY

My third-grade teacher was a Black woman, and I remember her teaching us about the Civil Rights Movement. She didn't sugarcoat anything. We read books and looked at pictures of people being hosed down. She taught us an accurate history of the movement—it was reality. It made me, at eight, want to go to the library and get more information and talk to my mom about it. I appreciate that I was told the truth, the whole history, and I was told it unbiasedly. I bring history into my class the same way. In my 10th-grade ELA class, we are reading *Stamped from the Beginning*, the Jason Reynolds adaptation. We are confronting history and racism, talking about and having honest conversations about it. I am, also, allowing students to grapple with their own identities and how they view people of other races and themselves.

YOLANDA'S CLASSROOM

An ELA teacher shouldn't read *The Great Gatsby* if they're not actually going to talk about the Jim Crow era. Gatsby is about race. Within the first few pages of the book, it clearly talks about a White America. I teach history by exposing kids to all of it. Sometimes all of it means that it's not going to put a particular event in a positive light or it's not going to put a particular person in a positive light, but I still want kids to know it and critically think. I want them to examine, to discuss and to be able to engage with it. I also want them to look at some of these people and see that they were flawed.

I, also, want students to be exposed to other [racialized] people's history. They can then start to make connections and see the systemic nature of racism that's embedded throughout history. Then, they realize this is not just about you and it's not just about me. It's about the structures in place that allow some of us to have a seat at the table while others don't, and it's about who gets to make those decisions.

LISA'S HISTORY

I went to school and grew up in a very homogeneous area. There were very few teachers that really talked about that [racism] until I had a combined history and English class with Mr. Rose. I will never forget, Mr. Rose. He was one of the first people, let alone teachers, to challenge our thinking by asking, *"You don't think that your experience growing up here in this area is different?"* It made us stop and look at the community. And we realized most of our caregivers were White flighters. And a lightbulb went off—oh, okay. And then we questioned: *What does that mean in a classroom? What does that mean as a person who's growing up to be a citizen of the world? And what are you going to do with that information?* I love that part of teaching. It's not just learning things. It's being a citizen of the world and taking what you learn and doing something better with it. That's why I love my American studies class. You're always teaching context. There's always the context something is written in, and there's also the historical context you have to understand—and the context changes, and you need to be aware of that. Students are, themselves, always changing and their understanding of the world becomes different with time. Ten years ago, students wouldn't talk about the things that are happening now in the same way because the things that are happening are different. That's a piece of history to, also, understand.

EBONI'S STORY

Eboni, a librarian in Texas, discussed how her familial history has impacted how she engages in the work of antiracism. "I wasn't supposed to talk about my dual nature. I was supposed to only be Black. I didn't even know my dad could speak Spanish until my grandmother came to visit from Cuba. I had to learn who I was and learn the language in order to be complete." Because of her personal history, Eboni ensures books in her library showcase with pride a wide range of racial identities.

It takes know-how

Can I trust you with a secret? I once bought an ELA unit from a site with teacher-created generic lessons. I will offer no excuse because I am not even sure why I did it. And, no, it was not worth it. The bundle was about 1,000 pages of prettily designed worksheets—one-dimensional, passive busywork. I learned my lesson. The purchase was antithetical to the type of analytical, critical and creative thinking the students and I needed and wanted. On its best days, my middle school ELA classroom was alive with energy and students challenging texts, themselves, racism, sociocultural, sociopolitical, socioenvironmental and socioeconomic issues and their view of the world. On those days and many others, I have been awed by the brilliance shared by young people, something those pretty worksheets could never do. Perhaps, you also have committed the cardinal sin of buying generic, laborious and uninspiring bundles from teacher sites; let's repent together and vow never to do that again. From that $20 purchase, I learned instruction cannot be bought. Intentional, thoughtful instructional practices designed with and for students raise consciousness, inspire and shift power in the classroom and that cannot be found on a checklist or a lesson labeled antiracist on a pay-a-teacher-for-their-worksheets site.

Antiracist teaching and learning take know-how. While talking to educators, I was struck by the focus ELA educators placed on what we teach. Many of the educators shared books they have included in their classroom libraries or as counternarratives to White canonical texts and talked about writing opportunities encouraging students to use their native languages. It was great to hear that educators are giving deep consideration to the texts they put in front of students and the honor given to various forms of racial identity. It was, also, interesting what I heard less of and that was *how* we teach as antiracist ELA educators. **The what cannot come at the expense of the how.** When we put a text that reflects a student's racial, linguistic and ethnic identity in their hands or tell them they can use translanguaging in their writing, this is one of many steps. It is not enough to choose a great text by a racialized author of the global majority or a White racialized author without considering the instructional practices that ensure students engage in learning, thinking and acting in ways that promote racial equity and subvert racism. As Jessica K. stated, the goal is for students to engage with texts and offer literary critique and use the skills of historiographers to understand and analyze texts for their present and past value. Of course, this will look different based on the age of your students; however, it is vital to antiracism in the ELA classroom.

How?

Our approach to our craft should be rooted in the students we serve. It is essential to recognize that each class is unique, and each student brings a different set of learning needs and interests to the table. Therefore, we should ask ourselves, "What do students want to learn? What do they need to learn? What can I learn from them? How can we co-construct opportunities and environments that promote constructive and adaptive thinking about complex issues such as systemic racism and oppression?" This is not prescriptive work—it's mindset, heartset and skillset work, but it is also not arbitrary. It requires an understanding of learning theories and best practices, an awareness of the numerous ways in which students engage with learning and an appreciation for the power of diverse perspectives and experiences. It is the recognition that learning is a continuous process of discovery, experimentation and reflection.

In our ELA classrooms, our effective antiracist pedagogy establishes a frame for engaging with all forms of literacy. This frame encourages students to think critically and analytically about race and racism as they read texts, engage in writing activities and have conversations with peers. Through instruction on how to analyze texts through a critical race lens, we help students better understand how power is distributed in society, how privilege and oppression manifest in different contexts and how they can address and resist racism in their own lives. We also build the capacity for students to understand the dangers of essentialism, the importance of intersectionality and the power of language in shaping our understanding of race and racism. By engaging with texts through a critical race lens, students learn to recognize and redress the subtle ways in which racism is perpetuated in our society. Table 4.2 provides a starting point for students to begin examining texts through a critical race lens.

One of the primary utilizations of this framing is critical literacy. Critical literacy prompts students of all ages—yes, early-childhood students included—to question and challenge language, power and their intersections in and outside of a text. Earlier in this chapter, we learned about the problematic history of literacy in the United States. Reading critically is a practice of resistance, an opportunity to grapple with the fraught history of literacy and literature to disrupt the status quo through interrogation of social issues and taking social action. Critical literacy is antiracist in its aims to challenge conformity, inequity and injustice. It is a form of literary criticism of which there are four dimensions (Table 4.3); however, these are not steps or a framework to be rigidly followed—don't put them on a worksheet and sell it. The dimensions represent interrogation points for students as they examine texts

TABLE 4.2 Understanding antiracist ELA through a critical race lens

Critical Race Lens A critical examination of texts (all forms) through a lens of race and racism.	◆ Exploration of how structural racism, White supremacy and other forms of oppression are represented in a text and in life. ○ How race and racism are used to perpetuate or challenge existing power dynamics ○ How texts reflect and perpetuate the effects of racialized power dynamics ◆ Analysis of history, language, form, content and characterization to gain a deeper understanding of how racism and other forms of oppression are woven into narratives ○ Including the intersections of race, class, gender and other forms of identity in texts ◆ Examination of how texts are situated within a larger sociopolitical and sociocultural context and how they interact with existing societal norms, expectations and power structures. ○ The ways in which texts reproduce or resist dominant ideologies and discourses ○ How race and racism impact the production, reception and interpretation of texts ○ How different media platforms serve to either reinforce or challenge existing representations of race and racism

TABLE 4.3 Critical Literacy

Dimensions	Key Attributes/Guiding Questions	Nonfiction Embedded Antiracism in Praxis Topic: Water Conservation	Fiction Embedded Antiracism in Praxis Theme: Identity
Disrupt the commonplace	Gain an understanding of history and historical impact Identify any hidden messages. *Are there messages that marginalize a person or people group?* Think about the way the text has presented the story/information: *What are some assumptions the text makes overall?* *What are some assumptions about the reader?* **Positionality** *What view of the world is the text presenting?*	*For early childhood educators* Texts: USAID (United States Agency for International Development) World Water Day Photo Essay 2019 and *All the Water in the World* by George Ella Lyon **Critical questions** Based on the photo essay, what are your noticings and wonderings? Who has clean water and who does not? Would your photo appear in this year's photo essay? Why or why not? How are you alike or different from the people in the photos? What do the pictures tell us about who has clean water and who does not? Do you believe the photos? What other information do you need to know about who has or does not have clean water? Based on the book, where does water come from? Who owns it? If water belongs to us all, why do you think some people have clean water while others do not?	*For early childhood educators* Text: *The Proudest Blue: A Story of Hijab and Family* by Ibtihaj Muhammad **Critical questions** Since we have talked about hijabs and why a person would wear a hijab, let's think about these questions: What do you know about hijabs and the people who wear them? What did you think you knew about hijabs and the people who wear them before our discussion? Why do you think Faizah and Asiya's classmates said rude and hurtful things about the hijab? The hijab is vividly described. What makes something beautiful? Who gets to say if something is beautiful or not? How do Faizah and Asiya define beauty for themselves? How is your experience different from Faizah and Asiya's and why? How might the first day of school be different for different people around the world?

(Continued)

TABLE 4.3 (Continued)

Dimensions	Key Attributes/Guiding Questions	Nonfiction Embedded Antiracism in Praxis Topic: Water Conservation	Fiction Embedded Antiracism in Praxis Theme: Identity
Consider multiple viewpoints	**Questions for critique:** *Whose perspective is shared?* *Whose voice is included and excluded?* *How does that impact the text and the reader?* *What other opinions might exist?* *Who is valued? Who is harmed?* *What counternarratives are present or absent?* *Who creates the problems?* *Who solves the problems?*	*For elementary educators* Text: Autumn Peltier's UN speech **Critical questions** *What do we learn about Autumn in this speech?* *Why is the topic of water important to her and her community?* *Autumn mentions her ancestors and her great-aunt repeatedly during her speech. What is the significance of including them?* *How might this speech be different if given by a non-Indigenous Canadian?* *Autumn mentions living like those in a third-world (developing) country. What is the impact of this comparison?* *What do we need to know to better understand the water stories of people in developing countries?* *Autumn mentions the water crisis in Flint, Michigan, a couple of times during her speech. What is the impact of adding their water crisis to her speech?* *What perspective is missing that you would like to learn more about?*	*For elementary educators* Text: *Yusuf Azeem is Not a Hero* by Saadia Faruqi **Critical questions** *Uncle Rahman says, "History informs our present and affects our future."* *What is the Azeem's history?* *What do others think and believe about the family based on history?* *How is this history complicated based on power and privilege in the United States?* *What is truth when we are analyzing personal and societal viewpoints?* *In this novel, how is Texas presented to epitomize America?* *Can you connect this representation to your reality?* *As a representation of America, what do we learn about Texans' view of who belongs and who does not?* *What complicates their beliefs?* *How does Yusuf resist being stereotyped?* *Who joins this resistance and how does that affect Yusuf?* *What included perspective helped you better understand the novel's central problem?* *What perspective is not included in the novel that might have added to your understanding of the problem?*

Focus on the sociopolitical	**Identify and interrogate the systems presented** *How are they positioned?* *What do they reveal?* *What are the problems presented?* Analyze the presence of power and privilege ◆ Through characters ◆ Through language ◆ What is communicated? Recognize, connect and dissect the problem *How does this connect to your life?* *How is it connected to a societal issue?* *What is it communicating about the issue?*	*For secondary educators* Texts: *Waves for Water* documentary and *Dry* by Jarrod and Neal Shusterman or *Not a Drop to Drink* by Mindy McGinnis **Critical questions** Identify the power structures/systems that keep clean water from the people who need it most. *What policies have been enacted?* *What is the impact of these structures/systems?* *Who is privileged within these structures/systems?* Waves for Water: Jon feels a responsibility to advocate on behalf of those without access to clean water. *What are our ethical responsibilities to those without natural resources?* All the main characters and the subject of the documentary are racialized White people. *How does the erasure of racialized people of the global majority affect the central message of each of these texts?*	*For secondary educators* Text: *We Are Not Free* by Traci Chee **Critical questions** Minnow and Shig's mother tells them to "gaman," which means to persevere. *In what ways are racially marginalized people existing in a constant state of persevering?* *Where is the hope in the Japantown boy's "gaman"?* *What other language throughout the text connects to power differentials?* Patriarchal societal expectations burden Yum-Yum. *What is the history of expectations placed on women in society?* *How do these expectations affect how she sees herself and how she engages in the world?* *What is the role of societal expectations in the lives of racially oppressed/marginalized people?* Stan faces myriad challenges. Analyze the role systems of oppression have on Stan's character and development. *What is the tangible and intangible evidence of his subjugation?* *In what ways are there ongoing assaults on Stan that would make him question himself?* *How are these types of assaults customary for racially marginalized people?*

(Continued)

TABLE 4.3 (Continued)

Dimensions	Key Attributes/Guiding Questions	Nonfiction Embedded Antiracism in Praxis Topic: Water Conservation	Fiction Embedded Antiracism in Praxis Theme: Identity
Taking action	Questions to consider: Is there an injustice presented? ◆ What is the desired change? ◆ How can you or your community participate in bringing about change? ◆ How has the language of the text promoted action or inaction?	*For early childhood educators* Create a class photo essay to educate family, friends and your community about clean water. *For elementary educators* Research places in the United States without access to clean water. Determine the best method of action to help bring awareness to the issue and the people. *For secondary educators* Research what clean water access policies exist. Read about the policies and the advocates lobbying for change. Interview them to find out how youth can help bring change.	*For early childhood educators* Teach your caregivers about the beauty of hijabs. *For elementary educators* Yusuf does not hide in the face of stereotyping and discrimination because he is Muslim American. What does it mean to support a people group that is negatively perceived? Create a class action guide for allyship. *For secondary educators* Invite community members or others into your classroom to learn more about the history of Japanese concentration camps.

and their larger meanings. When equipping students to read critically, there are some common practices of educators. They include (1) crafting lessons that reflect and build on students' lived experiences, (2) incorporating one or more of the critical literacy dimensions, (3) thoughtfully selecting varied texts and (4) having rich discussions and analysis that become increasingly more nuanced and complex with time and practice (Mulcahy, 2018).

Often, as educators, we feel constricted by curriculum when the truth is we can enact antiracist pedagogy within most curricula. We simply need to understand that our job is not to merely consume curriculum but to negotiate and navigate our curriculums in the best interests of students, "the point is not to teach a certain novel or a set of facts about literature, but to engage students in a dialogue, to teach them to find connections between their lives, literature, and society" (Christensen, 1992).

Everyday practices

It will come as no surprise to you that educators make between 1,300 and 1,500 decisions a day, and according to research, this is more than brain surgeons make on a minute-by-minute basis. Teaching ain't easy that's for sure. A lot of the things we have examined in this text thus far happen before we prep, plan, instruct and assess students. And rightfully so, unearthing the roots of our beliefs, interrogating our stories, setting a standard and culture of antiracism and understanding the historical legacy of literacy is the necessary prework before the classwork. With that prework underway, it's time to tackle the everyday practices we must make as antiracist ELA educators.

Listening
Listening to students is as important as the books we select and the things we write. **Actively listening to what our students are communicating through their words, intonations, facial expressions, gestures and other actions will give us ideas about what we can do for students, relationally and instructionally.** Listening is an opportunity to honor students' voices and build trust.

After listening to students, we should be asking ourselves the following:

- ◆ What are students talking about amongst themselves?
  - ○ What is their preferred language when communicating with peers?
- ◆ What are students communicating they need and/or want?
  - ○ How are they communicating this?
  - ○ How can I plan instruction and create an environment based on the knowledge gained through listening?
- ◆ What literacies (e.g., cultural, digital, informational, media, etc.) are important to students?
  - ○ Which literacies are students responding to and interacting with regularly?
- ◆ What language (words and expressions) are students using to talk about race and racism?
  - ○ What are students' reactions to local, national or global instances of oppression and racism?
- ◆ Who is disengaged and/or communicating verbally or otherwise that they need additional help?

From the teacher's desk

Nora F., an activist and high school ELA educator, advises her colleagues to listen more than talk.

> I listen. I try to listen more than I talk. And my students share all sorts of things that I would not have known. I was just coaching a teacher who'll be teaching American literature for the first time and I'm mentoring someone who's coming into the profession for the first year this year, and my advice to both of them was the same: My number one piece of advice is to always listen more than you talk, especially when handling sensitive topics, and ask questions, ask follow-up questions and don't feel compelled to always have the answers.

Related instructional practices (see glossary of instructional practices for more details):

- Conduct an empathy interview
- Organize listening circles
- Bring improvisation into the classroom

Localizing

We should also be attentive and acutely aware of what is happening in our school, the community and society at large. Being observant, racially aware educators will help us to consider the structural and societal forces students may encounter when they are not in our presence and their impact. Learning is not just happening in our classrooms. **Students are reading their world and bringing that comprehension into our literary classrooms.** To ignore the communities to which our students belong and are engaging in daily is malpractice.

We should be asking ourselves:

- How am I connected to and partnering with the community to which students belong?
  - Community organizations? School community? Parents/caregivers?
  - What is my understanding of the implication of local laws, practices, policies and values on students?
  - How am I bringing that awareness and understanding back into the classroom?
- Who from the community do I need to speak with to better understand my students' lives outside of the classroom?
  - How am I creating space to authentically discuss and write about their lives through various lenses?
- What is my awareness of how societal events, ideologies, structures, etc. impact students' view of themselves and/or the world?
  - How am I using my awareness to build solidarity among students and to inform my interactions with students as well as my instruction?

From the teacher's desk

Rachel B., a high school language and literacy educator and policy advocate, believes in keenly listening to what students are saying, how they are responding in class and what questions they are asking and connecting that back to their realities defines an antiracist ELA educator.

> *It has been looking at what my own definition of being antiracist is and realizing that sometimes that's really what my students need, and sometimes it's not and I need to pay attention to how they're responding. Thinking about the way that White supremacy has impacted every corner of our globe and the ways in which different ethnic, racial, linguistic, cultural, geographical groups have been experiencing White supremacy, and then interacting with other groups over time in the city of Chicago and in our building.*

Felicia H., an award-winning high school English educator, is a member of the local historical society to better connect to the community and bring that learning into the classroom.

> *We talk about our high school in my class, and what students observe here. We've compared our school to the school-to-prison pipeline, and we watched a few videos about what that means and how it was happening in schools across the country. Just this week, we looked at our school profile. We looked at suspension rates and who's represented in those suspensions. We looked at the school's performance on the SAT and another fitness performance matrix. We compared our disabilities statistics and so much more. Overall, I want to provide a space that is not everything that they've had for the last three years of English.*

Related instructional practices:

- ◆ Local field trips and invite community speakers into the classroom
- ◆ Cogenerative dialogues
- ◆ Student Study (see Chapter 5)
- ◆ Classroom community meetings

Learning

Everyone is a self-proclaimed expert—when the truth is everyone and no one is an expert these days. In my immediate family, there are a few know-it-alls. I won't name names, especially since by virtue of being a know-it-all, they already know who I am talking about. Before you can get a good word in, they have told you everything you should have known about the topic. And while this may make them feel good in the moment, those with expertise and deep knowledge are often not the ones jumping in to finish your sentence or correct you. They are instead learning with you and processing information with a beginner's mind, aka Shoshin. Shoshin is a Zen Buddhist concept meaning to approach everything with an open mind free of preconceptions. As antiracist ELA educators, we will need to be able to pivot as people, language and ideas evolve, and adopting a beginner's mind is key because this learning is ongoing. We can begin to practice this approach as we learn to deepen our understanding of race/racism. This learning is perpetual. Antiracist educators are constantly evolving their understanding of race and racism.

As we build our racial literacy through "noticing, analyzing, and proactively engaging with race themes" (Rolón-Dow et al., 2020) and structures affecting racialized people of the global majority, we gain the skills necessary to recognize how racism functions and thrives in our schools, curriculums, classrooms, policies and instruction. As we discussed in Chapter 3, racial literacy is key to building authentic critical care with and for students. It "requires us to rethink race as an instrument of social, geographic, and economic control of both whites and blacks. Racial literacy offers a more dynamic framework for understanding American racism" (Guinier, 2004), so we can craft informed, honest and meaningful learning opportunities with and for students.

Some of the skills inherent to lifelong racial literacy include the ability to

◆ engage in and navigate conversations about race/racism
◆ listen and gain an appreciation of varying racial experiences, perspectives and insights
◆ recognize how to ask questions
◆ develop a critical lens

The utilization of these skills leads to transformative teaching and learning. **Racially literate educators are not only more knowledgeable but also fully cognizant of how racialized students of the global majority are impacted by race/racism in school and their own positionality therein.** They are mindful of how and what they are presenting to students so as not to cause curricular harm and violence. They recognize that the educational system has been a major instigator of structural racism in the lives of historically oppressed racialized students of the majority, and they must be agitators.

As K–12 educators, we don't teach critical race theory (CRT), but as antiracist educators, we must know and understand the tenets of CRT and its theoretical frame to deepen our understanding of White supremacy and systemic racism in the United States, past and present. I am aware the mere mention of this may make you a bit uncomfortable, especially if you live in a state that is politicizing it. The fight against CRT is less about education than it is a political reaction to people, especially young people, across the U.S., exercising their voice and power to demand change in response to the murder of George Floyd and the hosts of injustices his murder and the litany of prior and subsequent murders revealed. Young people—some not even old enough to read the signs they carried—mobilized to change the status quo. Power and progress are always followed by resistance. CRT backlash is an attempt to erode progress.

To be clear, I am not asking you to teach CRT in your classroom. However, to be an antiracist educator is to understand how the discourse of race and racism enters and is examined in the public dialogue. It is also to understand how CRT applies to education.

From the teacher's desk

Jennifer S., a former middle school educator and currently an assistant professor of elementary education, discusses the current sentiment around CRT and its place in the antiracist ELA classroom.

Critical race theory is under the microscope currently in our country and we need to examine why. What about critical race theory is frightening and for whom? Teaching is a political act and it always has been, but few want to admit it. What you teach, how you teach it, whom you teach it to, and the methods that you use are all political tools as is your philosophy of teaching. Education has been a tool to maintain Whiteness in our country since the beginning of public education. Critical race theory is becoming a more popular tool in social justice educator circles to dismantle generational White supremacy. Critical race theory is so powerful that a handful of states have already forbidden teachers in their public schools to utilize this lens. What does one gain by continuing to perpetuate a zero-sum game?

The most important instructional shift toward antiracist pedagogy is for educators to start learning about and then applying critical race theory, including, but not limited to, the intentional use of counter-storytelling particularly related to our country's history.

Each of the tenets has an application in the American educational system and thus our classrooms.

◆ The education system is inherently racist because racism is endemic to all American systems.
◆ White epistemologies and curricula are privileged, claimed and owned in schools excluding other forms of knowledge.
◆ Curricular inclusions of diverse texts are essential to complicate and challenge master narratives.
◆ Standardized testing values and esteem the dominant group.
◆ Racialized students of the global majority are defined, categorized and labeled as underperforming in spite of the inherent inequity in the educational system and their bodies and beings are policed through school policies and practices.

From the teacher's desk

Anita B., an award-winning high school ELA educator, believes that when we don't exercise the skills of racial literacy and understand power and privilege, we are furthering White supremacy.

When we don't go to a place of antiracism which is a step further than culturally responsive—a step further than social, emotional learning, when we don't isolate race when we don't look at the impact and the unique lived experience and don't do our work to understand how the limitations and barriers of our lived experience manifest in power, we are stopping short of the real issue which is that this system is steeped in White supremacy. And how do you undo that? You have to decenter Whiteness and that's really scary to say, but it's even harder to do. And the discomfort that follows is even more jarring… To be a teacher is to hold a position of power, and people like to say that it's not or not understand or put that at the center of the conversation. We have power over the trajectory of people's lives. How we see them is how they in turn tend to see themselves and then the world, so not going to that place of antiracism doesn't undo anything. It just fosters a fallacy.

Related instructional practices:

- ◆ Autobiographical storytelling
- ◆ Add racial awareness to your lesson planning
  - ○ Problematize racism in the real world
  - ○ Provide opportunities for lateral and divergent thinking
- ◆ Develop discussion and inquiry prompts based on the tenets
  - ○ Engage in Power Analysis

Lobbying

Sometimes as educators, we relegate our roles as practitioners and our pedagogy to the four walls of our classrooms. How many times have you said or heard: "I'm going to close my door and do what I need to do?" While I understand the sentiment and have used the phrase myself in the past, antiracist educators do not have the luxury of closing their doors and simply teaching. **The how of antiracist teaching and learning exists inside and outside of our classrooms. If racism is ultimately about power, then we must consider who wields the power in our schools. Who makes the decisions? Whose voices are esteemed?** As anitiracist educators, we must be lobbying for change to power structures, and teaching our students to do the same.

In 2021, the National Association of Realtors spent over $44 million lobbying the government for improved access to home-ownership, fair housing regulations, community development and vitalization efforts and more. Lobbying is a successful means of advocacy. Real estate agents understood they could not just close the door and sell houses. They needed to utilize their collective power and agency to address the multiple and varied issues impacting their ability to do their jobs successfully. The same is true for educators. As we listen, localize and learn, we are gaining valuable insights that can help us challenge and change the system. This will also take a collective, concerted effort, and it does not matter where or whom you teach.

This may mean engaging in advocacy to reform the high rates and more harsh discipline for racialized boys of the global majority considering how these decisions are made. It may mean assembling a group of your colleagues, parents/caregivers and students to review the student handbook or code of conduct for language and policies that dehumanize or disenfranchise historically oppressed racialized students. This could be lobbying your school system to create antiracist professional learning communities. It could mean advocating for students to join curriculum committees or have a seat on the school board. Lobbying is the work of advocacy and action to contest the deficits and disadvantages power structures create. It is the brick-by-brick work of dismantling and rebuilding the system with students because nothing is for them without them.

From the teacher's desk

Jessica K., a 5th-grade literacy educator, instructional coach and policy advocate, poses some questions for us to consider about how our instruction highlights students' power to be lobbiers for change.

It's our personal responsibility to have an ever-growing understanding of systems and then to teach that to our students. I think a lot of it is personal learning, and what learning we're taking on, and how we are sharing that journey with our students and being upfront with the things that we thought before and have shifted because of our own learning growth. We have to ask ourselves: What is happening in my classroom space? What skills do I ultimately want students to lead with—beyond, can you read the book? I mean, obviously, you want them to do that, too, but that's just the start. When they leave you, I mean, after the school year, do students understand systems and the world and mechanisms of resistance as well as oppression in more complicated ways? I think about Hasan Jeffries [historian, educator and host of the Teaching Hard History *podcast], and what he told me when I was doing a National Endowment for the Humanities program with him which was* **always lead with resistance.** *Are you? Are you teaching students first and foremost, the mechanisms of social change and transformation? Are you asking students: How do you think we got here? Are you positioning them to be problem solvers? They will end up figuring out we got here because people organized because communities organized and because young people got involved. That's really important and powerful, too.*

Lisa T. connects this idea of lobbying back to the foundational work of her high school English classroom (and our ELA classrooms) and the history of the subject itself.

When you look at an English language classroom, you're looking at the power of language, but you're reading texts, and things that were meant to do something—books are political. They were written in a context, and they're written for a purpose. So if you're teaching students that, I don't think you can or should keep it as an academic exercise. We're not here to pick apart pretty language and admire it on a wall. We're here to look at that, admire that piece of it, but then think about what did it [the book and its message] do? What is it still doing? And what can we then do? The other piece I want my students to leave with is a sense that they have power to wield language and they have power to speak, whether it is a personal thing that they want to highlight or whether it is related to what we're reading. If it is Beloved, *and we're picking apart Morrison's language and the beauty of what she's saying, we're also needing to look at the fact that what she is speaking about is not done. She wanted this book to be this monument to slavery, and we still don't have one. The work is not done. This is not something that we can look at and say this happened, we're done with it. How can we take that text and give it meaning now and do something because of it? Books change you. Words change you. The only response to me is action in some way.*

Related instructional practices:

◆ Student-led professional development

- ◆ Organize a *Talk that Walks* Space
  - ○ A weekly space for students to surface ideas, concerns and generate actions to address each
- ◆ Equity pause

TEACHER LESSON IN SESSION

Briana M., East St. Louis Illinois

Briana is a fierce student and policy advocate as well as a nationally recognized, award-winning 11th–12th English teacher at an alternative public school. During her interview, I was struck by her passion and focus on disrupting racialized language and writing instruction and her wondering, *"What does it look like to teach, effectively, a language and a course that is steeped in racism itself, not just the language but also the literature?"*

HOW DOES WHITE SUPREMACY SHOW UP IN OUR CLASSROOM? WHAT DOES THAT LOOK LIKE?

I'm in a unique position in that I am a non-Black educator of color in [an] all-Black district. All of my administration is Black and 100% of my students are Black. Obviously, I am not Black, and so I think there's a very clear distinction between being a person of color and identifying as like a Black educator. And so yes, there's privilege that comes from being a non-Black person of color teaching English. I have the privilege, even though English is not my first language—my first language is Spanish, of being taught what would be called proper Standard American English. That's what we're expected to impose upon our students. For Black students, we also need to come to the understanding that Standard American English is not Black student's first language either. African American English is a legitimate dialect that has its own grammar rules and structure. It's culturally destructive to teach our students that their language is broken or incomplete. A lot of students absorb these ideas about their language or the way that they speak, not realizing that it's a commodity for society. We profit off of Black language. People make their livelihoods and base their personas off of Black culture and Black language all the time. Yet, in schools, we're teaching students "don't talk like that, or there's a time and a place to talk like that." I'm very much against code-switching as a means of telling students there's a better or a worse way of communicating, especially in English. It's very popular to tell students, specifically White educators, that "this is just more proper" or "this is the more academic way that we can communicate our ideas." What you're actually telling students in those moments about code-switching for academic purposes is that what they are doing is not White adjacent enough, and students need to change themselves in such a way to either be better understood or to have their ideas legitimatized.

I have conversations with the kids about what code-switching means to them: *How does it feel to be told there are certain places are spaces where they need to change who they are to be accepted?* And that's also a very hard concept for my students, specifically, to understand because East St. Louis is such a different place than the rest of the world. They're surrounded by people who look like and talk like them and who are comfortable with their identity unlike other places of the world, which actually does have diversity and is not a homogenous community, and not everyone is Black not everyone speaks the same dialect. They don't know what it's like for someone to tell them that they don't understand what they're trying to say or it's not legitimate. I'm having conversations and unpacking those feelings because we are about to send them off into different places outside of St. Louis where they are going to have to confront these things. And, also, I'm providing them with the language to be able to talk about those things. I think it's so important in these conversations. When we have these larger conversations that should have appropriate depth, we need to tell students how to communicate what they're feelings are and call these things out—it is White language supremacy that we're talking about, code switching is in subjugation of your true self. And ask them: *How does it feel for someone to be able to tell you what's the right choice to make?* I think people think that young children don't have the depth to be able to have these conversations, but oftentimes, it's that they don't have the vocabulary to talk about what they're feeling or what they're seeing. It's important to arm them because when the kids understand what's going on, they can speak more fully about their experience.

HOW DOES YOUR UNDERSTANDING OF STUDENTS' LANGUAGE IDENTITIES TRANSLATE INTO WRITING INSTRUCTION (ESPECIALLY GRAMMAR)?

Grammar, specifically, with Black students is oftentimes the way they're policed. Teachers make kids rewrite the same thing a million times because they "don't understand what they're trying to say," when they actually do. They just want students to write it in the White way. I do a lot of creative writing with my students. We do a trauma-informed writing workshop where students produce poetry of witness to take back their power over their own traumatic life experiences. It was important to accept their writing as whole. Kids already have a hard enough time producing writing that they feel proud of, and grammar, punctuation and writing structures are sometimes the first thing teachers use to say kids' writing is incomplete or that it's broken, and that's what needs to be worked on. There are so many other ways to approach kids' writing to make it more full, to help kids to more easily communicate what they're actually feeling and the purpose of their piece instead of just focusing on the spelling of their words and things like that. In my practice, I'm accepting students' writing because I understand what they're trying to say. When they're sharing with each other, they understand what they're trying to say. It takes away part of the community, especially in poetry, if you're having kids try to write in a certain way. It automatically takes away a group understanding because the teacher is asking students to write in a way that's not familiar or is not native to them.

I've seen very culturally destructive practices in English classrooms from teachers who are trying to model college prep classrooms. I've seen little tombstone posters in classrooms for dead words (words like *finna*). The words students will say but that teachers don't want in their writing anymore. Imagine being a student—this is what you know, and that's how you communicate best what you're thinking, what you're feeling, what you're seeing, and you see that word on a tombstone poster in your teacher's classroom. Teachers can automatically shut kids down with things like that. It's not conducive to a positive learning environment, and it's not conducive to showing students they can be their whole selves and can be brilliant as they are instead of how we want them to be.

SO YOU OBVIOUSLY TALK ABOUT WHITE SUPREMACY IN YOUR CLASSROOM. DO YOU TALK ABOUT SYSTEMS OF OPPRESSION? DO YOU SEEK FOR STUDENTS TO TAKE ACTION IN YOUR COURSE?

It's very important to talk about oppression with students within their own communities. I don't teach White students, and I don't teach non-Black students, so I think these conversations look very different and they look very nuanced in other communities. But I think something that I've been very up front and honest with my students about as a Hispanic person is about the anti-Blackness that I see in the Mexican community, specifically. I share stories about my dad and things growing up I've heard him say about Black people or that Mexican people cannot be Black—these culturally, destructive narratives. And it opens, the door for students, now that I've shown them an example to be intimately aware of what anti-Blackness looks like from Miss M's own experience that I now have an understanding of the definition of anti-Blackness. And they can ask themselves: *Have I seen anti-Blackness or oppression by other people of color in my own community?* I think it's false to tell students that it is only one group of people who can oppress us as people of color because we know that's not true. We work with people who are trying to change our students into something that they're not, and they are people of color. And so we talk about what colorism looks like? What do microaggressions in my community look like? A really good resource that my kids have loved over the years is spoken word poetry by Ebony Stewart. She recently released a chat book of her poems called *Home.Girl.Hood.* She talks about being the dark-skinned girlfriend in her friend group and what it looks like to have a group of friends who are White or friends who are lighter than you and to have pain that they truly can't understand. I have dark-skinned students. I have boys who fetishize light-skinned students. We have those conversations about how those types of things are problematic and how those are in service of these larger narratives of you're not White adjacent enough. Having those conversations and building them into the literacy classroom, I think is an easy segue because we talk about a lot of these bigger topics in English. There are so many amazing poets, so many amazing artists, so many amazing authors who have done some of this work that allow us to open the door for our students to have those conversations. And then obviously, writing is a space for kids to channel their thoughts and their feelings about those things, so we do those things in my classroom.

> **COMPREHENSION CHECK**
> ◆ How does Briana's writing instruction reflect an understanding of the racial and linguistic identities of her students?
> ◆ How are you challenged by her words and/or instructional ideology?
> ◆ How is Briana equipping her students with the language and emotional capital needed to contest racism?

Lisa T., a high school English teacher and policy advocate, shared that how we teach, especially writing, and the dialogue of a text is quite White-centric.

English for a lot of my students is their second language, so I start off all of my classes with a really explicit look at language, when we use language and how we use it in different contexts.

◆ How have you engaged in White language supremacy?
  ○ What do you need to learn and/or unlearn?

Make the SHIFT

Teaching is a high-demand and high-stress profession. Presently, we are working to reengage and socialize students and families who lived through a global pandemic and its resulting, and potentially ongoing, trauma. This is evidenced by a 2022 Stanford University study that found the stress and ongoing trauma of surviving a global pandemic have led to "poorer mental health and accelerated brain aging [by 3–4 years]" in adolescents (Gotlib et al., 2022). Additionally, a lot of us are teaching students who have lost critical instruction and are in need of a multitiered system of support. We are doing this while, also, learning and practicing how to keep students and ourselves physically safe within our school walls. We are doing this while having said goodbye to colleagues and friends who have chosen to leave the profession or whose level of stress is so debilitating that they are taking a break from teaching to heal. And we are doing this while being inundated with frequent media reports of a mass teacher exodus and

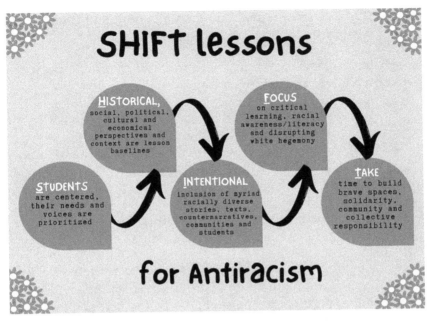

FIGURE 4.1 This graphic outlines the lesson principles necessary to SHIFT to antiracist instruction.

looming teacher shortage. We have a lot on our plates. In times of barely keeping our heads above water, we don't need someone to toss us a manual on how to swim. We don't even need swimming lessons—we need help staying afloat. We need someone to jump in and show us we can breathe while underwater.

I am not going to throw you a manual. Many of us have lesson plans we are required to enact or a lesson plan format we are required to follow. As my mother would say, we should not cut off our nose to spite our face. In most instances, we can salvage the lesson plans we have. We just need to SHIFT those lessons, rethinking and revising them. Figure 4.1 outlines what it means to SHIFT our lessons for antiracism.

Here is a more detailed look at the acronym SHIFT and what we are hoping to accomplish by shifting our lessons:

S—Students are centered, their needs and voices are prioritized

- ◆ Students act as co-creators and collaborators
- ◆ The classroom is democratized eliminating power structures

◆ Students (and educators) gain awareness of their social positions, identities and biases

H—Historical, social, political, cultural and economic perspectives and context are lesson baselines

◆ Texts, discussions and skills are relevant to students' lives, the world and offer salient solutions to racial oppression
◆ Historical truths and knowledge are foundational
◆ Educators are constantly growing their own historical, political, social, cultural and economic knowledge

I—Intentional inclusion of myriad racially diverse stories, texts, counternarratives, communities and students

◆ Meaningfully include voices and perspectives from racially oppressed people groups (in-text and in-person)
◆ Voices and perspectives challenge the status quo, racial inferiority, stereotyping, tokenizing and victimization

F—Focus on critical learning, racial awareness/literacy and disrupting White hegemony

◆ Acknowledge, analyze and challenge language, meaning and the causes and enduring impact of power, systemic racism and Whiteness (assessing of and for antiracist learning)
◆ Create opportunities to build agency, resistance and action
◆ Reimagine power, privilege and freedom for an antiracist future

T—Take time to build brave spaces, solidarity, community and collective responsibility

◆ Shared understanding and language for antiracism

Just as we have shifted our mindset, we must also shift our lessons. This serves many purposes. First, it disrupts White epistemologies. As educators, it is important to recognize that education operates and rewards White ways of knowing and being. The privileging of "the classics" (whose classics—I might ask) and the adoration of the written word are White constructs that inform power, hegemony and the epistemology of our classrooms, and, yes, all of **our** classrooms. Remember, our default operating system is one of White dominance until we program it otherwise. An antiracist pedagogical shift challenges White epistemology by questioning who creates, accesses and legitimizes knowledge (Harsma et al., 2021) and provides opportunities for knowledge to be gained and expressed in myriad ways. It also upends curricular violence and apathy. Within curricula, the devaluing and dehumanization of historically oppressed racialized people and the erasure of their context, perspectives and voices in classroom texts and discourse is an act of violence and control that furthers racial oppression and inequity and has lasting effects on students. One of the shifts we can make is to always offer counternarratives that "talk back" to narrow constructs of knowledge that foster and maintain White supremacy in schools (hooks, 1989). Ultimately, shifting our existing lessons frees us to reenvision with students how an antiracist future is purposed, potentialed and applied on a daily basis.

While surveying educators about their antiracist needs, many mentioned their struggle and desire to understand how to apply antiracist pedagogy to writing instruction, so I have purposefully featured a writing lesson (Figure 4.2) in this chapter. It is my hope that the SHIFT made to this lesson serves as a model for your own lesson transformations. As we fortify our antiracist knowledge and utilize SHIFT, it will become easier for us to adapt our mindset and instructional approach. The lesson in Figure 4.2 typifies a 1st-grade narrative writing lesson. I have used the SHIFT acronym to revise and enhance the lesson. It is annotated, so you can see the changes made and the application of the antiracist pedagogical *practices* of SHIFT.

Let's briefly examine the why behind the instructional shifts applied to this lesson. Before getting into the lesson SHIFT, one of the first things I do when given an existing lesson to teach is to build my own knowledge base finding where areas of White epistemologies, race/racism, power, privilege, freedom and joy are present or absent and what I need to learn and unlearn. When looking over this lesson, I found I needed to learn more about how narrative writing can be a source of power for students. Using the learning gained from *The Antiracist Writing Workshop* by Felicia Chavez, I knew I wanted to disrupt the notion of

Grade: 1st grade
Unit Focus: Narrative Writing
Mentor Texts: *Fireflies* by Julie Brinckloe & *Roller Coaster* by Marla Frazee

Common Core Standard: W.1.3
Lesson: Writing Small Moments

Formative Assessment	Summative Assessment
Writing notebook/portfolio	Published pieces
Questioning & discussions	

Essential questions: *How important are the small moments of our lives? What's the value of exploring those small moments in writing?*

Students will understand:
• Narrative writing has many forms.
• A small moment in your life can become a full story by elaborating and adding details.
• Writers carefully select and add details to their writing to express feelings and paint a picture for the reader.

Instructional Plan
1. Ask students to recount something that happened yesterday in class. Probe for more details.
2. Ask students to pair share what they believe a small moment is. Ask pairs to share their responses.
3. Record student responses on "Small moments" chart paper.
   a. Provide a working definition of small moments.
4. Read one of the mentor texts to students
5. Ask students to pair share again and redefine small moments explaining their connection to the text.
6. Add brainstorming definitions and moments from the mentor text to the chart paper.
7. Discuss the importance of details in narrative writing especially for bringing a small moment to life.
   a. Go back through the mentor text and search for the details. Think aloud for students highlighting where details appear and where they don't appear in the text.
8. Return to the event that happened in class yesterday.
   a. Ask student pairs to brainstorm details around that event.
   b. As practice, students write small using the classroom example.

Annotations:

1. SHIFT (I): Add *My Papi has a Motorcycle* by Isabel Quintero, *Jabari Jumps* by Gaia Cornwall and *When Lola Visits* by Michelle Sterling

2. SHIFT (S & T): Formative Conferencing small & individual groups, daily check-ins, sharing every day (aloud). Summative: Read aloud for audience. Write a foreword that tells why the story and perspective matter.

3. SHIFT (F): Add *Why is my story important to tell? What makes my voice unique?*

4. SHIFT (S): Ask students to contribute to this list (their wants and needs)

SHIFT by adding or replacing
- Share why writing is an exercise of freedom five examples (H) 5
- Discuss the power of story to define self (S) 6
- Meet the mentor authors (I & T) 7
  ○ Discuss authors and the importance of their story, voice and points of view as racialized people of the global majority
- In pairs, students create their own mini charts, read mentor texts and craft a definition of small moments and list of its characteristics. (S & T) 8
- Use student mini charts and findings to lead a guided study of language in the mentor texts (T) 9
- Students write collaboratively with provided opportunities for experimentation and innovation time and space to play with language (moving away from white normative writing and conventions) (S & F & T) 10

FIGURE 4.2 Typical 1st-grade narrative writing lesson annotated to incorporate SHIFT principles.

writing as isolationist or as an individualistic endeavor (a White epistemological construct) and instead lean into a collaborative, communal writing experience with constant opportunities for oral sharing and student ownership of their learning.

Narrative writing SHIFT:
SHIFT 1—Intentional inclusion of myriad racially diverse stories, texts, counternarratives, communities and students

- ◆ The addition of three mentor texts better reflects the identities and experiences of racialized students of the global majority
  - ○ Check the language and imagery of each text for accurate and authentic representation

SHIFT 2—Students are centered, their needs and voices are prioritized and take time to build brave spaces, solidarity, community and collective responsibility

- ◆ Revision of formative and summative assessments aligns to the goal of communal creation and sharing
  - ○ Connects writing and oral storytelling (privileges oral storytelling as an important mode of expression)
  - ○ Offers daily opportunities for students' agency through sharing and learning from one another

SHIFT 3—Focus on critical learning, racial awareness/literacy and disrupting White hegemony

- ◆ Additional essential question enables students to explore their own power and social agency with the goal of understanding how their voice adds to and/or challenges notions of storytelling

SHIFT 4—Students are centered, their needs and voices are prioritized

- ◆ Personalizes the learning experience for students by adding what is important for them to know to the list of enduring understandings

SHIFT 5—Historical, social, political, cultural and economic perspectives and context are lesson baselines

◆ Adding the discussion of writing and storytelling as practices of freedom connects them to a historical legacy of power and provides and opportunity to connect writing/storytelling to the past and/or present

SHIFT 6—Students are centered, their needs and voices are prioritized

◆ The exploration of identity and social positions and how they impact writing serves to affirm, celebrate and demystify difference and seeks to communicate "The myth of the race neutral writing classroom is largely informed by the colorblindness logic, a byproduct of meritocracy" (Pimentel et al., 2016)

SHIFT 7—Intentional inclusion of myriad racially diverse stories, texts, counternarratives, communities and students and focus on critical learning, racial awareness/literacy and disrupting White hegemony

◆ The use of racially representative texts to "challenge the hegemony of what counts as English language and English education" (Baker-Bell, 2020)

SHIFT 8—Students are centered, their needs and voices are prioritized and take time to build brave spaces, solidarity, community and collective responsibility

◆ Working collaboratively, students lead their learning through inquiry and choice

SHIFT 9—Focus on critical learning, racial awareness/literacy and disrupting White hegemony

◆ Comparing, questioning and critiquing language for critical literacy (disrupting the commonplace) and "to affirm students' linguistic identities, to aid comprehension of meaningful texts, to encourage collaborative inquiry with peers, or to illuminate linguistic inequities" (Brown McClain et al., 2021)

SHIFT 10—Students are centered, their needs and voices are prioritized and focus on critical learning, racial awareness/literacy and disrupting White hegemony and take time to build brave spaces, solidarity, community and collective responsibility

◆ Provides a democratized classroom environment for students with communal responsibility and the freedom to experiment with language and their voice

Pitstop

If we were in a classroom, this would be the perfect place to stop and make time and space to process the learning. I cannot help but do the same here. If you are like me, you are probably ready to SHIFT everything. I want to remind you that this is a journey, not a race. It is important that we remember antiracist teaching is larger than an acronym. It is not found in a prepackaged program or curriculum; it is a standard—principles, a mindset. When we shift our mindset and gain racial awareness and literacy, our lessons will naturally become aligned with our evolving consciousness. My hope is that you outgrow SHIFT and that your antiracist ELA lessons are responsive to and meet the need of your students.

◆ What is your understanding of how to SHIFT your lessons?
◆ What are the elements that most resonate with you? What challenges you?

The *Gatsby* effect

In almost every interview with high school English teachers and students, there was mention of *The Great Gatsby*. It often entered the dialogue as an example of a curricula relic and canonical demigod that empowers Whiteness as empirical and infinite. As a representation of the American Dream, teachers and students alike felt the deification the novel communicates and validates the American ideal as White, male and upper-class limiting the exploration of other voices and experiences and creating an illusion of a single, unified American narrative. In addition to offering critiques of the text, its characters, theme and relevancy, the text seemed to be a flashpoint for students and teachers on the current state of ELA and its ambivalence and ignorance in selecting texts, themes, assignments and assessments that are responsive to student's needs and desires. Their concerns speak directly to the enduring power of White racialized stories and authors in curricula that exist without reprove for their erasure and devaluing of racialized people of the global majority. A lesson SHIFT for *The Great Gatsby* was then compulsory, although I suggest replacing the text if that is within your power because the addition of young adult literature around a canonical text centers and presumes it as the "end goal for readers" and stops "short of actually disrupting the notion of the canon itself" (Toliver & Hadley, 2021).

The lesson in Figure 4.3 is one you may find in a 10th–11th-grade American literature class.

The American Dream is such an iconic and fraught concept. It will require a different framing and language to move students beyond its dominant narrative and get students questioning the concept and its validity for them and future generations. When approaching this lesson, it is important for us to focus, first, on our own unlearning and how we are expanding, contesting and reconstructing knowledge through the various texts. One small change I have made that has had a big impact on student learning and how they engage in a unit is being extremely selective and deeply considerate of the text that will start the lesson: *What does it say? Who does it speak to? How does it challenge students and create opportunities for new perspectives?* This initial framing of the unit will set the tone for the type of learning you want students to engage in throughout.

Unit Focus: The American Dream — Grade: 10-11th grade

In this lesson, students will examine the concept of "The American Dream" through various perspectives and define the concept for themselves.

Common Core Standards: RL 11-12.1-7

Anchor Text:	Supplemental Texts:
The Great Gatsby by F. Scott Fitzgerald	The American Dream: A Short History of an Idea That Shaped a Nation by Jim Cullen American Dream and Economy 2008 Speech by Barak Obama The Young F. Scott Fitzgerald a PBS Documentary

Formative Assessment	Summative Assessment
Annotations Small group discussions and additions to anchor chart	Create a visual display of your interpretations of "The American Dream" drawing inspiration from each of the texts. Comparative analysis essay

Essential questions: *What is the American dream, and how do people seek and achieve it? Who has access to this dream? Is this dream real and attainable for any or all Americans?*

Students will understand
- One topic can have multiple perspectives that affirm or contradict one another
- A claim can be supported through various forms of evidence

Instructional Plan

1. Brainstorm around the concept of the American Dream.
2. Introduce Jim Cullen's *The American Dream: A Short History of an Idea That Shaped a Nation* from the book.
   a. Student groups will read and analyze teacher-selected passages from the book.
   b. Debrief as a whole class and chart how the author would answer the essential questions.
   c. Create an anchor chart to track American dream ideals and to compare its key features in various texts.
3. View F. Scott Fitzgerald's PBS documentary.
   a. Discuss Fitzgerald's ideals of America and its possibilities.
   b. Discuss the who-text audience. The what- what other texts were being written around this time. What is this text in response to or in conversation with? The why- why this topic?
4. Read *The Great Gatsby*
   a. Annotate the text responding to how characters interact with and relate to one another and to their relation to society as a whole.
   b. Small group reading groups will discuss and compare the text to other texts and the symbols used in each to represent the American Dream.
   c. Add findings to a class anchor chart.
5. View President Obama's (then Senator Obama) speech on the American Dream.
   a. Reflect on the speech's theme and message.
      i. What is said and what is not said?
   b. Compare this assertions about the American Dream to those of Cullen and Fitzgerald.
6. Create a visual display of "the American Dream" that draws clear inspiration from the unit texts.
7. Small writing groups will brainstorm ideas and share evidence for the final writing assessment.
   a. Students will write a comparative analysis essay on the various textual interpretations of the American Dream.

Annotations:

1. SHIFT (P) Revision: In this lesson, students will examine role of power, privilege and meritocracy in shaping the American Dream from various perspectives.

2. SHIFT (D) Add the following texts: A Gate of a Country By Anna Quindlen, The America I Believe in by Colin Powell, Color of Fear Documentary Clip (What it Means to Be American), A Dream Deferred by Langston Hughes, American Like Me by America Ferrera, El Sueño de America by Esmeralda Santiago, Jaune Quick-to-See Smith Art piece Add it, but not without hope; student choice additions

3. SHIFT (S) Revise formative and summative assessments to include a student-led EdCafe. Multimedia presentations and written reflections

4. SHIFT (H & F) Replace with: Is the American Dream able to defined? is it an illusion? How does the dream shape and/or distort our reality? How do social and systemic oppression impact one's pursuit of the American Dream?

5. SHIFT (H & F) Add: Dominant narratives are often exclusionary and therefore incomplete

6. SHIFT by adding or replacing
   - Students will bring in an artifact (image, art, music, quotes) that connect to their dreams (S & D)
   - Teacher will share a multimedia presentation including historical artifacts of American identity and its dream. (H & D) 7
     ○ Students will write a reflection that compares their artifact to the historical artifacts.
   - Students will take the PBS American Dream Quiz and view one another. (S & P) 8
     ○ After taking quiz, students will craft questions to ask their peers to understand their results and reactions.
   - (textual) annotations will be related to social, economic and systemic power/privileges/oppressions and their impact on characters. (H & F)
   - Through the unit, students will create and led EdCafe sessions around a topic of interest connected to one of the texts (S & T) 9
   - Students will create a multimedia piece that challenges single voice narratives about the American Dream, or students can create a new concept beyond the dream for the future generation (S & F & T) 10

FIGURE 4.3 Typical 10th-grade lesson annotated to incorporate SHIFT principles.

Gatsby SHIFT:

SHIFT 1—Focus on critical learning, racial awareness/literacy and disrupting White hegemony

◆ Explicitly states the unit's objective of critical racial inquiry and analysis

SHIFT 2—Intentional inclusion of myriad racially diverse stories, texts, counternarratives, communities and students and focus on critical learning, racial awareness/literacy and disrupting White hegemony

◆ Additional texts allow for varied text types, perspectives and methods of engagement since texts have been "used to inculcate dominant ideologies as common sense" (Willis, 2008)

SHIFT 3—Students are centered, their needs and voices are prioritized

◆ The power of possession of their own ideas and voices as a means of fighting the dispossession of their bodies, minds, identities and spaces

SHIFT 4—Historical, social, political, cultural and economic perspectives and context are lesson baselines and focus on critical learning, racial awareness/literacy and disrupting White hegemony

◆ Recognizes historical erasure is also a means of erasing people, and therefore makes inquiry and a historical analysis of oppression focal

SHIFT 5—Historical, social, political, cultural and economic perspectives and context are lesson baselines and focus on critical learning, racial awareness/literacy and disrupting White hegemony

◆ Resists dominant narratives and offers entry for new and different narratives to expand knowledge and understanding that reveals oft-hidden knowledge

SHIFT 6—Students are centered, their needs and voices are prioritized & Intentional inclusion of myriad racially diverse stories, texts, counternarratives, communities and students

◆ Moves beyond student choice to students as central to the learning in the classroom—their texts create the learning and dialogue and construct the meaning of goals and dreams

SHIFT 7—Historical, social, political, cultural and economic perspectives and context are lesson baselines and intentional inclusion of myriad racially diverse stories, texts, counternarratives, communities and students

◆ Problematizes concepts for students: "A curriculum that supports critical thinking, problem-solving, communication, collaboration, and applications of knowledge to real-world problems is essential for today's society in which knowledge is expanding rapidly" (Darling-Hammond, 2017)

SHIFT 8—Students are centered, their needs and voices are prioritized and focus on critical learning, racial awareness/literacy and disrupting White hegemony

◆ Addressed students' efficacy and agency; disrupts power structures in the classroom and who has access to knowledge
◆ Provides space for peers to practice carino y confianza and validate one another's experience

SHIFT 9—Historical, social, political, cultural and economic perspectives and context are lesson baselines and focus on critical learning, racial awareness/literacy and disrupting White hegemony

◆ Engages critical conversations around race, justice and oppression

SHIFT 10—Students are centered, their needs and voices are prioritized and take time to build brave spaces, solidarity, community and collective responsibility

◆ Provides a democratized classroom environment for students with the freedom to choose their own topic of interest and lead an informative session that intersects with a concept from one of the texts

SHIFT 11—Students are centered, their needs and voices are prioritized and focus on critical learning, racial awareness/literacy and disrupting White hegemony and take time to build brave spaces, solidarity, community and collective responsibility

◆ Provides students with "the ways in which literacy can be emancipatory, a restorying that synthesizes, recontextualizes, and reimagines experience to create new narratives that reflect a diversity of perspectives" (Thomas et al., 2020)

WAYPOINT

Perhaps you have the freedom to create your own lessons and do not need to SHIFT preexisting lessons. Table 4.4 has some questions for you to consider as you create new anti-racist language and literacy lessons.

TABLE 4.4 Road map for teachers to reflect on how they can craft their own antiracist lessons through key questions

Critical Questions for Lesson Planning

◆ What have I **learned through listening, observing and direct communication** with students about their needs and/or racial awareness that is connected to this topic?

◆ How is the lesson's subject, context, theme, etc. **connected to or affected by racism** (any facet thereof)? *Hint: Racism affects everything.*
  ○ What additional knowledge do I need to understand this better?
  ○ After learning more, what is important, appropriate and applicable for inclusion in this lesson to better help my students understand race/racism, power, privilege, Whiteness, systemic oppression, resistance to racial injustice, agency to combat oppression, etc.?

◆ What **mentor texts** (any form of texts) by racialized people of the global majority would help to deepen this lesson, adding a **counternarrative or perspective?**

◆ How will this lesson **resist the status quo** (i.e., racism, inequity, White supremacy)?
  ○ Watch your language.
  ○ What is communicated and how? What is assumed? Is there evidence of biases (hidden and apparent)?
  ○ What are the normed understandings?
  ○ How? Why?
  ○ What is constrictive?
  ○ What is the rationale?

◆ How are power and/or privilege presented, addressed or ignored in the lesson? Who has it? Who does not?
  ○ How does the lesson create conditions to support students' enactment of their own power?
  ○ How will you **continually seek feedback** from students to understand their needs?
  ○ How will your assessment methods account for **an array of ways of knowing?**

THINK–ACT–REIMAGINE

Think – Act – Reimagine

Think	Act	Reimagine
What are the daily practices of an antiracist classroom? How you will SHIFT your instruction?	Rethink some of your lesson plans. Start incorporating the SHIFT principles into your lessons.	Your classroom as a brave and transformative space where students are themselves challenging the status quo.

FIGURE 4.4

DO NOW

◆ Write out your everyday practices. Do they align with listening, localizing, learning and lobbying?
◆ Select a lesson and apply the SHIFT acronym.

Resources

The Anti Racist Teacher: Reading Instruction Workbook by Lorena Germán

Coppola, R., Osorio, S., Taylor, K. & Woodard, R. (eds.) (2021) 'Antiracist Pedagogies', *Language Arts (NCTE)*, *99*(1).

Letting Go of Literary Whiteness by Carlin Borsheim-Black & Sofia Sarigianides

Literacy Is Liberation: Working Toward Justice Through Culturally Relevant Teaching by Kimberly Parker

Reading, Writing, Rising Up by Linda Christensen

Teaching for Change at www.teachingforchange.org

Section III
Climax

5

Student Impact

What are the effects of an antiracist ELA classroom on students?

It was wrapped in brown paper with a neat bow atop. It was not my birthday but a welcomed surprise to receive something just for me. I ripped the paper to reveal a book. The cover was simple, and the author's name, Toni Morrison, was as big as the title. My mother's friend told me the book was essential reading for young Black women, and she hoped I enjoyed it as my mother nodded in the background. At 16 years old, I rolled my eyes as this could certainly not compare to my mother's Harlequin romance novels I was secretly devouring. And I hoped after reading this book, I would not be expected to join their hours-long verbal treatises on any given topic. I thumbed through the pages of *The Bluest Eye*, and it seemed nothing like the aforementioned torrid novels to which I had become accustomed. I grunted a "thank you" and went to my room flinging the gift onto my desk. I mused, "Who brings an unsolicited present of a book and tells the gift recipient that all young Black women should read it?" I could not understand or appreciate the gift until years later when the book resurfaced, buried in a box of old notes along with other items of disregard. Having nothing else to read and past my romance

DOI: 10.4324/9781003296171-8

novel phase, I became engrossed in the dysfunction, pain and grief that Pecola and others endured and Morrison's prevailing message of the consequences of self-hatred. I'd never been confronted with the idea of Whiteness and Blackness so blatantly in writing. My mother's friend understood the likelihood that it would be assigned reading essential for a young Black woman in school was nil. She wanted me to hear a voice that would jar and spark a need to question the world and how I perceived and engaged in it. The gift traveled with me to college and spurred me to read any and everything Toni Morrison wrote. On so many levels, it was the gift that kept on giving: giving me the desire to read Hurston, Angelou, Walker and Baldwin, giving me the desire to discuss the pain of my ancestral past, giving me a starting point to closely examine Whiteness and its impact, giving me ideas to write and the freedom to play with words. I was, therefore, not surprised when my mother's friend had her article "Whiteness as Property" published in the *Harvard Review* years later. She'd written that into my heart long before she'd published the piece.

Alexa, tell me about Gen Alpha

Similar to my experience, young people may not always realize the profound effect literature has on them. It can be easy to discount students as social media addicts who are more enamored with living in an alternate reality than our present one. My mother's friend probably made a 1990s' era comparison to me and my addiction to music videos. Yet the truth is, students today are more informed and projected to be the best-educated generation in history. They are able to access the world in a matter of seconds which explains why they tend to lose interest if a task or assignment is longer than 15 minutes. Alexa has replaced the encyclopedia sets that adorned bookshelves and is more like a family member who has all the answers. And while the headlines lament technology and social media as disastrous to our mental and intellectual health, for example, "Is Google Making Us Stupid," this conjecture is not entirely accurate. Some research suggests the use of technology like Alexa enables our brains to focus on processing more complex tasks like problem-solving and critical thinking than on the menial information gathering Google and Alexa provide.

When I am having issues with any piece of technology in the classroom or a personal device, my students jump into action and can solve the issue faster than it would take to complete a request for tech assistance. As digital natives, this is first nature to them. While I amble around trying to click a million things to close a screen or open a program, they are screaming, "Just do this." It is the difference in the way our brains are wired. The chasm between generations is almost a tradition; the younger generation mystifies the older one and vice versa. Technology and social media are clear differences between Generation Alpha and subsequent generations, but it is not the only difference. To help bridge the generational divide, there are some interesting data points we should know about the newest generation of students we are teaching.

According to research conducted within the last 5 years ...

◆ 49% of 4th graders and 26% of 8th graders are happy at school most of the time
◆ 79.8% of high school students report feeling stressed in school
◆ 42% of 9-year-olds read for pleasure each day (disaggregated by race: 35% Black students, 41% Latine students, 50% Asian students, 48% Indigenous/Alaskan Native students and 45% Mixed-race students)
◆ 17% of 13-year-olds read for pleasure almost every day (disaggregated by race: 15% Black students, 10% Latine students, 28% Asian students, 19% Indigenous/Alaskan Native students and 23% Mixed-race students)
◆ 80% of students say they use social media every day
◆ 15–17 year-olds are engaging more in educational pursuits in the summer, spending an average of 39 minutes a day in July on homework or classwork
◆ 48% of post-millennials are non-White
◆ 77% of multilingual learners speak Spanish at home

Each generation, each child is different. These statistics are not meant to put today's students in a box or make them a statistic as is typically done, especially to racialized students of the global majority. The data points are meant to get us thinking about what we know about our current students and how the information presented corroborates or conflicts with our experiences.

COMPREHENSION CHECK

Let's take a moment to reflect:

◆ What are your initial thoughts about these data?
◆ Do these data connect to some or all of your students?
◆ How are the data different from what you know and/ or believe?
◆ What is a point that you can take and learn more about?
◆ What questions do these statistics raise for you?
◆ How can you use this data to better connect with your students?

Give them the keys

Our students are more than numbers on a page or members of a generational group. We might start there for a baseline under-standing but the best way to truly understand our students is to **see** them. For far too long, historically oppressed racial-ized students have been invisible in classrooms. This is true in schools with majority racialized students of the global majority or in schools with none. Think about it: there are few educational spaces where White perspectives are not present even in the absence of White people. For example, I taught in a school with no students who identified as Indigenous and very few students who identified as Latine or Black or Pacific Islander. I worked to ensure students heard the perspectives of people, young people particularly, from these racialized groups in other ways in the classroom, that is, published pieces, videos, collaboration with another school and so on. It is too easy for educators to render some people invisible just because they are not present in our classrooms while the reverse is unfathomable because Whiteness is the societal default. Making racialized Indigenous, Black, Latine, Pacific Islander and Mixed-race young people visible requires intentionality. The best knowledge we have as educators about students is our experiences with them and believing what they tell us and what we hear them say to others (as noted in the previous chapter). This means seeing them as individuals beyond racialized social constructs, and instead as learning collaborators and power brokers of their own destiny.

From the teacher's desk

Heather D., a high school English teacher, shares how she ensures she is not engaging in White saviorism. She wants students to know they are the leaders of their learning.

It's actually a big, big thing for me being the White teacher at a school full of minorities. I have almost this terrifying idea of ever being considered like that White savior syndrome. So letting students understand that this classroom and what we learned and what they do with it is theirs, so that what they bring to me is theirs and that they have full aspect is huge for me, because I've seen too many White suburban ladies holding up a flag and trying to take part in a movement that isn't theirs to own. And I tried to really push that I am not here to own any of their [students] education, any of their experiences, but to show them how to learn these skills to put their own experiences and education to work for them. And so, it just really bothers me when teachers want to control students. When I learned about White saviorism in college, the idea of Tarzan really stuck with me. I am not swinging in to rescue anyone because my students don't need to be saved. They just need a good education, so they can have the best lives so what they bring me is what I give them. Actually, I tell them when they say you gave me an F, no, you gave me nothing, so it always comes back to them being responsible for their education.

Nothing for students without students

Years ago, I started doing student focus groups. I provided lunch and invited some students to participate. Over lunch, I asked students questions about the class culture, their comfort level, things they'd like to see changed and advice on how to make the curriculum relevant to them. It was early into my antiracist journey, and I was realizing that by not inviting students into the conversation about the inner and outer workings of our classroom I was inadvertently communicating they did not hold power. Soon, students started inviting themselves to these focus groups. Those groups eventually evolved into students being co-teachers. Each unit, four to five students volunteered to be co-teachers and collaborators. They were responsible for helping me plan, teach and assess the learning in the unit. We would meet weekly. They took their responsibility seriously and I treated them as equals as we made decisions and they offered suggestions. We looked at the district curriculum and our learning objectives identifying the things we had to include, and then we'd get to work. We'd decide the best ways to assess the unit and how we'd share the teaching load. Their eyes would get large, and they'd be stunned that they really were going to have a say in what we were learning and doing. It was so cool to see the things they added to our units. Sometimes, it was a traditional text, and other times, it was a video game clip to add. In one unit, we incorporated various game shows into the learning. Collaborating with students was by far the best thing I tried. It rejuvenated my classroom. I was hooked and became intent on hearing from every student. I started conferencing regularly with students to ensure even those students who had no desire to co-teach with me could have their voices heard. My learning was immense, and I agree with Crystal Belle, the director of teacher education at Rutgers University–Newark, who says, "[S]eeing students requires teachers to recognize them as valuable contributors to the classroom space, as opposed to social, cultural, and academic burdens on the so-called master in the room—the teacher" (Brooks, 2021).

This step to decentralize the power in the classroom provided an opportunity for the student co-teachers to begin thinking in antiracist ways. I'd ask questions like, 'Whose voice have we not included? How should we include decisions about power and privilege in small groups about the Kurt Vonnegut short story "The Lie" and what other texts show the other side of education?' They developed a critical lens and began offering suggestions without prompting because it was the way they knew we'd approach our instructional plan. I'll remind you; 48% of the students in the building were White, 40% Asian, 5% Latine, 4% Mixed race and 3% Black. Antiracist teaching and learning can and should happen in any and all classrooms. When I shared teaching and learning power with students, I never imagined it would become a means of cultivating antiracism. It was a wonderful outgrowth.

Student collaborators

Just as I included the voices and ideas of students in our classroom, I could not write a text about students without centering their words and ideas. For this text, I interviewed several students from 7th to 12th grade to learn about their school experiences and their beliefs about antiracism in school. The student collaborators I interviewed were passionate about what they wanted to see happen in antiracist ELA classrooms. The climax of any story is the point of highest interest, the turning point. The words of the following students are the most important you will read in this book. After each student collaborator, I have included opportunities to process what you've read and consider how their words may serve as your instructional and behavioral antiracist turning point.

Note: *I edited student collaborators' interviews for brevity, and I have not changed their words except for removing the word* like, *for your sanity and mine, in* every *interview.*

Student Collaborator: Jocelyn V.

Jocelyn is a high school senior who loves science "because there's always a right answer to science and math ... unlike my least favorite subjects, English and History." Currently, she is taking EMT (emergency medical technician) courses at a local community college and will finish prior to her high school graduation. Next year, she will study forensic science in college. Jocelyn is social and enjoys time with her friends. In her large suburban high school of over 3,000 students, she is one of less than 200 Black students. According to Jocelyn, "this is the school that my parents have been wanting me to go to for a while now … it's supposed to be leveled up compared to other schools." The school is nationally ranked and has a reputation for academic success.

Throughout the interview, Jocelyn was candid, holding nothing back, often she'd say "let me think about that" before answering a question. She was so committed that after the interview I got a text from her asking if I wanted to interview a friend who could share a different perspective.

What are your favorite and least favorite subjects?

Science is definitely my favorite. There's always a right answer to science and math and there's always a formula to get to that answer. The best part is you don't have to relearn it over and over again. Because it's kind of like a stepped process, unlike my least favorites, English and History. In elementary school and middle school, teachers would teach us little bits of American history, but then when we got to high school, teachers were like, "Okay, so we lied about that. This is what really happened." And then you have to learn it all over again.

Why do you think you were taught an incorrect history at first?

Because no one wants to seem like the bad guy. We don't learn what actually happened and not just for Black history but everyone. Wars, for example, are not just Black and White other people fought too. Native Americans fought in wars, Hispanic people did too, and many, many people that didn't get credit, and that kinda gets buried. I guess it's because it's the dirty side of American history. Now, we want to say that racism is no longer a thing, and there is no such thing as color—really? I remember a girl whose mom complained because her daughter felt bad when we talked about race. The girl felt bad because she felt like it was her fault, and her mom said she shouldn't be learning this because her kid shouldn't feel guilty about something she didn't do. But then again, it's something we need to know. I think it's just a guilt problem.

When the whole Columbus Day thing changed, they said Columbus Day is no longer a holiday, but we're still learning in school that Columbus "discovered" America. And we didn't really talk about the whole invasion thing or the Native Americans or about forced religion, education and all that stuff. It was funny because my dad always said that he would teach me history at home because the stuff I learned in school wasn't true, especially Black history. At home, I learn a bunch of stuff that we are learning in schools, except I learn what actually happened—and not just the whole America is beautiful and we don't do anything wrong, kinda thing.

Let's talk about English class. In what ways has your English teacher presented history?
So English, I hate English. We've looked at history but not in history books. Instead, we've looked at it more in novels and stories. We've read, I can't remember a lot of the books' names, but I remember one was about a man who owned many slaves. I just don't like it because most of the books are written by dudes, old White men, who are telling the stories of people who actually struggled and so it's not really giving the whole picture.

Do you think when Indigenous, Black, Latine and Asian people are presented to you in your English class they are presented in ways that celebrate them or are joyful or are they presented in oppressed ways?
Actually, last year was the first time that we really touched on Black history besides slavery. We spent a few months talking about individual things people may struggle with in America. Then we had debates—no, not debates more like open conversations. It was cool because it wasn't just the White and Black kids who could talk about this stuff. It was everyone talking about their experiences, so I feel at least in my class we were trying to change what you're talking about a bit by talking about not just slavery, and slavery, and some more and more slavery. We have talked about the cool things that Black people did as well like inventing the wringer washing machine and rock music. We also read a story about a Hispanic woman who had moved to America and how she struggled to adjust because people discriminated against her. There were plenty of stories that we were able to relate to, so I thought that was really cool. Even though I hate reading, I found that a bit more interesting.

Did you talk about race specifically in the class? Was it a safe and comfortable conversation?

Well, sometimes, yeah. Race is always uncomfortable. Because I feel like whenever it comes to the word *race*, you kind of match it with racism, so people are very careful with what they say to you. Specifically, when we were talking about Black people or topics, I can tell people are just very on edge about what to say and how they word their responses around me. I think they think if they say one thing wrong, or you have a question, then you're automatically racist. That has kinda put up a few barriers. If you have a question, just ask your question. I'm gonna share my thoughts on it and that doesn't necessarily mean I am answering for all Black people. It is just kinda hard to have discussions because people are always being very cautious about what they say because they don't want to be called racist.

I did bring up systems of oppression in class one day. We were talking about racism, and I said racism is power because that's what my dad taught me. I gave the example of housing, and redlining—that was a system of oppression and racism because it was all based on power and keeping Black people out of certain areas.

Another time we talked about racism because we were having problems in our school with people using racial slurs. My English teacher, I think, was the only teacher that did this. She showed us a video that pretty much talked about how certain words are reserved for certain groups of people, and if you don't fall into that group of people, then it is not your word to say. For people that might be LGBTQ, they have their own set of words that they can use with each other, but outside of that don't ever use it.

Do you think that helped?

Yeah, maybe. We talked about it afterward, it was pretty bland conversation.

What could your teacher have done to make those conversations better and safer?

Smaller groups. It was a whole-class conversation and no one wanted to be the person to say something ignorant in front of the whole class.

Is race something you should talk about in English class?

If so, there are gonna be a bunch of parents saying, "Oh, no, the classroom isn't meant for subjects like racism." But how do you expect your kids to learn if they don't learn about it in school? That's why we have all these ignorant adults out here. That's why I like my generation because we are kind of trying to get it together because other people don't want to learn what they have to learn. I don't like to sit around and just do nothing. If something's not right, you've got to take action and change it, and the thing that you can do is educate people and to do that— we need to learn about it.

In what ways has your English teacher empowered you?

I was nominated for something by my English teacher. We have a student board at my school. You have to be nominated by a teacher and the board makes decisions for the school and brings things up to the principals and deans. My teacher said she nominated me because I like to get my point across and I don't like to just sit around and do nothing. I didn't do it though because I lost the paper, and I was too embarrassed to ask for another one.

If you could give advice to your English teacher, or other English teachers, what advice do you have for them?

Stop making your students read about old White men and books that were written 100 years ago. There's plenty of new versions of books that are talking about new and modern issues that you could educate your students with. Why are we still talking about old stuff? Like that one with the dude who had a lot of money and couldn't find the girl he wanted. [*Gatsby?*] Yeah, yes, yes. I don't want to hear about him.

Where do you feel safest in school?

It's actually not at my school. It's my EMT class at the local community college. I'm the only one from my school in the class and everyone is really nice. It's a break from the snobby people at my school.

As I interviewed Jocelyn, I could sense these were conversations she was comfortable with having as well as things she had considered herself or with her parents. While Jocelyn is sharing her unique experience, her words echo what I have heard from other students. I believe she is talking to all of us, and I hope you can take the time to hear her even if you teach younger students.

COMPREHENSION CHECK

After reading Jocelyn's words,

◆ I understand …
◆ I wonder …
◆ I will hold onto …
◆ How does Jocelyn's experience compare to the students in your class? Similarities and differences?

Jocelyn's reflection that classroom literature is filled with "old White men" is not atypical, especially for Black girls. In the article, "We Need More of 'US' in Schools," Delicia Greene (2016) affirms that "the push for canonical texts and the lack of culturally conscious texts has resulted in Black adolescent girls silencing their own voices; in order to accommodate dominant perspectives. This has also resulted in a tremendous gap between Black girls 'in-school and out-of-school literacies." Jocelyn noted that when texts and discourse were reflective of her racial identity, she was more engaged in class. The invisibility and the inaccuracies of Black people, in general, are contributors to Jocelyn not enjoying her English and history classes. What if Jocelyn's love of science was connected and appreciated literarily and her English teacher knew and understood the power, as did my mother's friend, Cheryl, of putting an Octavia Butler book in her hands or other science-related texts written by Black women? For a young adult who isn't fond of English, science-related texts could bridge her love of science and need for activism: "I don't like to sit around and just do nothing. If something's not right, you've got to take action and change it …" I wonder how reading a science fiction or a science-related text might challenge and encourage Jocelyn to find that "all activism is science fiction, for envisioning a world without oppression requires the active creation of socially just societies formed from innovative ideas and visionary possibilities" (Toliver, 2021).

Student Collaborator: Ryan M.

Ryan M. is a high school senior at the same suburban school Jocelyn V. attends, although they do not know one another. Ryan is on the executive board of his school's equity action committee (the same one Jocelyn was recommended for). He is a community activist having "interned for the campaign of the youngest Black woman ever elected to Congress." He considers himself an ally and is passionate about equity. In college, Ryan plans on majoring in biochemistry but is considering law post undergraduate school. He is a member of the school orchestra as well as a music honor society member.

Do you consider yourself an antiracist?

Yeah, I would think so, or I would hope so at least. I think I tried to be as much as I can. I definitely wouldn't say I'm a racist. One of the things that just happened recently was one of my cousins was talking about being pulled over [by the police] and getting a slap on the wrist. There were people of a different race there, and I was like, um, you probably shouldn't be talking about that because if they [people of a different race] get pulled over it's an hour-long stop and the police are bringing in drug dogs for no reason.

Do you believe you've been a student in an antiracist classroom?

It's always been ELA classrooms, really, for me, not as much my sophomore year because that was when I stayed online the whole year because of COVID. But my freshman year, I had a teacher who was Muslim. She was really good at being super relational. And also, even though our curriculum was a lot of *Romeo and Juliet* and *Of Mice and Men* and those books that are a lot older and that have a lot of just like White people in them, she made her own unit. We got to choose a book, and a lot of them were very diverse. The book I read was about a North Korean man and his escape from a concentration camp in North Korea or something that the government was keeping him in. That was just some diversity in a curriculum that was not super diverse. I remember that classroom was really good about talking about race. She would always bring in articles from the real world and talk about them, so I think even in a curriculum that's based on a lot of older texts that aren't super diverse you can bring stuff in and talk about it. This year, my English teacher who was also part of our student equity committee is really good about talking about race and brings in a lot of articles. We even read a book called *Between the World and Me*. When we read it, we talked a lot about race because that's really what that book is about and the ties it has to our country and the struggles of people. She would bring news articles, and every week we'd have to write about a current news article and our opinion on it or what was going on, and in those I always kind of found myself talking about race. I feel like my English classrooms have been really good about that, and knowing my sophomore year teacher, she would have been really good about it too, if we were in person, but I think with the weird Zoom schedule only meeting twice a week, we were rushing to get our basic curriculum done.

What do you think educators need to know or do in order to help students to become advocates for the demolition of racism?

They [English teachers] are always people who analyze the room. And I think that they always see who people are and they advocate for them. They're super good about being connected to culture. We did an editorial, and I wrote about unjust school systems, not with racism, but grading because it's super stressful. I wrote about how we'll have tests where they throw something you've never seen before on it and half of the test is like that. How is that even possible or fair? But one of the students wrote about the Palestinian conflict, and my teacher didn't say, "Oh, no, maybe you should write about something else." She just said do anything you want, anything that makes you angry.

Just think about who people in your classroom are and make sure they don't feel the need to conform to anything. They should be able to connect to their culture or their identities that may be different than other people. I think this is important. I think it was all the English teachers and some others that really wanted the equity committee created. Hopefully, that was on behalf of the kids who maybe hadn't had their voices heard because that committee is all about talking about really difficult subjects with people who are different than you. I think that is something really important for antiracism.

Have your English teachers been purveyors of truth? Have they taught you hard history and expected you to be a change agent?

It's really simple to teach truth—just state the facts of history. There's no reason to sugarcoat it and at my school they don't. Teachers at my school have been completely open to calling out racism or false tales of history we may have learned as children, but this doesn't happen in every school in America.

If you were given a chance to speak directly to ELA teachers, what would you say they have to do if they want students to be antiracists?

They definitely need to be present with their students. I remember sometimes in middle school I wouldn't feel super connected to my English teacher. But I feel like the last few years, our English teachers have been really good about walking around when we're doing silent work and even if you're doing group work, they'll talk to you about what you did this weekend or experiences that are going on in your lives. Every Monday, my English teacher this year would say, "What did you do this weekend?" People would say the most random things, and even if they were a completely different person than she was, she'd say, "Oh, that's interesting," or if it was someone's holiday that she doesn't celebrate, she'd say, "Oh my goodness, that's amazing. I've always wanted to go to a festival or something." I think connecting with your students makes them feel like they can trust you. Especially if they're feeling something is unjust, they come to you. That's extremely important; it's kind of a first step. Because if no one trusts any of the teachers at the school, they're not going to bring up anything they dislike, so connecting with your students is that first step, and making sure that everyone feels heard and that they can talk to you and express their beliefs to you.

Where do you feel safest in school?

I feel safest in collaborative classrooms. There are some classes where I just go there to learn, and that's okay, but classes where we actively engage in discussion makes me feel like I'm part of a unique community and that makes me feel safe.

Listening to Ryan, it was hard to believe that he and Jocelyn attended the same school and were in the same grade as their perspectives and experiences are quite different. Ryan mentioned his freshman English teacher who was Muslim and "super relational" went rogue, changing the curriculum to include a more diverse array of readings and authors. Obviously, this experience was memorable for Ryan and may have set the tone for how he perceived his future English classrooms. This also highlights an effective antiracist educational strategy: hire and retain more racialized educators of the global majority. The perspectives, experiences and racial awareness they bring to school spaces can be invaluable to students and the overall school culture since "teachers of color have been shown to increase student engagement, improve reading and math test scores, and boost college attendance rates for students of color while also ensuring White students feel cared for and challenged" (Rembert et al., 2019).

COMPREHENSION CHECK

Ryan's ELA educators have intentionally diversified text offerings and connected these texts to current events.

◆ What are the things Ryan's teachers do well?
◆ What are your suggestions for taking their antiracist pedagogy a step further?
◆ What additional steps can you take to ensure students understand racial justice and understand that antiracism is an action?

Student Collaborator: Kaylee A.

Kaylee is a 7th grader who likes golf, clay/3D art and badminton. She enjoys debates and is excited about her public speaking class next semester. She also enjoys designing houses and talking to her friends.

Kaylee attends middle school in the suburbs of a major city. There are just over 500 students in her 6th–8th-grade middle school. As is the case nationally, her public school student population is racially diverse (47% White, 30% Latine, 13% Black, 3% Asian and 4% Mixed race), and the teaching staff is overwhelmingly White and female.

Kaylee smiled shyly throughout the interview asking clarifying questions to ensure her understanding.

Tell me about your favorite class, and what happens in that class to make it your favorite

My favorite class is my math class because I like the way she [the teacher] teaches. She lets us talk to other people. She's not super strict about noise. It's just fun.

What's your least favorite class? What do you wish your other teachers would do?

Probably my social studies class because I just don't really like the way she teaches. I've never really liked social studies because it's a lot of memorizing. I sort of wish she'd let us talk a little bit more because she's super strict about noise. Last year was a little bit different because I had a super nice teacher and that made it more fun. There were less tests and more projects. But this year, it's more tests and more memorization.

Based on the definition I've given you, do you think you are racially literate? And if so, where does that come from?

I would like to think so because I want to be inclusive to everybody. I don't see why anybody would separate people based on their skin color. It seems sort of bad because why would you— there's no reason to. I learned it mostly from my parents and a little bit from school in grade school. They tell you to be inclusive in school and stuff, but they don't really touch that much on "don't separate people based on how they act or their skin tone."

My parents told me to be nice and respectful to other people, no matter how they look or who they are.

Do you think those kinds of conversations would be uncomfortable to have in school?

I don't really. I could see how other people could maybe think that. But I think learning about different cultures is really fun and really interesting. I've never like been told about it [racial literacy] before, so it's something new that I can remember for the next time it might be brought up. Race hasn't really been brought up too much.

How do you feel about people saying we should not talk about race because it makes people feel bad?

I sort of think it's needed to have a source of empathy and realize what people actually went through with slavery and that stuff was a thing. Because I think it's really important to know about it, and see why did they do that. Why did they have slavery? Why did they have the triangular trade? Why was it needed?

To be antiracist means you are engaging in action to challenge racism. Is that too big a responsibility to put on young people?

No, as a human being you deserve kindness and to be respected. Kindness is not enough, but I think it's an improvement, but there's still some things that you can definitely do.

Where do you feel safest in school?

The place I feel most comfortable in are my honors classes (ELA and Math) because it's mostly the same people I had honors classes with last year. I can connect with them the most because I've known them for years. Everybody in those classes are more or less friends, and nobody judges what you say as long as it's not hurting another person.

Kaylee takes pride in being in honors classes at her middle school, which she describes as a safe space because the students in these classes know each other from being in honors each year. Although not included in the transcription, Kaylee also mentioned that her honors classes had very few students from historically oppressed racialized groups. As a result, racialized students of the global majority do not benefit from the comfort, safety and camaraderie that Kaylee has experienced. This made me think of my eldest daughter's experience when we moved from a suburb that was racially diverse to one that lacked diversity. At my daughter's new school, there were a lot of excuses when I inquired about her being placed in honors classes as she had been in her previous school, such as needing her standardized test scores and enrolling for at least a semester in a non-honors course before placement could be determined. As an educator, I knew these were just barriers to entry. Statistics show gatekeeping in honors classes; for example, according to a 2020 Education Trust report, only 10% of 8th graders in Algebra I are Black, and only 18% were Latine. The report identified educator and assessment bias, inequity in resources and a lack of communication with families about advanced learning opportunities as factors that keep historically racialized students of the global majority out of honors classes.

COMPREHENSION CHECK
◆ What do Kaylee's words tell you about her learning experiences in school?
◆ How does her learning maintain the status quo?
◆ What is one thing Kaylee shared that stood out to you? Why?

Talking with Kaylee I was struck by the educational system's (curriculum, teachers, etc.) desire to preserve White innocence. Kaylee noted she's ready to discuss topics that highlight race, power and privilege, and yet that type of discourse and analytical thought is not happening in her English or other classes. If White racialized students are never asked to discuss race and interrogate their discomfort, White fragility and apathy, racism will continue to thrive.

Student Collaborator: Jaylen V.
Jalen plays youth football and really enjoys robotics. He is one of a small number of Black boys in his 8th-grade classes.

What's your favorite and least favorite subject?

My favorite subject is math. Because I never really learned anything bad, and I never have to do things twice. My least favorite is geography because there is tons of writing. It's difficult and takes a lot of time and is very hard to do. We're only doing stuff that we're not really going to need in life. School is supposed to help us learn and be better at what we want to do in life. Yeah, that's not happening. Geography needs to be done differently. Geography could be world experience and not just learning about the land and environment and all that–there's more to it than that.

Sounds like you have an issue with the way school is structured. Talk to me a little bit more about that.

I feel like I'm not allowed to do the things I want to do. I like to build stuff, but I have to wait until high school. People barely listen to kids. People don't really listen to you as much as unless you were an adult, so you can't really change things until you get to later on in life when you are more of an adult. No matter how you feel, you got to go with it. You can't go [and] just change it. You have to embrace it and try to go with how things are now.

Have you talked or read anything in your English classroom about race and power?

I remember talking about it in 5th grade when we talked about the civil rights movement. All we ever learn about is either the civil rights movement or slavery. That's basically it.

Would you want to know more?

Yeah, it's interesting, and I've never heard of it. I'd like to listen.

Do you prefer to listen more than to discuss? Would it make you uncomfortable?

I like to listen. We should learn about it [race and racism], but that shouldn't be the main focus, though. You should learn about it, so we can figure out the problem and try to figure out ways to fix it and change it to make a better future.

Why should we not focus on it?
Because there is a lot more stuff to learn and that stuff kinda makes people think things about the past and not today.

What is some advice you would give ELA teachers?
It's okay to try something new and make changes to the subject. That allows us to learn what we don't already know which means we learn more.

Where do you feel safest in school?
No place in school. That's an annoying question. I feel safe after school during my extracurricular stuff.

During the interview, Jalen was straightforward with his responses and sometimes quite emphatic. However, he did not want to talk about his ELA classroom as much as about the structures at school that make him feel powerless. Jalen expressed a desire to have a say in his educational experience, yet felt his ability to explore and express himself freely was limited. This is a common experience for Black racialized students, who often feel dispossessed of their own path, power and knowledge. Rather than being in control, these decisions are often in the hands of teachers, who tend to place Black racialized students in a box. This can have not only a huge impact on their academic experience but also on their emotional and mental well-being, as Black racialized students feel their needs and wants are widely ignored and unable to be met. This can lead to a sense of alienation and marginalization in the classroom.

As ELA educators, we understand the importance of tone in communication and Jalen's tone showed frustration with limited opportunities to pursue activities that interest him and with the idea that school is more about compliance than meaningful learning. He asked, "What is really the purpose of school?" Interestingly, Jalen shared that he enjoyed remote learning during the COVID lockdown because he is better at learning by himself. He said, "I've learned to build, I've learned a lot of stuff in science, I've learned a lot of stuff in math by myself. I've learned what I want to do in life on my own and how to fix things. And lately, I have been thinking about how I wanted things to be in the future. I've done a lot on my own." He clearly expresses school as a constriction rather than a source of freedom for him.

COMPREHENSION CHECK

Consider what Jalen says and doesn't say.

◆ Jalen believes it is important to talk about issues of race in the classroom but would only like to participate as a listener.
  ○ Why is this important to know and understand?
  ○ What may be some of his reservations about being a vocal participant?
  ○ How can antiracist classrooms be a safe space for students like Jalen who want to listen more than verbally engage?
◆ Jalen feels strongly about being dispossessed of his own learning pathways.
  ○ How might this sense of powerlessness affect his learning and motivation?

Student Collaborator: Christina S.

Christina attends a K–8th-grade fine and performing arts magnet school in a large city. She enjoys K-pop and spending time with her friends.

Tell me a little bit about yourself. What do you like to do?

I like to listen to music and read. I really like any genre of music except country, but I mainly like K-pop and hip-hop. Right now, I'm reading *No Longer Human* by Osamu Dazai.

What's your favorite subject?

Oh, right now it's currently math. Yeah, because it's really easy, and all my other classes are hard. Math is easy, and I actually enjoy learning it.

Talk to me about your English class this year or last year. What did you like about it? What did you dislike about it?

I did like a lot of the projects we did, and some of the topics that we learned about. Like during Black History Month, we had to do a project about a Black person that was famous–well not famous but had done something good. I liked that. I don't like that we did not get to pick out our own books a lot.

What made that assignment stand out to you? What made that one interesting?

Since I'm half Black, I really enjoyed writing about someone that's kind of similar to me.

Have you ever had a conversation or read a book in your English classroom about race or racism?

We've had a conversation once this year. It was about something that happened in school, so we had to talk about it as a class. I don't remember exactly what we talked about.

Do you think it is important to talk more about race and racism in school? Do you want to read books and have conversations so you can know what it means to be an antiracist?

Yeah, I would because there is racism around us. Students are obviously going to be diverse, so we need to talk about it. I think they [teachers] should let us voice our opinions and say how we feel, and listen to the stuff we say. We should talk about problems that are going on in the world and around us, even something in our neighborhood or anything, big or even something small.

What do you think ELA teachers need to know is important to you as a student?

Make me feel safe. I can feel shy and pressured, so I like nice teachers who understand that and I don't have to feel anxious.

Where do you feel safest in school?

In the lunchroom because I'm with my friends and I can be myself around them and not feel restricted.

Christina typified a middle schooler. Her responses were brief, and she could not remember the specifics of what was happening in her ELA classroom. I did get the sense that in her large city public school system the curriculum was more rote and offered less critical and creative thinking. Christina could not share a whole-class novel that she'd read this year or the previous year. Christina mentioned being Mixed-race and wanting to explore that part of her identity. Because this is not a visible part of her identity, her teachers would have to get to know this about her to fully understand Black history as important to her.

COMPREHENSION CHECK

◆ What are your thoughts about Christina's advice (connected to cariño y confianza)?

Student Collaborator: Londen S.

Londen is also an 8th grader at the same magnet school as her twin sister, Christina S. She likes drawing, listening to music and hanging out with her friends.

Tell me about what's your favorite class

Social studies or science because I like learning about past stuff. In science, I like doing experiments. My science teacher was my favorite teacher last year. She was the teacher who knew everything about the drama at our school and knows everything about people. She was just pretty cool.

What are you reading right now in your ELA class?

Well, we're not really reading any books right now. We are talking a lot about the government in our class.

What are you writing?

We're learning how to write down what people are saying really quick by drawing or writing it out in our own way. I really don't like English class.

What makes English a subject you don't like?

The teacher talks so much. She literally talks the whole entire class period, and we just read and discuss from the textbook. It is not fun.

What would make the class better?

Maybe not focus on the textbook and her talking so much. There is no art or videos or anything like that in the class. We just did a project that we got to choose. We had an hour to research and then we had to present it to the class and I liked that. I got to work with my friends and there was this pressure to hurry up and get it done, so we actually had to finish in a short time or take it home for homework.

Do you ever talk about race or racism in class or read books about it?

The only time was when we were talking about the Holocaust. I would be uncomfortable talking about it.

How could you talk about that and be more comfortable?

I don't know. I want to know more about cultures and stuff. I want to know more about my ancestors and stuff like that.

Where do you feel safest in school?

In the lunchroom because I'm with my friends and there are more of us than the teachers.

Londen was also brief in her responses. While she was clear about her likes and dislikes, she did not want to discuss the details of her classes. For her, antiracism was more about how she feels than what she learns. Londen expressed a clear discomfort talking about racism, indicating that such conversations are infrequent in school. However, she said she has these discussions at home and feels safe and comfortable talking about these topics there.

It is imperative that classrooms are safe spaces that elevate the voices of racially minoritized students, so their stories and perspectives are not silenced or filtered by Whiteness, and that all students regardless of race or other identities are able to enter and engage in constructive conversations around challenging but necessary topics like power, racial oppression and injustice.

Student discomfort can be quelled with proper planning and guidelines. Table 5.1 is a quick guide to leading race and racism-centric classroom discussions.

TABLE 5.1 Guidance for setting expectations, preparing for, beginning, facilitating and concluding productive dialogues in the classroom

Setting expectations*	◆ Everyone should be respectful to one another and acknowledge everyone's opinion ◆ Be an active listener 　○ Listen to understand, not to respond
Preparing for dialogue	◆ Utilize multimodalities to ground the topic and offer multiple entry points for students ◆ Explore language (privilege, oppression, racial animus, etc.) and its use ◆ Model for students how to reflect on their own assumptions and privileges ◆ Invite students to set goals and expectations for the conversation
Beginning the dialogue	◆ Start with an open-ended question to establish a basic understanding of the issue 　○ What does race/racism or justice/injustice mean to you? 　○ What is happening in the world today to corroborate or contradict what we have read or discussed? ◆ Invite students to share their experiences and perspectives 　○ How has your experience shaped your views? ◆ Plan thoughtfully to create meaningful dialogue that encourages all students to participate
Facilitating the dialogue	◆ Ask clarifying questions to ensure student understanding and thinking critically ◆ Ensure everyone has an equal opportunity to participate in the conversation 　○ Make sure no one is left out or silenced ◆ Keep the conversation focused 　○ Stay on topic and avoid getting sidetracked ◆ Encourage students to take different perspectives 　○ Avoid historically marginalized students from carrying the conversation load ◆ Allow for silence ◆ Check in with students periodically
Concluding the dialogue	◆ Take students' emotional and mental temperatures ◆ Allow time for processing and various methods of reflection

* These expectations should be regularly met by the teacher and modeled before being introduced to students.

COMPREHENSION CHECK
- ◆ How might the use of this guide help students like Londen (and Jalen) engage and push through discomfort?
- ◆ What hesitancies do you have about student comfort/ discomfort?

Student Collaborator: Natalie A.

Natalie is a high school sophomore. She is an honors student who enjoys baking, dance (hip-hop especially), spending time with friends, reading and public speaking when she is not playing on her high school's varsity golf team. She's thinking about pursuing a career in journalism or astronomy after college.

Tell me about your favorite class

To be completely honest, my favorite class is probably my dance class because I am very close with a lot of girls in there. It's a break from the school day for me because it's something I'm good at and something I really love to do. My teachers are really nice to me, in general, but if we're talking about actual academics, I'd probably say my English class because we talk about a really wide variety of topics.

What's your least favorite?

This one surprised me at the beginning of the year, I thought it was gonna be my favorite, AP U.S. History. I have always loved history. It was always my favorite subject in school. I was always really good at it, but I'm not. My teacher is fine. It's first period and the teacher, he's kinda got a bit of a monotone voice. The way it's described is a lot of memorization, and since it is an AP class it goes superfast. The book that I have to read is 30 pages of super tiny font [per night], and it's a lot of information all at once. I pick up on history stuff pretty well; we're learning about the Civil War right now, which is a very important topic, and I would like to say I know quite a bit about it, but it's a lot of new information compared to previous years, so I am not doing so well.

What do you wish would be done differently?

We kind of do the same thing in class a lot. We do play these review games, which are fine, but it's always over kind of the exact same few topics. Then the multiple-choice tests, which are what we mostly do, the questions don't exactly correlate, so if he could just advance on those topics a little bit more I feel like I would get more out of the class.

In that class, do you talk about things like race and racism?

We haven't a whole lot. We talked about the Civil War. I know we talked about slavery but not really in detail. It's mostly just all stuff in the book that you'd have to read. Yeah, it's kind of odd. It is talked about but in a very formal matter like how slavery and the slave trade impacted the economy, and not so much about slaves experiences themselves. It's not really the teachers' fault. It's just how the curriculum is. That book was made a long time ago. It's not relevant to today. We talk more about that kind of stuff in English right now. We're gonna be reading *The Crucible*. Previously, in the year, we talked a lot about the negative impact of stereotypes, and we watched a TED Talk by Chimamanda Adichie, "The Danger of a Single Story." We did a little unit on it, and I liked it because we got to talk about a lot of things during that unit.

How do your teachers empower you to be your best self? How do they empower you to be your best self to make society better?

They do push me to do my best and have always encouraged me that if I need help, to come after school to make sure that I get the information I need. Their office hours are always open. They're very welcoming and are like "Hey, if you need help, just ask. I've totally got no problem staying after school to help you." Especially my English teacher, he's pulled me aside and been like, "Hey, I know you're really busy with golf and stuff," because he's the boys golf coach. He kind of knows how busy it can get, and I was kind of struggling during that time. He told me, "I know how it goes. If you need anything tell me it's fine." My chemistry teacher did the same thing.

Natalie, it sounds like you're in a lot of advanced classes. Do you see people of other races in those classes with you?
Honestly, not as many. There are three to four people of color in most of my classes, but the majority are White.

Why do you think that is?
I don't know. My school is pretty diverse.

Do you think you're racially literate? Where does that come from or where do you think it should come from?
I would like to think I am. I mean, I do acknowledge how I, as a White person, have a lot more privileged than somebody else who isn't. And I understand how that may impact their day-to-day life and my day-to-day life. I've probably learned it from books and my parents. I've read books by Angie Thomas before, and I read those when I was younger so I feel like I have understood for a longer time. And I think that's really important. My parents taught me years ago.

And really, we haven't talked about being racially literate in school before I don't think. I feel like topics like that are kind of skirted around, like just leave it be because someone's gonna get offended or something, but I don't think that's how it should be.

I understand that there's a discomfort to having those conversations at school. But do you think there's value in that?
I do. I don't think there should be any discomfort. I think the kids aren't the ones that really have the problem with it. To be honest, I think it's more the parents. A lot of the people in my grade and even in younger grades like middle school and late elementary school, I think should be having conversations because of how important they are and to having that mindset growing up.

Do you think those kinds of conversations are more difficult then maybe perhaps a conversation about culture?
Yeah, I do. They do invoke more emotion. And we do—I would like to think as a society—think bad about that period of history.

Because of where we are now, we're like that's morally wrong, and why would somebody ever even think to do that? But at the time, it was relevant and at the time, it had a significant impact on society, so we have to kind of look back, learn from our mistakes and just grow. Advancements have been made, but there's still so much to work on. It's still happening, and if you're just turning a blind eye to that we're really not improving at all.

Are you reading books from various people of color?
A lot of the stuff I'm reading at my level is just all old White men. We read *Night* by Elie Wiesel last year. We read *Fahrenheit 451*, but that really doesn't have to do with race, it's more like the importance of books. Yeah, we read a lot of Shakespeare last year, too and *A Tale of Two Cities*. I think we're going to read *The Great Gatsby* this year. The classics are overhyped a little bit.

What do you want your teachers to know about your needs, so you are more racially literate in school and can engage in antiracist action?
I think they just need to talk about it. Honestly, I think that's a really important part of it, especially in English and History, those are really big because it is relevant. I mean, chemistry is just a lot of math numbers, but I do think it's good to learn and it should be integrated into our school curriculum a lot more.

Where do you feel safest in school?
In English class because I have a lot of friends in the class and it challenges me unlike pass English classes.

Natalie spoke with such confidence and presented as older as a result. I often did not need to probe her further because she was good at elaborating on her responses and holding the conversation. I could imagine her bringing great insights and depth to readings and discussions about topics that delved into race/racism.

According to Henry Giroux (1997), a preeminent critical pedagogy theorist and scholar, educators must create space "for White students to recognize their own agency and legitimate place with the struggle for social change and an anti-racist society." This means we need to create environments that challenge White racialized students to critically examine their own individual and collective privileges as well as be able to identify and understand the various systems of oppression that contribute to racism. Just as we need to ensure students feel seen and heard, students need the same from one another. Our English classroom provides the perfect context for White racialized students to engage in meaningful dialogue around diverse perspectives and develop racial humility and understanding for those experiences that are different from them. Natalie is eager to become an active agent of antiracist change. She just needs the necessary knowledge and tools to challenge racism in all its forms.

> **COMPREHENSION CHECK**
> ◆ What resonates with you from this interview?
> ◆ Consider Natalie's calls to action for educators. What can you heed?

Out of the box

bell hooks said education makes it possible for students to become more truly themselves. Each of the students I interviewed expressed in different ways they wanted to be valued for who they were as individuals. Whatever their racial identification, they did not want to be put in a box. However, the presence and persistence of racism in schools have done this very thing: Asian students as high achievers, Indigenous students as only existing on reservations, Black students as poor academic performers, Latine students as English language learners and Mixed-race students as outliers who should choose one racialized identity over another. Instead of being themselves, these students are expected to assimilate and acquiesce to Whiteness to become racially palatable. Racialized students of the global majority are fully deserving of being valued and esteemed as individuals outside of any box and not as the lies held therein. Normed stereotypes and deficit perceptions of racialized students of the global majority beget policy and praxis that cause harm and further subjugate them, for example, tracking, language remediation, low-quality drill-and-kill curriculum and instruction, a culture of low expectations. This promulgates the insidious belief that historically oppressed racialized students are the problem rather than products of a broken, White supremacist system.

This belief is rarely said aloud unless you are my former principal. While outlining the previous school year's standardized testing data and highlighting the achievement of each student "subgroup," she stated, "And, as we'd expect, Black students are not meeting standards." Yes, that was actually said aloud. I could not believe it either. I looked around the room expecting a collective gasp. Nothing, no challenge other than mine surfaced. Our students are not "subgroups," and the expectation of them not meeting standards should not be a presumed outcome; such dysconsciousness, or a lack of critical judgment, does not challenge or question inequity; instead, it regards it as a given based on White hegemony (King, 1991).

The by-product of such thoughts, stated or unstated, is internalized oppression. Internalized oppression occurs when racialized students of the global majority are repeatedly exposed to negative messages and misinformation. As these messages and misformation are repeated, internalized and accepted as true, they become part of a student's self-concept and can promote feelings of self-hatred, low self-worth and self-limiting beliefs.

The following are examples of internalized oppression and its impact:

1. When racialized students of the global majority are told or think they have to work twice as hard as their White racialized peers to be successful, this causes students of racialized global majority to feel they are actually not as capable as their White peers and perpetuates a cycle of self-doubt and low self-esteem.
2. When a student's language is policed, it can lead to students internalizing the idea that their language or ways

of speaking are wrong and inferior, leading to feelings of shame and lowered self-esteem.

3. Students of the global majority refraining from participating in certain class discussions because they believe any overt expression of emotion will result in them being labeled as "aggressive" or "disruptive," even if their peers are allowed to express their opinions. This can have negative effects on their academic performance and motivation.

4. As a result of a culture of low expectations and a lack of support, racialized students of the global majority give up on themselves believing they are incapable of academic success.

These are not failures on the part of students but the result of the boxes we attempt to place them in, limiting their potential, power and freedom. The solution is to simply remove the lid.

The following questions can help to combat internalized oppression in students and ourselves:

Learn and unlearn
- What myths, negative messages and misinformation could students internalize?
  - Have I taught my students to recognize these and understand how and why they exist?
- Do any of these inform my perception of or interaction with students?
- What am I doing to highlight the truth about racialized people of the global majority versus the lies?

Celebrate good times
- How am I consistently showcasing the brilliance and indelible contributions of racialized students of the global majority and their ancestors?

Watch your mouth
- How do my words and the voices of those included in the texts and classroom guests contradict stereotyping and inferiority?

○ What expectations or standards have I set and communicated with students?
◆ How do my words and those included in the classroom
esteem and value racialized people of the global majority?

Avoid bad influences
◆ What are you consuming that may feed you misinformation and lies about historically oppressed people groups?
○ How is it informing your worldview and understanding of racialized people of the global majority?

These questions are a starting point to being more conscious of
the ways we, as educators, help students and ourselves to recognize and refute internalized oppression. If we are to, as hooks
suggests, assist students in becoming their authentic and best
selves, then we must free them from constraints of any kind and
stop trying to fit them into predetermined boxes.

Go to the source

Anita B. an award-winning high school English educator and
instructional coach, helps her colleagues understand how systems of oppression operate in her school and the things students
may be subject to internalizing by going directly to the source.
She developed a student observation protocol (Figure 5.1) with
a colleague based on the book *Living the Questions: A Guide for
Teacher-Researchers*. Anita encourages her colleagues to shadow
a student for a day and record their observations with the goal
of developing a "deeper understanding of the student's school
experience, including their social interactions, and their experience with teachers and school staff" (Bucio, 2015). If you want to
better understand students, I encourage you to conduct your own
student interviews and engage in a student study using Anita's
protocol as a guide.

We are the lead learners in our classrooms, and the most
important subject we can learn about is our students. I asked
educators: *What are you learning about antiracism for your
students?*

Student Study

Observation & Analysis

As you shadow a student for a full day, you must take meticulous notes as an observer—raw notes (Shagoury & Power, 2012, p. 148-149). Write down and record absolutely everything you observe, record the time it happens, and avoid deciding whether something is important or not in the moment you are observing it. Your notes should include details from every period of the school day including lunch.

The goal of this observation is to gain a deeper understanding of the student's school experience, including their social interactions, and their experience with teachers and school staff. Write down anything and everything that you notice.

After you complete this observation, immediately do the following:

1. Draft a short <u>memo</u> using the compass, agreements, and conditions (Shagoury & Power, 2012, p. 150-151) which reflects on the experience of observing the experience of this student. Also be sure to capture any burning issues or ideas you had along the way as you completed this portion of the assignment. Your memo should be completed before you go to bed on the day you completed your observation—this is an important detail. (You will submit this memo to me along with the more formal analysis paper and your raw notes.)

2. <u>Cook your notes</u> (Shagoury & Power, 2012, p. 148-149) and begin to analyze your data. Simply, you will annotate your raw notes with questions that push and expand your thinking, and you will look for trends. These questions or trends can be abbreviated to codes. A code in qualitative inquiry is most often a word or short phrase that symbolically assigns a summative, salient, essence-capturing, and/or evocative attribute to language-based or visual inquiry.

3. **Write your analysis as soon as possible.** By waiting, you will lose memory of your experience, your initial thoughts, and more generally, momentum and inspiration. Reflective Analysis of student observation In a short analysis, unpack the codes that emerged as you cooked your notes, and describe why and how they emerged. Then describe how this information might impact you as a teacher—and any other implications your findings might have for both policy and practice. Here are few guiding questions to spark your thoughts about what might come out of this experience, and what you might take up in analysis.

Describe your student.
How did they feel that day?
Did the student change throughout the day?
When were they engaged the most? When were they least engaged?
What were the strongest influences in this school day?
What worked well for this student throughout the school day?
What was problematic within the school day?

*** Feel free to provide information beyond these questions. These questions were just meant to provide you with some ideas of what you might want to include.***

FIGURE 5.1 Student Study Protocol.

Here are some of their responses:

To not make assumptions about what you think people think, is huge. I think at the risk of painting with a broad brush, and including myself in this, there's sometimes this idea that being an anti-racist educator means like saying great things about Black people. And one, a lot of people are very anti-Black when they themselves are also Brown or multiracial or from all corners of the world. Also, working in a community that is really homogeneous whether it's almost all Black or almost all Latino or almost all White or almost all East Asian is not the same thing as working in a culturally diverse environment. Recognizing that what one thinks one knows is nope—I know, my experience, the end, full stop.

Also, to ask students questions instead of assuming that they're going to care about an issue that I think that they're going to care about or that they're going to have the same opinion. Many of my students are very law and order because they want to feel safe. They were completely mistreated in their native homes, and they don't feel safe here, either. They were told that they should be safe in America, so they want to trust that the police are the people who keep them safe.

I am also figuring out how do students view each other. The way my Black American students and African students speak about one another is some of the most painful student-to-student negativity that I hear. But I think it really crosses all of the different American kids, all of our different international kids and our refugees and our immigrants. There's so much friction between those groups that no one talks about. It's really complex. Letting students lead in seeing the complexity, and not just barging in with I'm going to be so antiracist and Black Power and Black Lives Matter. It has to be I know what my values are, and I know where I want us to go. But I need to really listen to how my students respond and ask them questions. Because how else do we keep each other safe in a conversation? How else do I respect what their opinion is while also asking them to consider something else? How else do I keep them safe out of the classroom? So we don't have half of a conversation, and they leave and say something in the hall that's deeply offensive and can also get your ass whooped.

~Rachel B.

I've learned throughout the years a lot about language. If you were to say a girl's thick, one kid would think, yeah, she's thick, and she's beautiful. And another kid would be like, no, I don't want to be called that. Different cultures, different students, different genders of kids think differently or are having different conversations about words. I've also learned that some kids may say that something doesn't affect them, saying, "Oh, it's okay. It's whatever." And other kids are really affected by. I'm also learning that some kids may not be offended by something because they might have been shielded and not realize that that's actually something that's not okay and terrible,

and nobody's really gone through that with them. It's realizing that not everybody knows what you think a kid should know. You have to remember that kids don't know things until they're taught them.
~Maggie B.

I learned from my students that in neighborhoods that are heavily Mexican American the N-word gets thrown around among Mexican American students on a level that both our Black and our White students were not prepared for. And our Latinx students were like, what? There is a multidimensional miscommunication about language that a number of more diverse high schools in the area have really struggled with how to address. It becomes even more awkward to address when so many more teachers and admin are White, and not from those communities, so when you talk about recruiting teachers of color, yes, please, yes. That's something we've learned from our students, and that we've learned that we don't have the answers for at least not any easy answers.
~Nora F.

WAYPOINT

If we are not centering students in our antiracism efforts, we are not engaging in the work we need to do to achieve transformative justice and racial equity. We must be students of our students. Their voices, ideas and experiences are essential to this work; they are this story's climax. Listening to their perspectives and experiences allows us to understand the complexities of racism and oppression and to develop better strategies for addressing them. It also encourages them to become active participants in the process of social change.

THINK–ACT–REIMAGINE

DO NOW

◆ Research various student interview methods (i.e., empathy interviews)
◆ Determine a method you will use to learn about students' perspectives and experiences

◆ Watch the "Who Gets to Thrive" webinar series (see Resources)

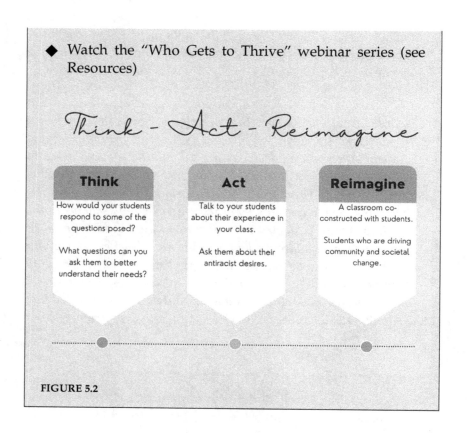

FIGURE 5.2

Resources

Cornelius Minor 'Becoming a better listener' at https://fb.watch/iqYULeNeAU/

Not Fire but Light: How to led meaningful race conversations in the classroom by Matthew Kay

Science of Learning and Development Alliance 'Who Gets to Thrive' Webinars at https://soldalliance.org/uncategorized/who-gets-to-thrive-the-science-of-learning-and-development-as-a-tool-for-anti-racism/

Section IV
Falling Action

6

Beyond the Noise

How should I handle praise, criticism and build community?

Is she really even teaching? No one said it to me directly, but it was the talk around the building that some of my teacher friends warned me was circulating: *You're being talked about a lot on the first floor.* The first floor is where the big, bad, almighty teacher resided. You know, the one teacher who is the self-proclaimed epicenter of all knowledge, all good teaching, and who everyone knows is also the source of all criticism, all gossip, all judgment and all the mess in the school. The one who is so busy minding everyone else's business that you don't know if they are really even teaching. Within weeks of starting at a new school, my euphoria was dashed by having my instruction and the rapport I was building with students questioned. The rumor mill was abuzz with tales of students in my class being too loud and too happy. While I was intentionally creating a safe and welcoming space, I became persona non grata by the teacher bully and his minions. There was always some new rumor about what was going on in my classroom although none of my colleagues had ever stepped foot through the classroom door. The micro and macro aggressions were enough for me to start to question myself: *Did I need to adjust how I was doing things to quell the*

DOI: 10.4324/9781003296171-10

*barrage of whispers in the hall or awkward glances from my new col-
leagues?* Not one to back down easily, I decided that teaching is
about joy and passion. I had to stay the course and rise above the
noise. Was it easy? Heck no. I felt the need to constantly justify
my praxis. I felt I had to as my mother would say "jump higher
and spit farther" than my colleagues to show I was a thoughtful, well-informed and intentional educator. Not only was I the
target of the ire of a bully and his minions, but I was also working for the first time in a majority White, affluent community
that was itself suffering from Whitefluenza, the spread of racism, classism and other forms of bigotry. I was contending with
parents/caregivers who were accustomed to new teachers being
young White racialized women, so they questioned *everything*
about me from my credentials to the content of my courses; they
hurled derogatory language at me, including calling me "girl"
on several occasions to "keep me in my place" when they did
not agree with a grade or disciplinary consequence. There were
so many microaggressions that I lost count. Even after years, the
remnants of both of those harms with the occasional whispers of
"she's not following curriculum" or "who knows what's going
on in there" lingered on because that which we don't understand—we villainize in education.

The villain drives the plot

If colleagues and parents/caregivers don't understand your
antiracist journey, you may be perceived as the villain. Your
centering of joy, counternarratives and instructional disruption of Whiteness in how and what you teach may cause you
to be whispered about in the hallway, the teacher's lounge or
in the community by parents/caregivers. **Your challenging of
policies and practices reinforcing systems of oppression that
enable racial inequity may be viewed by some as anarchy.** This
is messy work that some people will not understand or know
how to support. And yet, we will need to help bring folks along
with us and help them understand the premise and necessity
of challenging a dehumanizing system and show others how to

support us. This means we have to take both criticism and praise in stride and in both instances continue (when safe) to engage and teach justice, equity and antiracism to students, adult detractors, performative allies and those admirers desiring to start their anti-racist journey. At any given point, we might be engaging some or all of these ideologies. It is an unfortunate current function of our society that many presume expertise without knowledge and experience. Frankly, many people believe they know our profession better than we do, and these sideline noneducators have a lot to say about any and everything. This is something with which we will continue to contend; today, it's antiracism and tomorrow it will be something else because change scares people; not everyone, not even the majority of people, but a handful of folk will be led by the fear of change. However, we cannot be. While I was a teacher policy fellow and advocate, I learned I have a responsibility to help facilitate change and elevate the profession for those who think they know it from the sidelines. If antiracism depends on the partnership and collective work of educators, students and the community (Kincheloe, 2007), then we must be bridge builders. If not us, then who? Sometimes we will be both the villain and the hero.

A hero's journey

Engaging in productive disagreement is not something to run away from but toward. It is important to note the keywords in the previous sentence are *productive disagreement*. Surely, there will be times it's necessary to disengage and channel our efforts elsewhere for our mental and physical health. There have been times when what was productive for me was silence and rest for my own self-preservation. As a Black woman, I no longer waste my time and energy with people who are stuck in their own ignorance or simply feigning ignorance for a reaction and attention. However, there will also be times we must leave our circle of support (that was my second-floor teacher friends) and push ourselves to listen to critics (the teachers on the first floor) to understand their points and often their pain. Some disagreements can be dangerous, and some can lead to pro-ductive discourse. I decided to leave the safety of the second floor when I was ready and considered it safe for me. I recommend you make a similar assessment when you're testing the waters to see if you can teach others who disagree with your antiracist teaching. For me, engaging the teacher bully revealed his own insecurity and his desire to utilize his power to subjugate and judge others who he viewed would be easy targets. He'd banked on anti-Blackness in a historically White environment to lead others to, without provocation, question my teaching and if "I fit in." I learned all this by listening to him during the purposely brief interactions I initiated. I asked him questions about his classroom and I listened. My mother always taught me that when you actively listen, you'll eventually hear the truth. He enjoyed being heard and would often want to laugh and talk when the conversation was about him. Even as he feigned camaraderie, I heard fear: fear of not being considered the top teacher, fear of difference. My desire to build an environment of belonging in the classroom and my very being was threatening to this educator. How dare I smile at young people during the first week of school—blasphemy. How dare I enter a new school confidently—blasphemy? How dare I not kiss the ring of the teacher bully—blasphemy? I wish there was a happy ending to my story, one in which the bully and I become friends and he learns from his mistakes. There is no such ending. He continued to be problematic until his retirement. The hero in any situation brings healing to themselves and/or others. I chose myself in this instance. I chose to resist by not giving him my energy. There have been times when through questions and listening I've chosen differently because I heard something that told me the other person and I could find agreement and learn from one another. After listening closely to the teacher bully, I surmised I was not going to be the best person to educate and change this teacher's behaviors or beliefs. The choice is always ours. A hero makes brave choices in order to provide help. Whether villain or hero, our instruction and advocacy cannot be dependent on others' labels of us or our work or students' work because, in the long run, our antiracist journey drives us to be brave enough to confront broken systems that harm and blame affected people.

From the teacher's desk

Several ELA educators I interviewed shared their own hero's journey. They shared their advice and thoughts about how they have navigated challenging environments:

> I've worked in two high schools. In my first three years, I worked at a high school that was predominantly White. The school wanted to work toward, at least in the English department, an equity mindset and antiracist teaching focus, but they just weren't ready. They're trying to talk about race with books like To Kill a Mockingbird, and here I am saying, we can read better books. And me, I was like, well, I'm gonna just do what I want within the system. That's the thing, I did what I wanted within the system. I felt I was supported as a teacher but the system was not supportive of what I wanted to do. If I wanted to bring in a better book than To Kill a Mockingbird, then there would be a discussion about "that's the books we teach," and bringing a new book would be a whole thing that would need to be approved by these people. And we knew, these people might not approve of it. At my last school, I could not teach All American Boys and definitely not Stamped—could not teach it. If I wanted to bring it in and buy my own copies that'd be fine, but I don't think the system would have supported it. My current school and the system support it. I could say, "I want to teach Stamped, and I need 50 copies,' and they'd be like, 'I got you.' The books would be ordered and arrive by the end of the month. If I said, hey, the n* word is used in this book. There would be a plan. They'd be like, 'We're gonna make sure all teachers understand this is something we do not use in school even though this is a word some people may use elsewhere. It's something we choose not to say even if it's in the literature.' That's an example of how I feel more supported by the system. I don't have to say anything, and yet the people in charge make me feel I can teach, I can be an antiracist teacher in whichever way I please, and not just me as a Black male teacher, everyone in the department can if they so choose, so I feel supported in the system.
>
> ~ Dillin R.

Follow the work and writing and thinking of people who challenge you and challenge what you think you know about your *job. Have conversations with colleagues that challenge you also. Especially for White teachers, that's really important because White teachers can comfortably fall in with colleagues that support what they feel they already know, but I think we need to spend as much or more time with colleagues of color, not that it's our colleague's job to teach us and, man does that fall on teachers of color, way, way, way too often, but White educators should be listening and learning from teachers of color. I'm thinking of the educators and thinkers and writers I follow on Twitter, who present me with really challenging ideas and really caused me to rethink a lot of things. And keep reading people that challenge your ideas and go to professional development opportunities that aren't just telling you more about what you already do. Be in some uncomfortable spaces. White teachers need to be the only White person in the room sometimes. We need to read about educational experiences that are absolutely nothing like our own. For example, in Chicago, I almost don't want to talk to anyone who hasn't read* Ghosts in the Schoolyard *at this point. If you haven't, you don't understand school in Chicago and you don't understand how this works. You don't understand we're still doing the same thing. Keep challenging yourself, and never totally have 100% of your footing because if you do you get way, way, way too comfortable.*

~ Nora F.

We are constantly having to prove ourselves. I still don't always feel I have a seat at the table. And a lot of times, that's really tough. I'm not trying to change people, but I'm trying to get them to understand. I recently had a conversation with someone who essentially said to me, "Well, the way you do things," and I go, "Wait, the way who does things? The way you do them? The way culturally you do them?" Because this person was trying to give me the right way to do things, and these are the wrong way to do things lessons. I needed to correct that. Our job is to model for our students, and if you put students through the lens of your lived experience, you've erased them and their experiences. I find myself having more of those conversations, but I've also found myself ignoring or moving past them because I just can't keep educating

White people. I just can't do it. I formed a group last summer with White women and women of color. We read Ruby Hamad's book, White Tears, Brown Scars. *The book was very powerful because she [the author] provides a global historical lens about the experiences of women who've been marginalized throughout history. I wanted to show that this was beyond America, beyond us, that this piece around grappling with race and identity and antiracism and othering is not unique to America. The White women in the group had to think about their positionality in a way that I've always had to think about mine. Sometimes being type A and passionate about teaching is interpreted as she's angry. She's the angry Latina. And again, we get back to—this is how you're supposed to behave. And I just go, whose narrative is that? That's not my narrative. Navigating that is hard, especially when some teachers are uncomfortable because they haven't done the work. Because they haven't felt they needed to do the work, they've been in positions where they don't have to. I say go read Ghouldy Muhammad, Dena Simmons, Bettina Love, all these people are great. Listen to them. Go on Twitter. Brown and Black Twitter is amazing for educating you.*

~Yolanda W.

I was talking about wearing our hoods up [on the anniversary of Trayvon Martin's murder]. And I called people out. One of them was the social studies teacher, and I told her if you don't find this movement to be important, especially during Black History Month, I don't really know what type of history you're teaching in your classroom. I'm a very blunt and out-there person. I'm also okay with calling people out for things people should be called out for, even if it's in the work setting because I feel we're shaping minds; we are shaping the youth. If they're not getting it at home, we're responsible to do it in the classroom, so I feel it's okay to be called out for those things.

~Maggie B.

One of the hardest schools for me— I didn't finish the school year there and I'm not ashamed to admit it and I was for a while, was the school full of White liberals. My big thing is I can handle outright racism man, at least then I know where you stand. But it was the "Hmm, actually ..." and the "Really, I think we should" and the undercutting of ideas or the "They're not ready for this" that exhausted me. I was like, listen, they [the students] can because they live with it—that's life. That's the reality of what our kids go through and what they think, so we need to talk about that. We need to put it all out there, so we can make changes and adjustments accordingly. I struggled more with thinking I was in a supportive environment and letting my guard down as a Black person which we don't get to do, and we normally don't. But I was like, you know what, they say they believe what I believe okay, I can let my guard down for a minute. Wrong. Wrong–false. It was the hardest thing—even more than when I worked for one of the charter networks that I believe only reinforces the school-to-prison pipeline.

~Jordan L.

My new school is far more supportive and community-oriented than my last one. I find that there are more folks with whom I can readily connect who are continuing to cultivate antiracist journeys beyond the classroom—they do this in their personal lives. It is crucial to have an honest, engaged, evolving community because it keeps the work honest and relevant while also keeping the work away from the performative realm. It's tough work. It's messy work. It's not perfect, but the community makes learning and moving forward from missteps and difficulties possible. This work cannot be done in isolation. It requires a community. I am lucky to be back in a space where my colleagues legitimately support one another in this work.

~ Holly S.

Never scared

One of the biggest deterrents to antiracism, personal or pedagogical, is fear. When I asked over 50 educators what barriers kept them from engaging in antiracist work in their classroom or school community, the most common response was fear, the fear of pushback from colleagues, parents/caregivers or administrators and fear of doing it wrong. This response comes as no surprise since students and teachers have been used as political pawns and learning and teaching have been exploited for political theater and currency. To further feed this fear, more than 35 state legislatures have sought to constrict academic freedom by restricting humanizing and antiracist teaching in schools. Some proposed state policies have gone as far as refusing to grant funding to any public school teaching that causes "discomfort, guilt or anguish." If anyone thought teaching was apolitical, then these efforts by state legislatures have certainly debunked that myth. Teaching is inherently political, and these state actions affirm that our classrooms are also political spaces where "power is exerted, resisted and yielded to in every classroom; every classroom is situated within an institution, state, and nation—all locations in which resources, knowledge, and access must be negotiated" (NCTE Standing Committee on Global Citizenship, 2019).

The texts we read, the policies we adopt, the courses we create and teach, the way we grade are all political decisions.

The origin of the word *politics* is a reminder that there is more to the concept than the current partisan viewpoint. At its root, politics is the power and authority to make decisions and allocate resources. We need look no further than the disproportionate distribution of resources, school segregation, standardized testing and so on to see the power of politics in education that maintains school inequity.

Every day, we are upholding democratic values with an understanding that "politics must be part of our classrooms if we are to empower students to dissect and challenge rhetoric, understand and discern democratic ideals, and be active citizens who work in service to humanity" (Rembert, 2021). Indeed, the adage is true: every educational decision is a political one. Yes, my decision to have a conversation with a colleague that questioned why she'd told students they should not speak in their native language in class was a political one. Maggie B.'s decision to organize a hood's-up day to commemorate Trayvon Martin was a political one. The decision of a teacher at Heather D.'s early childhood school to have her students create a public memorial to Breonna Taylor featuring their artwork and subsequently discuss with the kindergarteners the reasons adults would deface their memorial was a political one. Dillin R.'s creation of a Stories of the African Diaspora course at a predominately White racialized school was a political act. The texts we read, the policies we adopt, the courses we create and teach, the way we grade are all political decisions. We make these decisions understanding the range of societal beliefs and experiences related to power, privilege and oppression and how these shape our lives and how our responses and actions shape social, political and economic systems. And thus, by making critical, necessary decisions, we are challenging politics and its policies that have denied access, questioned belonging, restricted power and perpetuated inequity.

As educators, we have a responsibility to foster the intellectual and political development of our students. To do this, we must be willing to make educational decisions informed by the personal, social, political and cultural needs and identities of students. This means asking ourselves questions like those Facing History posed to educators: *"How do politics (membership, power, and belonging) show up in my classroom, and do I interrogate this? How can disagreement be rooted in love? And when it's not, where and how do I stand up against what is bigoted and exclusionary?"* (FitzGibbon, 2020). We must resist the attempts to instill fear and manipulate us into believing that these decisions are politicizing our classrooms. We must recognize that the aim of this fearmongering and undermining of our autonomy is to make us so tenuous that we cannot make the essential changes needed to challenge oppressive structures. We must be willing to have difficult conversations about race, privilege and power dynamics in our classroom, PTA, staff and board meetings. We must also be willing to open these same spaces to students, so they can freely engage. It is through the constant exploration, analysis and deconstruction of racism and White supremacy that we can in community with students gain the understanding necessary to construct something new that sees and serves everyone. Think of it like a person who has been climbing a mountain for many days but has become scared to take the next step; if they had the courage to take that final step, they would reach the summit and be able to look out on the world in a new way. Just like that final step, dismantling oppressive systems and taking risks to transform education requires courage and a willingness to take the leap.

> **COMPREHENSION CHECK**
> ◆ Can you name your fears associated with antiracism?
> ◆ What is your understanding of the politics of education?
> ◆ How are the inequities in schools (your school specifically) tied to politics (access, power and resources)?
> ◆ How do the social, political and cultural identities of students shape their education?

Louder for the people in the back

Our silence maintains the system of racism. To be an effective educator, and I contend effective in any profession, is to never let our fear silence us. **Antiracism calls us to be vulnerable and to push *through* our fears. It is ultimately about trust, either you trust the impact of your voice and actions or you don't. If the latter is true, why are you an educator?** It is disingenuous to want change and to also be scared to confront and speak out against any obstacles to that change. This is not to negate the fact that talking about race and racism can be challenging. Yet, we must be willing to not be stymied by self-imposed discomfort and take risks and make mistakes, in order to continue to grow and challenge the status quo. And White racialized educators, particularly, must be mindful to not give into the entitlement of racial comfort. When you (White racialized educators) center yourself and your comfort levels, you are inadvertently spawning a dangerous cycle of systemic racism and oppression. This entitlement can lead to the whitewashing of curriculum and the histories shared in your classroom. It can also lead to tokenizing, infantilizing and marginalizing racialized students of the global

204 ♦ Falling Action

majority and not giving them the same respect or opportunities as their White racialized peers. And it can lead to the exclusion of racially diverse perspectives, experiences and knowledge-building, which can lead to oppressive mindsets and practices. To move away from these practices means continually asking yourself: What am I communicating and what do I believe if/ when I esteem my comfort over my racialized students, parents/ caregivers, colleagues, friends and others who have been histori-cally oppressed? How can I challenge the ways I have been con-ditioned to feel, think and act?

In addition to the aforementioned fears that silence us, some of us hold the belief that we lack the knowledge and skills nec-essary to engage in race-centric dialogue. As a result, we opt for silence that presumes safety and neutrality. However, nothing is neutral—especially in education, and suggesting such, is itself an advantaged position to take. To quote Nobel Prize winner Elie Wiesel (1986) "neutrality helps the oppressor," and there-fore choosing neutrality is a privilege. By not taking action to oppose racism, our inaction can have the same result as actively supporting it since our silence can be perceived as agreement, thus allowing racism to continue without challenge. There is no neutrality, safety or comfort for students, particularly his-torically oppressed racialized students, in our silence. Not one teacher or student I interviewed spoke about students fearing instructional shifts toward antiracism. Instead, their fear was that we do nothing. In Chapter 5, Natalie A. stated that "if you're just turning a blind eye to that [racism] we're really not improv-ing at all." In our avoidance of difficult and necessary conversa-tions about race and racism, we are failing to realize that they are already part of the dialogue and ethos of our classrooms. When I walk into a room, the discourse of race enters with me. When students enter the classroom, the ethos of race is already present because as racialized beings, race is never absent. And so, our silence is itself dialogue. If you have let fear and silence speak for you, the solution is simple. Educate yourself (check, you are doing that right now). Enter the conversation. Begin normalizing conversations about race, racism, inequity and jus-tice in your personal life and then in your classroom. The path of antiracism has "tacks in it, and splinters, and boards torn up, and places with no carpet on the floor—bare" (Hughes et al., 1995) but that does not deter us. We face our fears and overcome them in the courageous pursuit of equity and justice.

From the teacher's desk

Jessica K., a 5th-grade literacy educator, recalls her former principal's public exercise of fearlessness that shifted the culture of her school and teaching.

> *Society tells you that you should keep your blinders on, but I think that it comes down to White folks in spaces who are committed to the work and who then model it for other White folks: owning it–owning it upfront to others. My former principal, who was a White man and amazing principal, definitely went through a journey and a process and didn't get things right every time but I remember him owning it. One time, he stood in front of the entire staff and said these are my biases. These are all of them, and for 20 minutes, he shared every bias he had. We're all like—okay, it was a new thing. I was sitting thinking: I can say this publicly? I can have honest conversations with friends about this? About what I am thinking? You can just air all your dirty laundry, and people will respond to it in a really positive way? Yeah, there was definitely discomfort, but I kept thinking this doesn't have to be something that we have to be afraid of. We don't have to hide it. By putting it out there, we're doing something about it. It was so powerful. It shifted something inside of my brain. That 20 minutes transformed my classroom because then I started talking to my students about things: things I would not have shared before, things that made me vulnerable. I've created a safe space and community, and we can have very honest conversations about race because I saw that was possible.*

My parents always told my brother and I that a closed mouth never gets fed. They were encouraging us to be vocal and direct about our needs and desires in order to attain them. Jessica's former principal desired to challenge his staff's social consciousness by deprivatizing his biases. He was initiating a dialogue about the meaning of honesty and vulnerability and their consequences while also making space for the faculty to do the same. Following his example, they could remove their masks and face a messy and uncomfortable truth, knowing that even if it felt difficult, they would have support from their colleagues. Neither the principal nor Jessica would have known that such a shift in the school's culture was possible if the principal had remained silent. He opened his staff up to the possibility of doing things differently by sharing all his biases with them. His courage had a ripple effect, resulting in Jessica creating another layer of cariño y confianza with her students. Also, because he shared his biases, Jessica's former principal was accountable for them and thus more likely to recognize and work to consciously disrupt them. While this process of deprivatization can push the limits of our comfort zone, it is a necessary one in order to collectively unshroud our internal and external White supremacy. Perhaps, it is not a 20-minute confession in front of all your peers. Maybe it is a candid conversation with your JEDI (justice, equity, diversity and inclusion) buddy because when we are regularly sharing our goals, struggles and desire to learn and unlearn, we "reinforce the reflective habits of mind necessary for overcoming deficit orientations" (Brown McClain et al., 2021).

Heather D, former pre-K educator and antiracist administrator, shared the benefits of having a DEI (diversity, equity and inclusion) buddy.

> We've got a number of mechanisms here to get people in these conversations. There's a group of DEI partners which is totally voluntary, and we're working on making it a more formalized part of our school culture. It works like this: everybody who wants to participate is paired with a partner at the beginning of the year. The goal is to have a thought partner who you can meet with regularly to help you process or just discuss DEI related things in the world or in your classroom. It is someone who holds you accountable and asks you the hard questions to push you. I have done that for my DEI partner as we have had a lot of conversations about the violence against the Asian American community this year.

Dust your shoulders off

Despite our best efforts, it is impossible to satisfy everyone. There will inevitably be a colleague, a parent or caregiver, an administrator or a stranger who does not appreciate our anti-racist efforts. No matter how hard we try or how many antira-cist actions we take, there will always be someone who doesn't agree. This could be a colleague who does not think our actions are enough or a parent or caregiver who thinks we are going too far. It could be an administrator who doesn't agree with our approach or a stranger who believes our efforts are misguided. No matter how well intentioned our actions may be, there will always be someone who finds fault with them. Don't be discouraged; it can be hard for people to accept change, especially when it comes to racism because it is a foundational principle of this nation and as natural and free-flowing as the water we drink. Therefore, it is important to stay resilient and not let the negativity of these detractors derail our antiracist efforts. We can take the criticism into account and use it to improve our approach, or we can simply ignore it and continue to do what we know is right, based on our reading, listening *and* being in community and solidarity with racialized people of the global majority. When faced with this criticism, it is important to remember our own values and why we are doing what we're doing. We must remember our ultimate goal is to create a fairer and more just society for all, so dust your shoulders off, stay focused and continue the fight.

Figure 6.1 is a guide for handling objections to antiracism in the classroom. It is an adaptation of a protocol created by my husband, Marcus, for his upcoming book on negotiation and objection handling. While it may seem contrary, the pushback we receive from antiracist detractors is an exercise in negotiation. The Four A's protocol provides a structured approach to handling such negotiations predicated on listening, keeping the lines of communication open, interrogating and understanding the other person's perspective and collaborative problem-solving.

Four A's *for handling objections*

the objection
- This demonstrates you are listening.

What I heard you say is the classroom reading of "Me and White Supremacy" made your child uncomfortable.

with the person's right to object (not the objection)
- This deescalates the situation by finding common agreement.

Yes, addressing your child's discomfort is important.

follow-up questions related to the objection
- This encourages the objector to interrogate their thoughts, ideas and/or beliefs.

Is it just that your child was uncomfortable or are you questioning the validity of the text?

the objection and potential resolutions
- This allows a pathway to repeat the cycle or offer a solution

.The text is part of the school curriculum. I can share some of the learning outcomes and ways it will be used in the classroom.

FIGURE 6.1

The Four A's of handling objections to your antiracist pedagogy

1. **Acknowledge** the objection.
   - ◆ Most people just want to be heard, so take time to actively listen and not defend. If possible, provide physical cues that you are listening/engaged e.g., slight nod of the head, leaning forward, taking notes. As you are listening, you will also want to be aware of the emotions behind the words of the objector.
2. **Agree** with their right to disagree.
   - ◆ Acknowledge and validate the feelings of the person pushing back. The objector is likely not expecting your agreement even if it's just you agreeing with their right to object and not the objection itself.
3. **Ask** relevant follow-up questions.
   - ◆ Questions allow us to continue listening. They also provide space for the objector to interrogate their own thought process. You may through questioning

have the chance to uncover the *real* problem or need. According to Marcus, this is important because "you can't address the unknown and the worst objection is the one you're unaware of."

4. **Assess** what you've heard, and if you're confident you've identified the objection, offer information and collaborate on a resolution.
   ◆ Share facts, stories, examples that help your objector better understand.
      ○ Avoid teacher talk or jargon that may become fodder for debate.
   ◆ Seek a mutual resolution. As you understand the root issue behind the objection and/or need, you will want to also engage the objector in brainstorming possible solutions.
      ○ Present your solutions in the form of questions to engage the objector as a collaborator in this negotiation because when your objector is part of the problem-solving process, they have ownership in the outcome.

I would love to tell you that going through these steps solves the problem or that you will get to each step in the order they appear. The protocol is malleable, and nothing is foolproof. Sometimes you will go through these steps and both you and the objector will be satisfied and the process ends. Other times, you may have to ask more questions and acknowledge new objections. Other times, emotions and misinformation will hamper negotiations and no solution will satisfy your objector. Be prepared for it all, but know your efforts are not in vain. They are creating a dialogue and pushing people who have been swimming too long with the current of racism.

Students
By proxy, our students are on this antiracist journey with us. Some students may be further along than we are, while others may be just discovering that the path exists. As we learn and grow, so should our students. And while change can be intimidating for

some of our colleagues, administrators, parents/caregivers, our students are ready for it. As evidenced in Chapter 5, applying a critical antiracist lens has inspired Jocelyn and Ryan to challenge their own assumptions and those of their peers. They value the honesty and open discourse antiracist pedagogy encourages, as well as the opportunity it provides to learn about race, systems of oppression and the oft-untold contributions of racially excluded people. Admittedly, not all of our students will be as comfortable as some of the students in Chapter 5 in confronting their biases and privilege. Yet, as we build capacity, empathy and solidarity, we are making room for our collective antiracist knowledge and ideals to become acculturated.

From the teacher's desk

Lisa T. explains why antiracism is necessary for her students and how she handles students who are at different points on their own antiracist journey.

With my students, I think the biggest thing I always go back to is the idea of empathy. I understand that that becomes a squishy thing, and people think [it] is very feelings based and all these things. And it is, but empathy also very much has a critical thinking aspect. We just started our immigration unit in American studies, and we always have these big questions to answer. Our guiding question is: Who is an American? And because this is also very immediate and timely, we watched a short clip of people being bussed up and flown to Martha's Vineyard. Some kids made comments like, "Well, if these people wanted them here," and "They are here to take our stuff." And hearing those responses I always say, "What personal experiences have you had that make you think that? Where did that come from? Say more about why you think this way. What individual experiences, examples, can you point to because other people in this room have also shared that they're not originally from here, so explain your individual reason or experiences? Not what you have heard, let's think and speak as individuals with experience and knowledge." It's always hard because you don't want to give kids a platform to say just anything. You want to call it like it is, and say, when necessary, that this is not how we talk about other people here or this is offensive in a lot of ways for individuals in this room. I like to always start first by questioning students because the other concern I have is, I want those students to still be in the conversation. The worst thing that can happen is that they leave the conversation and shut me out. And they're thinking, "Well, this teacher's on her ..." So I try to keep them in the conversation to build that empathy by asking them to tell me more about what experiences make them feel that way. And by personalizing it, and maybe asking: "How would you respond to a classmate who just told you last week that her family came here from Syria?"

Dillin R. shared how being a Black man and antiracist educator impacts students' conversations about race in his classroom.

If you see a Black dude in front of you talking about race, well, he might know a little something about that. So I feel like I often do not get much pushback when it comes to people asking me questions or being inquisitive about something regarding race. It's also the relationship I tried to build with the students. I think they're more comfortable being like, 'Can I say this? Is this cool? Is that racist?' Or bringing up things they think involve race, so we can have a discussion about it.

Just recently two students in my class were going back and forth about something that one thought was racist. Instead of being like, "Hey, guys, be nice to each other. Don't do that," and moving on with the lesson, I stopped class right there and addressed it. To some people, it may seem like it's an argument with students saying not nice words. We had to address that somebody felt offended because of something involving race. And then move to how can we have conversations about that to create healing? Instead of, immediately, accusing somebody of being racist, and even if they were not, it's always best to ask questions, especially if you can get them to realize what they were doing is racist. It's important to stop, pause and ask questions: Why is that racist? If they can't give an answer, maybe it wasn't, or if they do have an answer and they hesitate, we can talk about the reason why they're reluctant to say that's racist. It's about having a conversation, and it's uncomfortable but you gotta be ready to be uncomfortable.

Colleagues

Sometimes the call is coming from inside the house. It may not be your students or your administrators, you may receive your most fervent opposition from your colleagues. Perhaps, they are questioning the posters on your walls as did one of my colleagues when I posted a picture online of my classroom adorned with "We the People" images that made visible racially and ethnically excluded people, including a young Muslim woman wearing an American flag headscarf. Maybe it comes from your canon-worshiping colleagues. The ones who vow to never stop reading Dr. Seuss even after learning about the racist imagery and ideas in many of the texts because they like dressing up in their Seuss costume each year. Some of my colleagues could not fathom why I happily abandoned *The Adventures of Tom Sawyer* and several other arcane short stories and instead opted to read more relevant and diverse literature with students. They expressed concern that I was not equipping students with the skills they needed to succeed in high school, as if only reading the "classics" provided students with the ability to think critically and was a barometer of academic success.

Table 6.1 offers an example of how I might engage with colleagues who oppose my classroom texts.

Although the opposition may continue, my attempt to resolve the objection is to center the most important stakeholders in the conversation—students. As an antiracist educator, I am constantly gathering, assessing and responding to feedback from students both formally and informally in order to inform learning *and* to use as evidence for those opposing antiracist praxis. Student thoughts, feelings and words should supersede all opposition.

Administrators

Jessica's former principal and Heather D. are not the norm. They are school leaders with a keen understanding of the ways race impacts students' lives and outcomes. They are constantly reflecting on how their schools, the educational system and its norms perpetuate racism. They are asking the hard questions: Who is the school serving? Who is it not serving? Why? In what ways is the school reproducing the racial status quo? They are not admiring problems but combating systemic racism with systemic antiracist ideologies, practices and policies. When making decisions, they consult affected racialized people groups,

TABLE 6.1 The 4 A's Framework for handling colleagues' objections with scripted responses

Acknowledge	*The problem is that you believe the texts and discourse in my classroom do not include canonical texts and therefore lack rigor.*
Agree	*I hear you. Yes, **I would agree** that students need to think critically for today, tomorrow and beyond.*
Ask	*Are you saying only the classics provide rigor? **Why do you say that? Can you share an example with me?***
Assess	*Have you ever read* Possessing the Secret of Joy *by Alice Walker? In high school, I read Shakespeare, Dickens, Brontë and Hawthorne and not one of those books challenged or encouraged natural criticality. It was that Alice Walker book that circulated through my friend group that I read with a dictionary nearby, annotating, questioning and researching to fully understand it. It is not considered a canonical text. Yet, I saw myself in it and I wondered about places in Africa and their traditions and the whys and hows of things that happened in the book. What book did that for you?*
	That is what I am attempting to do in my classroom. I want books to spark something in my students. I want students to be eager to talk about the texts we read, and books other than classics have merit and can generate the deep thought I want from students. I think they are demonstrating this. I can share their feedback with you. Would you like to read their responses about the text we are reading? You are also more than welcome to come in the class to listen and hear directly from students.

The bold words represent stems you may want to add to your objection script.

taking into consideration power dynamics, their own positionality and the operationalization of Whiteness. They understand their own social and racial identities and name them. Heather D. often says her desire has always been to be a "hood educator" who teaches and influences students who share her social and racial identity, and she understands the power of that proclamation. Unfortunately, the probability that you have a school leader with the same level of knowledge, courage and commitment as Heather D. or Jessica's former principal is unlikely.

According to a recent EdWeek national survey, 59% of school administrators lack the training and resources necessary to successfully promote antiracism in their schools. **Are your school**

leaders equipped to lead this work? If not, they may not understand your antiracist journey and question your race-conscious instruction. I personally experienced this when one of my former principals "warned" me to be "cautious," presumably due to pressure from parents/caregivers who believed that being "colorblind" was best for their children. It is admittedly more difficult and sometimes scary to adapt curricula, change policies and engage students in antiracist action like the kindergarteners in Heather D.'s school did without administrative support. If your school leaders are unprepared and/or intimidated when it comes to addressing the structural causes of racism in the school community, you'll have to start with the basics.

1. **Make connections.** Working to build relationships with administrators can help collaboration and understanding. Find common ground between the values and desired outcomes of leaders and what you are doing in your classroom. Repeat school leaders' own words back to them related to student success when you are sharing about how your instruction benefits students. Use the school's mission statement or desired outcomes to demonstrate how your pedagogy aligns with academic and social goals.

2. **Lead learning.** When in doubt, do what we do best— teach. If your school leaders are in that 59%, they need to be educated. Ask questions to gauge their understanding of systemic racism and its reproduction in schools. Share your knowledge about the effects of Whiteness on students. Offer resources from school leadership journals and organizations so that your administrators can observe the antiracist efforts of other school leaders in similar positions.

3. **Share success.** Invite school leaders into your classroom to see your antiracist instruction and students in action. This may ease their fears and discomfort. When you receive feedback from students or when you share information with parents, share this with school leaders so they hear from all involved parties.

4. **Be patient and persistent.** School leaders often work in silos and can be slow to implement change. Be consistent in your messages and don't give up.

School leaders are accountable to many stakeholders, including students, parents/caregivers, educators, the school board and the larger community. To manage the various expectations of these stakeholders, they need the tools, understanding and support of their superintendents and school boards, as well as the commitment of teachers. To meet these demands, school leaders will need to continually educate themselves and share their knowledge with others. This will enable them to effectively manage expectations, create successful outcomes for all stakeholders and extend necessary support to antiracist educators.

From the teacher's desk
Jennifer R., a former high school English teacher who works currently as a Director of Equity and Belonging in a high school, discusses how leaders can systematize the work of antiracism.

It's a systems thing. We're working on how are we empowering our people who are with us, and giving them opportunities, helping them to shine and making them those champions. We're doing curriculum review right now, we really haven't done that here. It's really outdated, and I love that the Curriculum Director embedded Gholdy Muhammad's pursuits. Our department is sharing with staff the [Culturally Responsive] teaching and leading standards that the colleges are using. And then there is the new Danielson model to adopt and use. If we're not holding people accountable for that kind of stuff, then they don't really ever have to learn to do it. But if it is, "Oh, I'm getting reviewed on that," then that's the real important part. It really is about how we are supporting and pushing people who are in it to win it, championing them and giving them that platform. And then how are we making it a part of our system with our leaders knowledgeable, and everyone knowing that those are our expectations. I think then it makes it harder to just say, "I don't want to do that or this." A lot of what happens in schools is that people are more autonomous, and they can fuss about things, but when this is in your review it has to be explicit. My work is getting us there. Our leadership team

is making a lot of changes. We are embedding this work everywhere.
So we can say: "This is in my portrait of a graduate. This is in my
portrait of a student. This is in my portrait of a system." Then staff
can say, "Oh, okay." That's different than it not even being said at all.
It's everyone's work, and then in the work, it's showing up in a lot of
ways. It will take time; it's constant work.

Parents/Caregivers

A 2020 Pew Research Study revealed that 80% of people in the
United States believe racism is a problem, yet many of those
same respondents have taken no action and have a limited
understanding of what it means to combat it. This illustrates
why, as we strive to educate students on systems of oppression, structural racism and Whiteness, it leaves some parents/
caregivers feeling uncomfortable and threatened. This is especially true for White racialized parents/caregivers who have
little to no experience with systemic racism and thus have a low
threshold for the racial humility and discomfort that the work
of antiracism requires. They may disregard antiracism as radical
since it demands drastic personal, social and political changes.
As educators, we must be prepared to address the backlash that
may come from parents/caregivers who consider your antiracist
instruction as radicalization. This kind of uninformed backlash
can impact students, our overall classroom environment, as well
as our own job security and mental health.

As we provide antiracist instruction, we must recognize that
it can prompt parents/caregivers to confront their beliefs, biases,
bigotry, power and privilege—a daunting task that may cause
them to be anxious, prompting emails and phone calls. They
may feel that while adults are able to face and seek to understand
race, equity and justice, these concepts are too complex and emotionally fraught to be discussed in the classroom. In Chapter 5,
Jocelyn reported that a parent or caregiver expressed concern
that their child was being taught to feel guilty or ashamed due
to race-centric instruction. This objection demonstrates a lack of
understanding in distinguishing between personal and structural racism. Therefore, we may need to add parents/caregivers
to our list of learners. As we share information with them about

the learning and happenings in our classrooms, we should also provide parents/caregivers with resources (e.g. the parent/caregiver guide in Table 6.2, which can be tailored to your teaching context) to aid their understanding of antiracism in our classroom and quell any trepidation that reasonable parents/caregivers may be feeling.

TABLE 6.2 Parent/caregiver guide to understanding antiracism in ELA*

Purpose	Antiracist instruction creates equitable, inclusive learning environments and encourages critical thinking about equity and justice. It teaches students about different races and ethnicities, beliefs and histories, helping them understand the importance of respect, empathy and being a changemaker.

Understanding difference	History
	◆ Providing perspectives and information to understand the origins of oppression, its evolution and the distinctions of human difference across time and contexts
	  ○ Develop an understanding of the complexities of race and its effect on individuals, communities and society
	Texts
	◆ Understanding and analyzing our differences through stories, experiences and language
	  ○ Read, listen and view texts by a diverse array of authors who have varied, relevant and meaningful perspectives
	  ○ Build critical thinking and literacy skills (to create better readers and thinkers)
	    ■ Reflect on the ways language, race, history and other social identities have created social barriers and how that impacts us

Learning about ourselves and others	Our stories
	◆ Learning from and about one another
	  ○ Understanding of difference based on our individual identities
	  ○ Provide an inclusive and safe classroom that encourages understanding, empathy and humility in our words and actions
	  ○ Disrupt bias and stereotypes
	  ○ Encourage respect and appreciation for one another and self

Creating better leaders and citizens	Our future ◆ Sharing what it means to create change and make the world a better place for its citizens ◆ Empowering students to be problem-solvers and upstanders

* Know the legislation in your state before providing any resources to parents/caregivers.

Some parents/caregivers may not understand the purpose and value of antiracist teaching and be confused as to what it looks like in action. It can be intimidating to share our antiracist ELA classrooms with parents/caregivers, as they may not agree with our teaching methods, and we might worry about receiving criticism or negative feedback. Understandably, those of us at the beginning of our antiracist journey are likely to feel especially apprehensive. To alleviate this fear, we must remember that parent/caregiver feedback is normal and to be expected. To ensure reasonable parents/caregivers understand and develop, we must be prepared to have open and honest conversations with them. For those parents/caregivers who are not open to reason, I suggest that you seek out the support of your school leaders, as it may be difficult to find a resolution on your own and you do not want to deplete yourself trying.

From the teacher's desk

Mark L. is a recently retired educator who shares what he learned about how to handle parental/caregiver resistance after more than 30 years in the classroom.

As far as the resistance, of course, it's going to start with parents. But a lot of times, and this baffles me and is a frustration of living in a social media world, a parent will post something, let's say on Facebook with pride, but one of their family members will become an alarmist saying, "Oh my gosh, they can't do that. That's illegal. That's critical race theory. I'm going to call the school board." And the next thing you know there's a person complaining about you or about your building to the school board that has no skin in the game. They just saw something that they were appalled by because they don't understand it. That's the most frustrating resistance. In reality, does it stop what I'm doing? No, it's just a stumbling block—a hurdle. Those people, they're out there and they're gonna find me. They're gonna find us. It is what it is.

The people that I believe deserve the most respect, the most communication, the most openness are the parents because they're concerned about the type of education that their kid is getting. And let me just, I'm sure you know this, but let me just get it out of my system—we're moving away from textbooks because of the internet and all these fantastic new online programs that do an amazing job.

Therefore, politicians have less say and control of what should be put into the textbooks. And as the politicians are losing control, we're starting to see less trust and more pushback from the communities at large. The curriculum can now go in various ways, and once we ditched textbooks (I did that like 15 years ago), we could see the true nature and art of teaching where we're meeting the students where they are, hearing and feeling their needs, and changing things on the fly, as opposed to, we finished chapter one, now it's time to go to chapter two.

When I meet resistance, I have a couple of rules: no emails, no texts or emails. I'm not talking to anyone where my words can be misconstrued. I want to meet face to face. I want to sit down and as often as I can I want to have the student available, too. I want to be completely open and honest with parents, and I want them to feel heard. It is less about an us versus them kind of thing. I want to get rid of the divide, and partner with them, educating them about what I'm teaching, my reasons why and how this will enrich the student in various ways. I want them to feel the process and realize that it's not scary. It's just an opportunity for each one of my students, as individuals, to make up their own mind, and bring in the worldview or to create their own worldview. Parents have said, "Well don't present things to my kids before they're ready." That tends to be easily erased when the parent sees that I'm not trying to tell your kids to think one way or another. I want them to see the truth, the facts—as factual as they can be. Ultimately, I want them to compare their real world with what they're learning and come up with a worldview, so they can start to then put their belief system together. Then, I ask parents: Do you want your child to create their own belief system to open their eyes, decide what fits them and their personality and where they're going in life? Or do you truly want them to just follow what others say? Very often, after just a little reflection, parents will tell me, "Well, I don't have all the answers. I don't want my kids to just be stunted by what I feed them because maybe I'm wrong. I strongly believe this but maybe I'm wrong." So it's that face-to-face conversation that makes it really real. You have to take out the defensiveness and that is so hard sometimes because parents come in defensive, but you just have to meet them with calm and a let's learn from each other attitude.

TEACHER LESSON IN SESSION

Shannon B., Indianapolis

Shannon B. has been an ELA and humanities educator, an instructional coach and, this school year, an administrator.

HAVE YOU ENCOUNTERED ANY CHALLENGES TO YOUR METHOD OF TEACHING FROM ANY STAKEHOLDER, WHETHER THAT BE STUDENTS, THE COMMUNITY, OR EVEN COLLEAGUES?

We did a semester-long PD [professional development] on Zaretta Hammond's book, *Culturally Responsive Teaching and the Brain.* We read it as a group and broke down chapters. I incorporated a lot of understanding of diversity and equity into our reading of that text. I encountered [resistance] from people who were from very different backgrounds. You kind of expect it from the White savior teacher types, but there were others who I was like, wait, you're from this community and you're talking like this. There was a mindset by some of the teachers that "I pushed through and was able to make it, so I want to push these kids through and help them make it." And definitely, some thought well, "That's not a teacher's job," which I found really fascinating. And then, of course, there were people who expressed being uncomfortable and not wanting to talk about race at all.

I had a lot of one-on-one conversations with one member of my team. I actually had many conversations with her where she and I sat down to talk about it one-on-one. In those instances, she would agree: "Yes, it makes sense." But as soon as we were in a big group and a colleague called her out, asking: "Why aren't you saying anything? I'm curious what your thoughts are." She'd say, "Well, I just get uncomfortable talking about race." And I just had to say, "Huh, why is that? Because you and I have one-on-one conversations all the time." And she replied, "Well, I just don't feel my words are gonna be understood when I'm in a big group like this." And she is a White woman. And I think the reason why she feels uncomfortable is because she's in this almost White fragility mindset where she can accept that racism exists but believes she is not part of the problem, and so she doesn't really want to help come up with any solution.

WHAT ADVICE WOULD YOU GIVE EDUCATORS WHO ARE ON THIS JOURNEY AND WHO HAVE COLLEAGUES WHO ARE MAKING IT DIFFICULT?

I would advise that we first acknowledge that everyone is in a different place—acknowledging that we might feel the urgency or that we do feel the urgency. I've taught in education for 10 years, and I can tell you, I felt that urgency my very first year, and I still do. When I think back to those kids I taught 10, nine, eight years ago, I think we did them an injustice. The fact that it's not fixed and they are full-grown adults now is a problem. But at the same time, I have to take a step back when I have conversations with current coworkers and staff reminding myself that they weren't in the classroom 10 years ago. Many of the educators I'm currently working with were students 10 years ago, so they don't have the context that I do in understanding this. They're coming from a different perspective. Therefore, I need to help them understand that there are other perspectives other than their own, and I need the help of experts that look like them. Because I'm Mixed-race many times I can have those conversations, but as soon as race comes up, I'm othered. I'm married to a White man, and he and I have had many conversations where we're talking about a mutual person that we both know, and I tell my husband I need you to go have this conversation with them because if I do, it will be perceived as coming from the assertive Black woman place, even if I speak to them as a person with expertise.

He can have the conversation with them as someone from their demographic. In a lot of ways, that has worked. It gets really tricky, especially in small schools and communities, because, a lot of times, this person doesn't exist. I have also realized it can't be someone in a position of authority and from their demographic. It has to be someone on their level and from their demographic, and also someone they respect.

As a person who works toward antiracism, I have trouble calling myself an antiracist educator because I'm still working on being more antiracist. As people who are working to be antiracist educators, we have to be willing to recognize when we're not going to get through to someone and pass the charge to someone else.

COMPREHENSION CHECK

◆ What is your initial reaction to Shannon's words?
   o How did you react in your body?
   o What does your overall reaction suggest or reveal to you?
   o Was there anything she said that made you uncomfortable? What was it? Why?
◆ Are there connections you can make to what she shared?
◆ How might you apply her advice?
◆ What are you taking with you from Shannon's spotlight?

Sit down—be humble

Do you know that one teacher in your school who, no matter the subject of the professional learning, says they have been doing (insert topic and side-eye) for years? They are the ones who proclaim they were antiracist teachers before it was even a thing or popular (insert eye roll). Don't be like them. You can't co-opt this lifelong journey for a photo-op. It's not enough to look the part, use the terminology and then go and do the same stuff you've done for years. Be honest with yourself: You need the PD. You aren't a founding member of the antiracist club. You haven't reached destination antiracism because hint: look around, none of us have.

On the other hand, it's a marathon, not a sprint. We don't need antiracism done speed dating style. Doing a bunch of things without full knowledge and intentionality is akin to all the organizations who raced to write antiracist and equity statements that are collecting metaphorical dust on their websites. Don't be like them. This isn't magic wand–type work. To undo and reprogram our racist operating system is deep, complex and important. Resist the temptation to wag your finger at others who haven't started their journey when you're just at the half-mile marker yourself. I understand the desire to *do something* but slow down. Without racial literacy and intentionality, you're likely doing more harm than good and no better than those at the starting line.

You also don't get to sit on the sidelines because you don't even teach racialized students of the global majority or you're not problematic so someone else can figure that out or you're going to let historically oppressed racialized teachers carry that load. Like the colleague in Shannon's story, choosing to disengage and let others take the journey while you linger at the rest area is not being on the journey at all. You don't get to ride the coattail of others. This is not a free ride. I'm not saying that we should all be going at the same speed. Everyone will have a different pace; however, it's important that we monitor ourselves and not become complacent. Remember, we are often standing in the way of our own progress.

Finding your people

We were created for interdependence, so it's essential to find your people to stay motivated and learn on this journey. Who is part of your antiracist ecosystem? Is your teacher best friend or work spouse joining you? Are there a few people in your department or grade-level team you can collaborate with and learn from? Thanks to the internet, you don't have to be in the same state or even the same country to connect and learn from like-minded people and experts. In this book, many teachers referenced finding antiracist teachers on Twitter to follow and learn from. It worked for me. I've learned immensely from #cleartheair and #disrupttexts. When I began this journey, I joined Twitter chats to ask questions and gather resources. I also took advantage of professional organizations and various professional learning opportunities, attending conferences, watching webinars and engaging in as many other activities as I could. Through these efforts, I was able to connect with people and find antiracist community and solidarity.

Here are some ways to find an antiracist community:

◆ Search online for antiracist organizations and networks in your area or use social media to connect with other antiracist educators.

◆ Attend events or conferences related to antiracism or connect with other educators through professional development workshops and seminars.

◆ Join an antiracist book club or discussion group to get involved in antiracist conversations.

◆ Join local antiracist organizations and groups that are doing the work to dismantle racism in your community.

Finding your antiracist community is just the beginning. Being in antiracist solidarity comes with responsibility and accountability. It means actively listening to, understanding and promoting the experiences and perspectives of educators from all backgrounds and identities, recognizing and challenging systemic racism and developing and implementing antiracism in all facets. It also means advocating for and supporting the rights, voices and needs of racialized educators of the global majority and other marginalized communities. It is important to acknowledge that finding an antiracist community is not easy. It requires dedication and commitment to the cause, but it is more than worth it in the long run.

WAYPOINT

While I, personally, struggle to call this work radical—to me there is nothing radical about humanization, justice and equity, I do understand that challenging and attempting to change a deep-seated and institutionally embedded idea (lie) that has become a categorical belief existing since the Portuguese rounded the tip of Africa is a mammoth endeavor that requires radical pursuit and purpose. We will have to become teachers of students, colleagues, leaders and parents/caregivers at times on this lifelong journey. We cannot get lost in the sauce, or the moment, and forget to humble ourselves and stay curious.

THINK–ACT–REIMAGINE

Think - Act - Reimagine

Think	Act	Reimagine
How can treating objections as a negotiation change the way you approach these conversations? Who's part of your antiracist ecosystem?	Start collecting feedback and keeping data related to your antiracist pedagogy. Adapt the parent/caregiver guide to antiracism in your class.	Antiracist solidarity as more than a network of learning and support but as an opportunity for you to support and engage in antiracist action with and for others.

FIGURE 6.2

DO NOW
- ◆ Tab the Four A's protocol and write out some sentence stems to practice.
- ◆ Begin the work of finding your people.

Resources

Racelighting is a concept that J. Luke Wood expounds on at
    https://racelighting.net/
A Social Ecological Model of Antiracism at https://cssp.org/
    resource/a-social-ecological-model-of-racism-anti-racism/

Section V
Resolution

7

Beyond Race

What are some additional benefits of an antiracist ELA classroom?

Tired of existential threats to their bodies, their freedom and their livelihood, eight Black feminists united in 1974 to form the Combahee River Collective (CRC). Drawing inspiration and their name from Harriet Tubman's command of Union soldiers who organized a raid that freed more than 700 enslaved people along South Carolina's Combahee River, the women of the CRC were also revolutionaries seeking liberation. They understood that their freedom did not depend on fighting one battle but many as they existed in intersecting and interlocking forms of oppression. Simply put, these revolutionaries understood that as Black women, who are often the most societally maligned, they would always be fighting racism with one hand and using the other hand to fight sexism, homophobia, classism, capitalism and other isms.

CRC member Audre Lorde (1983), who was a writer, poet and activist, once said, "[T]here is no hierarchy of oppression. I cannot afford the luxury of fighting one form of oppression only. I cannot afford to believe that freedom from intolerance is the right of only one particular group." It stands to reason, then, that the CRC worked tirelessly to create a multifaceted approach

DOI: 10.4324/9781003296171-12

to liberation, one which recognized that all forms of marginal-ization were interconnected. These Black feminist activists cre-ated a movement and model for intersectionality, challenging the notion that all forms of oppression had to be addressed sepa-rately. In doing so, they revolutionized the way that social move-ments address liberation and social oppression.

The women of CRC have provided us with a framework for antiracist intersectionality that affirms people existing in their complexity, free from oppression and from having to choose between or among their identities. They show us that the work of antiracism is also antisexist, anticolonial, anti-ableist and so on. We cannot afford the luxury of *not* including all forms of dis-crimination, oppression and exclusion in our classroom culture, texts, policies and actions.

With liberty and justice for all

Our desire for racial justice and equity does not stop in our schools and classrooms nor is our quest for justice singular. Audre Lorde (2015) reminds us that "there is no such thing as a single-issue struggle because we do not live single-issue lives." We exist across lines of difference. Therefore, our antiracist inquiry, dis-course and praxis create opportunities to teach and learn about differences, the forms of social oppression caused by those differ-ences, how they intersect and how to use this knowledge to strive for justice for all. **This means our antiracist ELA classroom must also make space and opportunity for students to understand that societal systems of domination do not occur in a vacuum, and it is impossible to effectively study and disrupt racism, power, oppression and privilege without also interrogating and challenging the multiple "isms" that hold them in place.** It is our standard of antiracism that readies students to explore the tensions of these "taboo" topics and interlocking oppressions, important and proximate to students' lives and identities. It is no surprise, then, that our ELA classrooms become proving grounds to flatten out our differences, develop our critical consciousness and examine race and other marginalized identities and contexts. Thus, creating antiracist ELA classrooms that promote freedom in all forms—personal, academic, and intellectual—rather than those that replicate dominant narratives and power structures. As bell hooks (1996) contends, "the classroom remains the most radical space of possibility in the academy." In such classrooms, students and teachers find revolutionary spaces that equip us to understand and challenge injustice and control and revelatory spaces for freedom dreaming, to envision new futures and possibilities for a world without oppressive constraints. The opportunity to cast a shared vision for a liberated, celebrated and joyous future in community with marginalized people is the epitome of solidarity and power.

Examining the acculturation of Whiteness and the resistance of racialized people of the global majority serves as a treatise for all oppressed people. In a society that norms White, cisgender, neurotypical males, everyone else becomes the other. Reinforced by individual and institutional systems, this normalization of superiority allows social oppression to thrive, which promulgates widespread harm. There's a saying that a rising tide lifts all boats and while an economic metaphor, it is applicable in this context because when we take action to end racism, it can create a ripple effect that can benefit other groups who are also affected by the same oppressive forces. This can be seen in movements such as the civil rights movement, where the successful challenge to racial oppression benefited not only Black folk but also other marginalized groups such as women, Indigenous people and people who are differently abled.

Jessica K. said, "It's our personal responsibility to have an ever-growing understanding of systems and then to teach that to our students." She also asks some important "how" questions about intersectionality in our humanities classrooms.

How do we become intersectional? How do we actually make sure that the identities even within one race are complicated and complex? And who are the people that we're bringing into the classroom space and sharing with students or providing them opportunities to share with us?

No hierarchy of oppression

Deepening the dialogue of antiracism with students means exposing them to the myriad ways hegemonic systems marginalize people. This includes anti-Blackness, ableism, classism, heterosexism, capitalism, imperialism, colonization, citizenship status and other forms of social oppression. Through learning about the complexities of oppression that exclude and hierarchize based on myriad identities, the nuances of discrimination and its multiple manifestations and the people who resist and show us what justice looks like, our antiracist classrooms can emulate the radical human understanding, shared respect and dignity and collective responsibility modeled by the CRC.

Anti-Blackness

We live in a nation whose very foundation was established on anti-Black racism. Think of it as part of the building code of the United States. Every structure of government, from our political to economic systems and all forms of human relationship from social to cultural, were coded to dehumanize and disenfranchise Black racialized people. This code has, for centuries, been used as the foundation of domination and oppression, giving birth to Whiteness.

By definition, anti-Blackness is "an embodied lived experience of social suffering and resistance … in which the Black is a despised thing-in-itself (but not person for herself or himself) in opposition to all that is pure, human(e), and White" (Dumas & Ross, 2016). It is essential for us and students to understand that much of the racism in the United States, historically, presently and personally, is predicated on anti-Blackness. Thereby, an understanding of anti-Blackness helps us more fully comprehend Whiteness since Blackness and Whiteness are foils, neither existing without the other (Yancy, 2017). If Whiteness is an individually framed social, political, and cultural construct that privileges and prioritizes people who are racialized as White, and Blackness is a collectively framed social, political and cultural construct predicated on subjugation and the erroneous assumption of racial inferiority of people racialized as Black, then anti-Blackness is rooted in the same idea of racial superiority that Whiteness is based on, and it serves to uphold Whiteness as socially dominant. This elevation of Whiteness and casting of Blackness as inherently inferior reinforces White supremacy. By perpetuating a racial hierarchy, anti-Blackness ensures that Whiteness is normed and that Black racialized people and their cultures are seen as deviant and to be feared. However outdated, oppressive and unjust, this American building code still dictates the operation of structural racism, governing everything from education to housing to employment to health care to laws and policing and the effects of which are seen in every corner of society, shaping the lives of Black racialized people in profound and devastating ways.

The institutionalization of anti-Blackness in schools creates a hostile environment for Black racialized students. This is evidenced by punitive and exclusionary disciplinary measures and the police-state-like atmosphere of close monitoring and presumed wrongdoing they endure in school. Author and researcher Benjamin Blaisdell (2020) asserts that "Black students do not even have to do anything wrong to be hyper-surveilled: … the Black body is condemned before it even acts; it has always already committed a crime."

Anti-Blackness is also pervasive in our curricula and instruction, manifesting in the inequitable distribution of educational materials and supports provided to schools with predominantly Black student populations and the failure to address racism within the curriculum and overall school environment. Curriculum and instruction often reflect the experience and ways of knowing and being of Whiteness without consideration to the experiences and epistemologies of Black racialized students. Additionally, anti-Blackness manifests in the assessment of Black racialized students, resulting in a disproportionate representation in special education and a lack of representation in gifted and talented programs.

As educators, understanding the history and manifestations of anti-Blackness in our schools and in our society is not an option but imperative for justice, equity and the safety of Black minds and bodies. This knowledge must be codified and shared with students, examined and dissected in every text and every lesson placed in front of them. Anti-Blackness is the building code of the United States, and encoded globally, and until we recognize that, we cannot effectively address the systemic racism and oppression that permeates our institutions and our lives.

Disability awareness and justice

Globally, one in six people identify as differently abled. And while this statistic suggests that being differently abled is common and normal, ableism thrives. Incorporating disability awareness and justice into our antiracist pedagogy is therefore not supplemental but vital to making visible our differently abled students and their experiences while empowering all students to think critically about ableism and how it intersects with other forms of oppression. Introducing students to disability justice reframes the conversation; it focuses on building a community of allies, recognizing that many types of bigotry and intolerance, such as racism, sexism, homophobia and classism, intersect with and amplify ableism. In our antiracist and anti-oppressive classrooms, students can grapple with how disability is represented in text, media and popular culture. By amplifying the perspectives and voices of those living with disabilities, we redefine the concept of "normal" and "ability" so that disability is not viewed as misfortune or a shortcoming but rather as a natural part of the human experience.

Table 7.1 highlights texts to begin this dialogue. Many of these texts are written by own voice authors who are challenging deficit and exceptional narratives.

As you engage students with these texts, the following framing may be helpful.

Introduce the text
◆ Introduce the author
  ○ Is it an own-voice author (writing as a member of the community) or an outsider? How does that affect our reading and analysis of the text?
◆ To what conversation (present or past) is this text attempting to add commentary?

TABLE 7.1 Texts to begin, many of which are written by own-voice authors challenging deficit and exceptional narratives

Elementary	Middle Grades	High School
I Talk Like a River by Jordan Scott	*Insignificant Events in the Life of a Cactus* by Dusti Bowling	*The Boy Who Steals Houses* by C.G. Drew
My City Speaks by Darren Lebeuf	*El Deafo* by Cece Bell	*The Words in My Hands* by Asphyxia
I Am Not a Label: 34 Disability Artists, Thinkers, Athletes and Activists from Past and Present by Cerrie Burnell	*Real* by Carol Cujec	*The Silence Between Us* by Alison Gervais
	The Chance to Fly by Ali Stroker and Stacy Davidowitz	*Challenger Deep* by Neal Shusterman
Charlotte and the Quiet Place by Deborah Sosin	*Show Me a Sign* by Anne Clare LeZotte	*The Pretty One: On Life, Pop Culture, Disability, and Other Reasons to Fall in Love with Me* by Keah Brown
We Move Together by Kelly Fritsch	*Breathing Underwater* by Sarah Allen	
Pixar Shorts:	*Out of My Mind* by Sharon Draper	*The Pedagogy of Pathologization: Dis/Abled Girls of Color in the School-Prison Nexus* by Subini Ancy Annamma
◆ *Loop* ◆ *Float*	*A Kind of Spark* by Elle McNicoll	
	The Learning Network (*New York Times*)	TED Talk:
	◆ Lesson of the Day: "Making Music Visible: Singing in Sign"	"Purposeful Steps Away from Ableism" by Alyson Seale

Humanize the story/experience

◆ What impact does this text have on students' lives and identities?
◆ What are the potential challenges and strengths of the people or characters in the texts?
  ○ What are appropriate responses from the reader?

Impact of social oppression

◆ What forms of oppression and systems are acting upon, influencing and/or shaping the experiences of differently abled people in the text?
  ○ How does the person/character react or respond?
    ■ Examine and explain your thoughts and reactions to this response.

Resistance
◆ How does the person, character or author redress oppressive ideas or notions of being differently abled?
  ○ How is normal defined or redefined?
◆ Who are the power brokers in the texts?
  ○ What can you learn or unlearn from them?

Action
◆ What individual and collective actions are possible to bring justice and/or awareness?
◆ What else can you read or learn to better understand this perspective, and how it is marginalized or celebrated?

Queer-affirming classrooms

Literature has long been a source of insight into the human condition, but queer students have often been denied access to this gateway. Over the past decade, we have seen an improvement in the quality of queer literature, but policy bans and restrictions, as well as parental/caregiver fears, continue to limit queer students' access to literary mirrors. In 2022–2023, a great deal of anti-LGBTQIA+ sentiment has been demonstrated by the abundance of oppressive legislation on both the local and state levels. According to the ACLU, more than 80 anti-queer school bills were proposed by states. This concerning statistic and the discriminatory policies it begets could profoundly impact our ELA classrooms, limiting both what we teach and how we interact with students. As a result, there is an urgency to our cultivation of learning environments in which students have access to inclusive and affirming queer literature positioned in our curricula to create a safe space for students to explore their identities, examine the differences between gender and sexuality and foster an environment of acceptance and respect. Our queer-affirming classrooms should empower every student to develop an understanding of their own identity and make informed decisions about their own life.

The benefits of a queer-affirming classroom extend beyond humanization, providing students with critical skills. These skills include the following:

- *Critical thinking*: Students can use critical thinking skills to unpack and challenge dominant norms and narratives, assumptions and beliefs that may be oppressive or exclusionary.
- *Critical humility and empathy*: Students can learn to be empathetic, open-minded and understanding of others, regardless of their gender identity or sexual orientation.
- *Perspective-taking*: Students can practice perspective-taking to understand and appreciate queer viewpoints and experiences.
- *Unlearning bias*: Students can learn to become aware of their own biases, understand the causes of these biases and develop strategies for mitigating the effects of these biases.
- *Allyship*: Students can learn how to create and maintain environments of respect, support and advocacy that are free from judgment and discrimination, irrespective of gender identity or sexual orientation.
- *Embracing difference*: Students can learn to celebrate different gender identities, sexual orientations and gender expressions.

These skills are necessary to counter the harm and erasure experienced by queer students in school. According to the Gay Lesbian and Straight Education Network (GLSEN) 2021 National Climate Survey of over 20,000 students aged 13 to 21, integrating queer texts, discussions and actions into our antiracist ELA classrooms is essential to create safe and inclusive environments. The survey revealed that queer students experienced an increase in homophobic and derogatory remarks made by teachers and staff around gender expression from 2019 to 2021. Noteworthy for us ELA educators was that 72% of queer students reported that no LGBTQIA+ topics were included in any of their classes (Kosciw et al., 2022), hence the importance of introducing concepts like queer justice to students. Queer justice is an intersectional concept that acknowledges the complexity of oppression, particularly as it relates to sexual orientation, gender identity and expression, as well as other marginalized identities. It challenges the assumptions and systems of power that create and maintain oppression, demanding that we move beyond tolerance and respect to actively work for liberation and justice for all people. Queer justice lessons move beyond additive voices to curricula. They focus on providing students with opportunities to explore the nuances of the queer experience and examine the power of language to both oppress and empower. They also show students how to use language and storytelling as tools for understanding and advocating for the queer community.

Here are some suggestions for incorporating queer justice throughout your antiracist ELA classroom:

1. Add more queer voices into the curriculum. Invite local LGBTQIA+ activists to speak. Include prompts for students to write in response to queer issues.
2. Incorporate queer perspectives into existing material. For example, when reading texts written by cisgender, heterosexual authors ask students to consider how the story might differ if it were told from the perspective of a queer character.
3. Integrate queer language into everyday instruction. For example, use gender-neutral pronouns (they/them/their) when referring to people and include this language around your classroom or when discussing families refer to them as "families of all kinds," rather than simply using the word *families*. This also means making sure all classroom materials are free of gender-based assumptions.
4. Provide a safe space for queer students to be seen and heard. For example, set up a weekly discussion group or check-ins where students can talk about their lives and how their identities intersect with the material being taught or a class advisory group that vets texts and offers texts and lesson suggestions.
5. Examine queer history and activism. Have students research queer rights movements and discuss how these movements have successfully created change.

Table 7.2 features queer-themed texts for your classroom.

TABLE 7.2 Queer-themed texts for the classroom

Elementary	Middle Grades	High School
Federico and All His Families by Mili Hernández	*Too Bright to See* by Kyle Lukoff	*The Darkness Outside Us* by Eliot Schaefer
When Aidan Became a Brother by Kyle Lukoff	*Last Night at the Telegraph Club* by Malinda Lo	*Lark & Kasim Start a Revolution* by Kacen Callender
Grandad's Camper by Harry Woodgate	*Almost Flying* by Jake Maia Arlow	*Say it Hurts* by Lisa Summe (for mature students)
Julián Is a Mermaid by Jessica Love	*Hurricane Child* by Kacen Callender	*A Queer History of the United States for Young People* by Michael Bronksi
Pride: The Story of Harvey Milk and the Rainbow Flag by Rob Sanders	*The Last Cuentista* by Donna Higuera	
My Maddy by Gayle E. Pitman	Pixar Shorts:	*Tomorrow, and Tomorrow, and Tomorrow: A Novel* by Gabrielle Zevin
A Princess of Great Daring! by Tobi Hill-Meyer	◆ *Cariño* ◆ *Out*	*All Boys Aren't Blue* by George Johnson
This is Our Rainbow: 16 Stories of Her, Him, Them, and Us by Katherine Locke		*Gender Queer: A Memoir* by Maia Kobabe
Pixar Short:		The Learning Network (*New York Times*)
◆ *My Shadow Is Pink*		◆ Film Club: "Here I Am" ◆ Lesson of the Day: "Queer Kids, Nerds and Sword Fights: It's the Hot School Play"

Pitstop

There is a long list of other identities that experience social oppression that can and should be explored in our ELA classrooms.

◆ Make a list of others and start adding texts and lesson ideas.

◆ Open this discussion up to students. Learn about the identities they would like included in the classroom.

As we continue to grow our understanding of social oppression and its implications in our educational spaces, we should also reflect on the texts in our classrooms and libraries. Assessing the texts we make available to students is essential to demonstrate our commitment to providing affirming, non-oppressive and critical perspectives.

Librarian Sarah R.-W. believes you should include students in the assessment of texts by asking them to read the books on your shelves and critique them using the following guiding questions, and if students say the book needs to go, it goes.

◆ Do you like the book?
◆ Can you relate to it?
◆ Is the representation authentic?
◆ Is the language accurate and affirming?

Shayla E. had students who were in an independent studies class do a diversity audit of all the school's humanities courses.

◆ How can you get students involved in the assessment of books, curricula, policies and so on on a classroom and a school level?
◆ How does such involvement reinforce antiracist and anti-oppressive ideology for students?

For transgressing's sake

To transgress means to push the boundaries of what is accepted or expected, so when bell hooks encourages us to "teach to transgress," she is offering us a powerful proclamation of love and defiance. She (1996) reminds us that "in the process of teaching, we learn to recognize our own limitations and move beyond them." Similarly, in as much as *The Antiracist ELA Classroom* is about teaching students, it is really more about teaching ourselves. We are pushing the boundaries of our knowledge and the boundaries of an educational system that has relegated, erased and oppressed myriad people groups. We are understanding truths and sharing those truths with students in accessible, intentional and meaningful ways. We are understanding the different paths to freedom and guiding each student down their own unique path, understanding that each presents differing opportunities and obstacles. Because ultimately, it is our job to share power with students and show them how to create the world they want to live in. This will require interdependence and some thinking shifts on both our parts.

From the teacher's desk

Briana M., a multi-award-winning high school English educator, shares some of the thinking shifts she and her students are making.

I'm adding layers and nuance to conversations that I think are often missing for kids. They oftentimes feel, especially Black students, that they are the only oppressed group, and therefore they don't understand what solidarity means. It's always presented to students as an oppression Olympics where XYZ was always treated the worst. And so when we're talking about sexual orientation, when we're talking about race or we're talking about gender, whatever the case may be, it doesn't allow nuance for students. Acknowledging the nuance is saying, "Hey, this is a gray area right here, so let's talk a little bit more about this." That's pushing the critical thinking for students, instead of expecting students to accept binary thinking that it's either this or that. I push my students a lot to think about and better understand what does it mean to have solidarity with a certain group. As English teachers, we can tie these conversations to theme, and really push students to think about what can I learn from these events that have happened to other people, even if I'm not one of them. It's also covertly teaching them empathy—that we can feel for other people, whether we know them personally or whether we have been through their exact same situation or lived experience. It's important to analyze that without that understanding, we are moving closer toward living in a world that's devoid of empathy and to discuss what's at stake if we don't understand that people's lives are different. That people are different. I want students to know we can still learn from people who are different than us, and that learning from other people's stories has a purpose.

I also try to teach my students that we only can live and understand things from our lived experience which always is incomplete because I'm only me, and you're only you. This is why sharing stories in an English classroom is so powerful. By sharing stories, our life and our understanding of the world becomes more full when we engage in conversation with others about what they have been through, and how it is or is not similar to us and why we should care. And I hate to say it, I love my kids so much, but there's so much apathy that I've seen. I'm really trying to combat that at all times, and show them we can be so much better than we are. It takes us wanting to care.

Decolonizing ELA

As educators move toward more inclusive, human-centered, intentional and historically accurate pedagogical approaches, we must be increasingly aware of the need to decolonize our classrooms. To support in this effort, there are many 5- to 10-step methods, checklists and other resources available to help decolonize our mindset, curriculum, policies and the literary canon. While these are worthwhile endeavors, a close examination of these methods reveals that they are more analogous with deepening social justice and cultural responsiveness than the act of decolonization. As Tuck and Yang (2012) explain, decolonization is distinct and not synonymous with fixing all of education's ills. It is an active process to undo the legacies of colonialism, dismantle its power structures and reclaim Indigenous rights and sovereignty. It is not simply a distant, figurative idea—a metaphor, as Tuck and Yang assert—but a personal and political act of liberation and transformation. Since settler colonialism is an active and current structure, decolonizing must also be an active, targeted process in our classrooms.

Because the foundation of learning is rooted in Indigenous knowledge and practices, decolonizing our ELA classrooms, once again, starts with us and involves recognizing the roots of colonial power, analyzing how it has informed the way we think and teach and making a concerted effort to confront and challenge our own internalized colonialism and reframe our mindset. For ourselves and our students, evaluating and rethinking the values of our colonially built and fortified educational system is the continual work of decolonizing ELA.

In our ELA classrooms, decolonizing the classroom means exploring and incorporating Indigenous ways of knowing and learning and supporting the resurgence of Indigenous identities, languages and cultures. This means we must both recognize and question the power dynamics behind the ways knowledge is prioritized, produced and presented in the classroom. Decolonizing the classroom is an ongoing process that requires active acknowledgment of the ways in which Whiteness and colonialism are embedded in educational systems. This means actively challenging the curriculum and ethos of the classroom to center Indigeneity and provide an accurate representation of the past and present stories of Indigenous people. When we begin a literary lesson in November with picture books of the first "thanksgiving" that feature a communal celebration that did not happen or an American literature class with colonial literature or postcolonial literature that ignores settler colonialism, we are essentially rendering Indigeneity moot. To decolonize the classroom, we must understand the history of settler colonialism and its current functioning in society and share that understanding with students. This requires creating learning environments that not only dismantle the history of erasure but also allow students to explore and discuss the complexities of colonialism.

Tuck and Yang's "Decolonization is Not a Metaphor" provide some enduring understandings to guide our decolonization of ELA (2012):

◆ Colonial oppression must be confronted and dismantled in order to achieve decolonization.
◆ Decolonization involves a restructuring of power and a redistribution of resources.
◆ An understanding of the history and legacy of colonialism is necessary to understand the current state of the world.
◆ Decolonization requires critical reflection and analysis from both individuals and institutions.
◆ Decolonization involves challenging the status quo and existing power structures.
◆ Decolonization is an act of resistance and self-determination.

Globalizing racism

Today's students are more globally conscious than ever before, likely because they are living in an era of unprecedented global migration. A survey conducted during the 2019–2020 school year found that more than half of all students in the United States had discussions about global issues in their classrooms. As educators, it is our responsibility to help students understand the global complexities of racism and antiracism. As global citizens, students should recognize the effects of racialized systems of power and how these systems impact people around the world differently. By studying racism on a global scale, students can gain a better understanding of its subtleties and the various forms it takes. Ultimately, this will help them develop more effective strategies for combating racism around the world.

The global implications of racism are far-reaching and damning. Imperial and colonial empires have left a legacy of racial and ethnic caste systems, destroyed land and lives and led to a dispossession of identity worldwide. To help students understand the interconnectivity between racism, capitalism, colonialism and imperialism, we must equip them with the tools to dissect and deconstruct these systems.

Here are a few strategies:

◆ *Use primary sources.* Have students explore and discuss a variety of texts, images and artifacts, illustrating historical struggles and current issues related to global racism and antiracism.

◆ *Analyze intersectionality.* Explore the ways multiple forms of oppression, such as race, gender, class and sexuality, intersect and interact with global racism and how that differs from place to place.

◆ *Examine institutions.* Examine the role of institutions such as the police, education system and justice system in perpetuating racism globally. Asking questions like How are they structured? What values do they promote? What policies do they have in place to sustain and perpetuate racism?

◆ *Increase connectivity.* Connect the classroom to the real world by discussing current events, visiting cultural sites, inviting guest speakers to the classroom or doing virtual classroom meet-ups to collaborate and dialogue with other schools around the world.

◆ *Create and implement action plans.* Work with students to develop plans of action that they can take to address global antiracism.

To create a truly antiracist future for all, students must understand the global struggle against racism and build solidarity with those fighting it around the world. By connecting our struggles against racism and forming coalitions of support, students learn how to recognize and respond to global racism as informed and engaged global citizens.

TEACHER LESSON IN SESSION
Felicia H., Windsor Connecticut

Felicia H. is an award-winning high school English educator. She currently teaches 11th graders, her favorite grade "because even though it is an intense year for them, they seem to be ready" and she likes the curriculum, which allows her to really delve deep and push her students' thinking. Felicia's work inside and outside of the classroom embodies the everyday practices of an antiracist ELA educator and classroom.

WHAT DOES BEING AN ANTIRACIST EDUCATOR MEAN TO YOU? WHAT DOES IT LOOK LIKE?

I'm going to directly oppose anything that's racist. And so for me, and in the context of where I am and where I'm teaching, the pieces that feel racist are the structural design of classes. The structure, I don't want to say the structural design of the curriculum because it has been revised, especially thematically, to explore multiple voices and perspectives, but it's still left up to the teacher; you have to be intentional. [In the curriculum] the tasks ask students to do this critical thinking about something but that something is still left up to the teacher, so if you were to teach *Gatsby* and then a number of other White authors for the year, you could. For me, it's about the choices students have, and I am also thinking about the experiences that students are having in front of me. Are they only being forced to write essays in this one way? Are they using certain language in group discussions and another language for writing? Are they only looking at the stories of these particular people? Or do they have options? I know this lends itself to cultural competence; it's important because they don't have those options in other spaces. They don't read all these different authors within a year or explore these lenses in other spaces. It becomes, for me, about which ways can I essentially look at this system and disrupt the curriculum, the experiences that they're having in the classroom and then the way that they get to think about text and American literature.

THAT SOUNDS LIKE IT GOES BEYOND REPRESENTATION. DOES IT?

I want students to understand that systems of oppression exist. I want them to have power and agency. Overall, I want to provide a space that is not everything that they've had for the last three years of English because they're gonna leave my space and go onto English 12, and then go to the same thing [non-antiracist instruction]. Hopefully, when they go back into those spaces, they question those spaces; like "Do I have a choice here? Can I read someone else besides Ernest Hemingway? This is old and irrelevant to me." That's the goal.

HOW DID THIS JOURNEY BEGIN FOR YOU?

I feel like it's been a forever thing. When I came into teaching, I came in wanting to teach in two specific school districts I knew were predominantly black with middle-class families but where students were getting subpar education. It was intentional, definitely intentional for me. I ended up spending the first five years of my career at the school where I student-taught. It was a traveling-based school called Global Experience. We went to Australia, New Zealand, China and South Africa. I learned so much through those experiences. Every place we visited, we would create some project-based lessons. Students went out into the communities and learned, and there was always some service-oriented component like building for Habitat for Humanity. Every time we went to a location, whether it was New Orleans or a village in South Africa, there was always this desire to learn and investigate: How did these people get here? Who are the Indigenous people of this place? And let's find them. Let's go see the Aborigines. I mean every place we went we found the people and their history from Hawaii to spending time with the natives in New Zealand. Even when we went to L.A., we took a tour that started off in this small town that still exists today. It was the first original town in Los Angeles, and it's completely populated by Latine community people who were originally there. It kinda became a passion of mine in terms of critically analyzing a people and their history. I became really focused on exploring the stories that were not being told.

YOU MENTIONED COLONIZATION. HOW DO ANTIRACIST PEDAGOGY AND DECOLONIZING OUR LESSONS CONNECT OR DO YOU SEE THOSE AS SEPARATE?

I feel like they are definitely connected. If my goal is to essentially go against and find ways to make these practices and policies and experiences not be just the same old White lens, then I need you to understand that this idea of Whiteness started with imperialism and colonization. When I taught world literature and *Things Fall Apart*, that definitely exposed that everything we are hearing, seeing and that we're consuming was designed intentionally to oppress you or to only give you certain limited information—which is oppressive. It's still a cycle of oppression for you to stay in and that is related to colonization. I see the relation [of antiracism and colonization] if we think about who arranged and set up school systems and policies: the no-hat policies, hair discrimination, the bells, all the required permissions. All of these practices are related to upholding European standards. My students recognize this. Hair discrimination was big for them this year along with redlining and mental illness. These were the things they were thinking and talking about most, and they are connected to both.

WHAT'S YOUR FAVORITE STRATEGY TO USE AS AN ANTIRACIST EDUCATOR?

Every time they look at anything, they always have to apply a lens that asks them to think about people's voices and experiences and the why. The why is always in there. It's never just here's the information that was designed by whomever that you must understand. It's always, here's this text, let's see all the information we can explore within it including the information that is not provided. It's really focused and includes using their voices to write stories to share. Then they may facilitate and lead discussions and lessons around social issues. I would say one strategy I think that lends itself to antiracism, in a way that is not problematic, is to always have students think about what lens can we put on to examine this text. Let's not just take one, the one that was written or the one that is depicted; instead, let's apply a few different lenses and carry that throughout the year.

> **COMPREHENSION CHECK**
> ◆ What is something that Felicia said or does that resonates with you?
> ◆ Felicia is intentional in her praxis. In what ways are you intentional in the texts you select, the choices given, the discussions held?
> ◆ How might you be even more intentional and shift your praxis as your antiracist knowledge is evolving?

Learning approaches

When guiding students to an understanding of racial and social oppression and their intersections, it may be advantageous to use a few of the learning approaches that promote collaboration, critical thinking and action. Table 7.3 lists some approaches with explanations and examples.

Holly S. is an award-winning writer, high school English teacher and community college instructor who believes in the innumerable benefits of service learning.

The service-oriented work in which my students and I engage is always student-suggested, student-planned and student-led. If the students offer service, it must be rooted in connection with the communities served. I go through lessons explaining saviorism and quid pro quo service, and I offer ways for students to reflect on their intentions with their proposed service project ideas. This helps students check any privilege or savior lenses through which a project may stem and then provide alternative ways to consider with whom, when, and why a different approach or relationship building may need to happen prior to engaging in a service project. The students often learn about intersections of race, socioeconomic status, gender and cultural upbringing. It connects to antiracism because these approaches uncover the various, more subtle forms of racism and White supremacy that are masked in aid and service work.

TABLE 7.3 Learning approaches for racial and social oppression and their intersections

Approach	Explanation	Example
Problem-based learning	Utilizes real-world problems to engage students in critical thinking and problem-solving	Use Lupita Nyong'o's *Sulwe* to delve into the problem of colorism.
Interdisciplinary learning	Encourages students to explore a concept from multiple perspectives, such as history, science and English. By looking at the topic from multiple angles, students can gain a more holistic understanding of it.	Investigate the Stonewall Riots *English:* Read and analyze Marsha P. Johnson's speech at the Christopher Street Liberation Day rally *History:* Examine the cultural and political context of the Stonewall Riots including the gender and racial politics of the era and the impact of the 1969 civil rights movement on the queer civil rights movement *Science:* Explore the biology of gender and sexuality, and how gender and sexual orientation are understood in different cultures and societies Reflect on the ways that the Stonewall Riots are part of a larger narrative of queer resistance and the ongoing struggles for LGBTQIA+ rights and representation
Inquiry-based learning	Explores topics by asking questions to develop an understanding of the issue. This type of learning allows students to construct their own knowledge and gain a deeper understanding of the topic.	Texts: *Things Fall Apart* by Chinua Achebe and "The White Man's Burden" by Rudyard Kipling Generate ideas, questions and critical dialogue around the colonial theft as metaphor (going beyond material goods)

Design thinking	Iterative design process of defining and solving problems	Text: "I ended up on this little island: Migrants land in political drama" article from the *New York Times* Use the design thinking process to create possible solutions to this problem
Service learning	Combines meaningful community service with instruction and reflection to enrich learning and communities	Read, analyze and discuss *Omar Rising* by Aisha Saeed Volunteer at a mosque during Eid or host a community talk about Islamophobia
Place-based learning	Engages students in an exploration of their surroundings that encourages student inquiry, research and exploration through hands-on, real-world experiences	Read *Illegal* by Eoin Colfer and Andrew Donkin Visit a local Refugee and Immigration Services office or a U.S. Citizenship and Immigration Services Office to hear about their processes

WAYPOINT

By not examining our social identities, privileges and positions, we may bring an unacknowledged bias and misconceptions to our teaching and learning. This is liberatory work for students and ourselves.

THINK–ACT–REIMAGINE

Think - Act - Reimagine

Think	Act	Reimagine
What are the intersections of your own identity?	Create a list of missing perspectives in the texts, guests and classroom visuals.	Laws, justice and protections for all oppressed people.
How are you and your students impacted by social oppression?	Learn about these perspectives and begin to add them into your lessons.	

FIGURE 7.1

DO NOW

◆ Note where you can add various forms of social oppression to your lessons
◆ Take time to learn about various forms of religious oppression, class oppression and more

Resources

Affirming Identities resource from Building Equitable Learning Environments Network at https://library.belenetwork.org/resources/affirming-identities-learning-condition-guide/

Resources https://www.dismantlingracism.org/resources.html

- ◆ Cycle of Oppression
- ◆ White Supremacy Culture
- ◆ Indigenous Ways of Knowing

https://www.nafsa.org/ie-magazine/2021/11/2/social-justice-pedagogy-conceptual-framework-all-international-educators

8

Looking Back and Thinking Ahead

How do I evaluate the antiracist classroom and keep moving forward?

Let's end with a story. Many years ago, a young man along with many from his small village were taken from their land caressed by mountains and majestic skies to be schooled far away. Whitecloud left his family, his language and his home. He is gone so long that he forgets the smell of the smokehouse and the sound of the wind on the water. He longs for it. He is tired of being "civilized." Civilized enough to be controlled. Civilized enough to not care for his neighbors. Civilized enough to miss the beauty of nature right in front of him. Civilized enough to parrot responses back to a teacher without thought or conjecture to achieve high honors. Civilized enough to know when his teacher speaks of Indigenous people as savages that he must let him believe he is right.

Everything Whitecloud is taught and the way he is taught are alien to him, requiring him to lose parts of himself. He is shrinking and almost invisible. He no longer remembers who he is, and there is no one to remind him. Perhaps, he has become all they say and fear about "Indians." Perhaps, he is lazy and untamed. Perhaps, he is not.

The rustle of falling leaves and the beating of drums beckon him home. He travels for days anxious for his return. Drawing

DOI: 10.4324/9781003296171-13

and redrawing the memories of home in his head. Exhaling at the sight of the mountains, his feet know the land. And yet, does he? Does he know the land? Does the land know him? Are the blue winds dancing for him? Who is he? Is he the White man or the "Indian"? Who is to decide?

Much like the experience of Whitecloud, students have far too long been "civilized" by dominant historical narratives, White-centric cultural norms, instruction and policies. In many ways, our students, too, have been rendered powerless, invisible because we have stolen their identities and erased critical dialogue about why this happens. We have not been concerned about their need to understand and function in a society running on a white supremacist operating system. We have not noticed the harm of Whiteness as we continued teaching the assigned texts, following the zero-tolerance discipline policy, forcing them to speak the dominant language and omitting race from discussions of curricula, assessment and student success (Hill, 2022). Who decides to stop this harm? We do.

Throughout this book, we've learned that we must create a culture of *cariño y confianza* and to have honest, liberatory, human and systems-centered classroom conversations that critique racial stratification and dominance, inequity and injustice. We have learned that we must create antiracist ELA environments and lessons that provide a safe space for students to express their lived experiences and to build the intellectual and emotional capital necessary to understand and contest racism, oppression and their effects on the world around them. We have learned that our enactment of power, policies and practices must also be rooted in equity-mindedness, which is itself antiracist. We have learned that no one student should lose themselves and be left to wonder who they are and where they fit on a mythologized racial hierarchy. The questions Whitecloud poses to himself should not be the fate of our students.

The long haul

One of my favorite literary lines is from Lorraine Hansberry's "A Raisin in the Sun." One of the main characters, Walter Lee

Younger, is trying to convince his wife and other family members that he has devised a plan for a solid business venture. He declares to his wife Ruth, "[T]his aint no fly-by-night proposition, baby" (Hansberry, 1997). Well, ELA educators, this ain't either. As we learned throughout this book, antiracist teaching and learning is not fleeting. There is no runners tape for you to run through or a proclamation from Siri that you've arrived at your final destination. Since there is no end in sight, our satisfaction will have to come along the way. A friend asked me as I was writing this book, "I wonder what it would take for you to feel more joy in this process." I wonder the same for you on this antiracist teaching journey. Your trek may be long and arduous, so you may need to find points to stop and smell the flowers, and don't despair, there will be many. So celebrate as you go. Cheer when your students apply a critical race lens to a text without prompting or when they are having independent conversations like Priscilla's kindergarteners. Jump for joy when they are writing in their authentic voice to disrupt Whiteness like Briana's students. Smirk when your colleague visits and comments about the depth of student engagement and criticality.

Remember, this is mindset (knowledge and thoughts), heartset (feelings and beliefs) and skillset (praxis) work that will not happen overnight. There are levels to this. We have to peel back a lot of layers of self, building our own consciousness and then fortifying our racial literacy and historical knowledge. We cannot teach what we don't know, and the truth is most of us have learned history and literature through a lens of Whiteness. And since we teach how we were taught, we have unintentionally replicated harm, so we need to continually interrogate all aspects of our praxis from setup to assessment. Shifting our thinking and making ourselves uncomfortable along this journey is neither fast nor easy.

This week, I attended a professional learning session in which Dr. Tia Brown McNair, equity expert and author, shared that the work of racial equity and justice is transformative and not transactional. This has stuck with me as I think of the transformative nature of antiracist teaching, learning and leading. I define transactions as immediate exchanges, whereas transformation is a process of change occurring over time. Very often, our lessons and practice are transactional. We want a product, and students want a grade. Conversely, we say we want this work to be transformative, but our commitment to this learning is often transactional. We want lesson plan formats or a reading list, so we ignore Chapters 2 and 3, which require too much self-work and cannot be implemented tomorrow. And we say we want antiracism to grow in our schools, and we may lead a professional development session or two but do not invite ongoing reflection, dialogue or an open door for our teacher friends to see our praxis in action and discuss the hows and whys that could invite them on this journey. Our words and actions must align with transformation and not transactions.

As we strive to move beyond transactional teaching, learning and leading, Estela Bensimon's term, "first-generation equity practitioners," aptly captures this work's nascent state and long-term impact. According to Bensimon (McNair et al., 2020), first-generation equity practitioners are passionate learners and listeners willing to confront challenges, create new models and strategies for equity and prepare this work for future generations. Is this you? Are you a first-generation antiracist educator? What are the responsibilities that come along with preparing this path for future generations? How are you moving away from a traditional transactional teaching, learning and leading relationship? How are you allotting yourself the time and space to be intentional, a requisite of transformation? Our dedication to this work is paramount for an antiracist future and means committing for the long haul.

COMPREHENSION CHECK

◆ What additional parallels can you draw between the current state of teaching and Whitecloud's experience?
  ○ What have you learned in this book that can disrupt this trauma?
◆ Check in with your mindset? heartset? skillset?
◆ What do you think it means to be a first-generation antiracist educator?

Being a student

When people ask me what I do for a living, I sometimes tell them I'm a professional student. As first-generation antiracist educators, we have a lot to learn and can't expect this knowledge to fall into our laps. It is incumbent on us to actively seek knowledge, vet it and then study it. I mean, really study it as we did in college with a highlighter and pen in hand (yes, I know I am dating myself). We know that students usually do not learn something in one exposure or from one modality, and neither will we. **Reading this book will make us more knowledgeable, but we are going to have to read more, listen more, discuss and analyze more to continually progress on this journey** (see Table 8.1). When we engage in this level of study, we will see that being an antiracist educator goes beyond our ELA classrooms. We can then advocate for antiracist institutional changes, such as recruiting and retaining racially minoritized faculty, the inclusion of ongoing professional development that addresses systemic inequities and injustices and policies that equitably allocate funding and resources (Harsma et al., 2021).

From the teacher's desk

For Ashley M., being a student of antiracism is being reflective and engaging in self-inquiry. Her learning is metacognitive and evaluative to inform her practice.

It's multipronged in terms of how I am personally reflecting on my own development. For example, I helped start the antiracism committee at our school, and we created a survey that just asked people to reflect. It asked questions like, How comfortable are you having certain conversations? Where did you take X risk? Did you try having one difficult conversation last year? So, if you did have one last year, and you've already had three this year, you can see that. Those things are pretty easy for me to measure.

I am definitely just really conscious of moments where I will lean in and have a difficult conversation about race, like about how we have a teeny tiny percentage of Black students and Black boys at the school, but somehow they're the majority in the office. That's also really easily measurable because I know when I'm having those conversations and when I'm not. I'm often reflecting on why.

TABLE 8.1 A study guide for antiracism

Read	View
Racial Innocence by Tanya Hernandez *Asian American Histories of the United States* by Catherine Choy *Freedom Dreaming: The Radical Black Imagination* by Robin D.G. Kelly *Not "A Nation of Immigrants"* by Roxanne Dunbar Ortiz *Doing the Work* by W. Kamau Bell & Kate Schatz *The Antiracism Handbook: Practical Tools to Shift Your Mindset and Uproot Racism in Your Life and Community* by Thema Bryant & Edith Arrington *Me and White Supremacy: Combat Racism, Change the World and Become a Good Ancestor* by Layla Saad *My Grandmother's Hands: Racialized Trauma and the Pathway to Mending our Hearts and Bodies* by Resmaa Menakem *Dying of Whiteness How the Politics of Racial Resentment Is Killing Americas Heartland* by Jonathan Metzl *Playing in the Dark: Whiteness and the Literary Imagination* by Toni Morrison *Cutting School: The Segrenomics of American Education* by Noliwe Rooks *Four Hundred Souls* by Ibram Kendi & Keisha Blain *The Sum of Us* by Heather McGhee	*How to be an Antiracist*. 2019. Ibram X. Kendi & Jemele Hill. Aspen Ideas Festival. "How Studying Privilege Systems Can Strengthen Compassion." 2012. Peggy McIntosh. TEDx. "What's Missing from the American Immigrant Narrative." 2020. Elizabeth Camarillo Gutierrez. TEDx. "The History of White Supremacy." 2017. Adriane Lentz-Smith. National Humanities Center Education Programs (Webinar). 13th. 2020. Ava DuVernay. Netflix. "What It Takes to Be Racially Literate." 2017. Priya Vulchi & Winona Guo. TEDWomen. "How to Deconstruct Racism, One Headline at a Time." 2019. Baratunde Thurston. 2019. TEDx. "How to Recognize Your White Privilege—and Use It to Fight Inequality." Peggy McIntosh. TEDx.
Listen	Enroll
"Be Antiracist" with Ibram Kendi "Pod Save the People" with DeRay Mckesson "Seeing White" with John Biewen "About Race" with Reni Eddo-Lodge "1619" with Nikole Hannah-Jones "All My Relations" with Matika Wilbur (Swinomish and Tulalip) & Adrienne Keene (Cherokee Nation) "Asian American" with Ken Fong "Intersectionality Matters" with Kimberlé Crenshaw "The Red Nation" with Nick Estes "Teaching While White" with Jenna Chandler-Ward	Zinn Education Project PD Rachel Cargle's: #dothework or The Great Unlearn courses Novia Reid's: Antiracism & White Privilege Monique Melton's: Antiracist 101 Crash Course Austin Channing Brown's: ACB Academy Layla Saad's: Good Ancestor Academy Paul Gorski's: Equity Literacy Institute

I'm also a note-taker, so I'm probably journaling, reflecting and thinking about how I can set myself up personally to continue to do better and have the skills to do so. I, also, think about being part of a larger educator community and ask myself questions like: How can I support my school to be in a better position? How can I support the development of those around me? And then, measuring the student experience, of course, because ultimately that's who I serve. I have a weekly student feedback form that asks: Hey, how are you feeling about this? How is this going? So in addition to informal conversations, I have data that I can track to notice trends. I am always analyzing, "oh, this subgroup of students is feeling this way, what can I do to address that" or "At the beginning of this school year, we didn't have this issue. It's maybe caused by this, and how can we address that?" And doing the same thing with families and taking seriously the idea of measuring impact as we seek to develop. Because if I am just "developing" by reading a book, and thinking, "Yay, go me, I read a book on antiracism but it's not translating to my practice, then that's not pedagogy—it's theory."

COMPREHENSION CHECK

Ashley is constantly questioning her role as an antiracist educator and her pedagogy. Let's explore how we can do the same.

- How are you interrogating your positionality and pedagogy?
- What does it mean and look like for you to be a student of antiracism?
  - How are you making time to process and analyze your learning?
  - Who are the people you are learning from and having deeper conversations with?
- How are you taking this knowledge and turning it into critical practice in your life and work?

Evaluating ourselves

In Chapter 1, we learned that antiracism is an active verb, requiring continuous effort. To combat racism effectively, it is not enough to have a set of antiracist beliefs; instead, we should be setting goals, tracking our progress and determining what's next. **One of my teacher mentors always taught me that great educators are reflective and evaluative hour by hour, not weekly or yearly.** When we don't take the time to think about instruction, its content and delivery, we are making the learning experience about ourselves and our control rather than the students. The process of looking inwardly and soliciting feedback and reflection from other stakeholders is one of trust. Do I trust that what I am currently doing is serving students? If not, then it is likely that I do not want to hold that mirror up to myself. If I don't want to hear from students and families, then it is likely because I don't value them or trust that I have adequately served them. Ashley's example demonstrates that our reflection should also be expansive and consider how our actions affect our colleagues, families and students and lead us to adjust our behaviors, practices and the questions we are asking ourselves and others. While it will take effort and may be uncomfortable, this is the type of reflective practice that will help us to identify our successes, obstacles and areas for improvement and make us great first-generation antiracist educators.

From the teacher's desk

Holly S. holds herself accountable by evaluating her teaching and this journey.

I constantly evaluate myself as an antiracist educator. I look at which voices, perspectives, cultures and experiences are present in the course material. I try to identify whose are missing and how I can remedy this. I review language and phrasing in the work and assignments provided. I reflect on how I address racist, misogynist, homophobic, culturally insensitive comments made by students and staff—Did I speak up? Did I invite a conversation about it? Did I ignore it? How can I do these things better? If I failed to act, how do I remedy my inaction? I will have conversations with trusted colleagues and see how I can do better.

An aspect of antiracism upon which teachers need to focus more is that it's a journey, not a destination. It's not a hashtag or a label for a social media account. It's continual action, research, assessment and application within and beyond the classroom. The work evolves, and as such, we must evolve, too. The work does not end with reading all the books, joining a book club, or flying a flag in a classroom—those are places where the work can begin, but truly, the work must begin internally. It needs to be part of all our lives and not only when it's trendy, comfortable, or convenient.

For early childhood educator and leader Heather D., self-reflection and evaluation start with setting goals and sticking to them.

For me, there has to be some kind of goal every year, I have to set a goal and check in with myself about it. Because living life does get in the way of all these things, especially during this pandemic, there's always this sucker punch coming. You cannot effectively measure your growth without having set a goal in the first place. The goals have to be attainable and you have to have check-ins to know you are working toward them. Be intentional or nothing will be accomplished.

Shannon believes data-driven self-evaluation can lead to deeper self-reflection and change.

Data can hide the real truth, but it does give you at least a starting point. I have spent a lot of time looking at my students' scores and looking at my students' feedback to me and to my principal. My school is one where the principal or administrator comes in and does teacher evaluations at the end of the year. They'll ask students questions like was this teacher helpful to you? Do you feel like you learned from this teacher? It sounds weird, but the administrator is the one who administers the survey, not the teacher. The teacher is actually asked to step into their office or leave the classroom entirely. It's not part of the teacher's evaluation. This data is given to the teacher to help them grow and understand where they're at. It's part of coaching conversations with their instructional lead, but it is not part of their final evaluation and doesn't count toward their pay or anything like that. I use that data as a teacher along with the data of how well my Black students did in my class.

I'm constantly trying to assess based on data and what happened every year. I think it's really important to also have conversations and be reflective. I'll be the first person to say I've made mistakes before, so many. It's important to have those moments of self-reflection and make them intentionally. I live a pretty good distance away from my school, so I drive 30 minutes to and from school every day. And I purposely don't listen to podcasts on the way home. I listen to them on the way to school but not on the way home. On the way home, I spend that time reflecting. Then when I'm sitting in my driveway, I spend five minutes jotting down how today went, the things that I need to follow up on and how I'm going to progress tomorrow based on today.

COMPREHENSION CHECK
- What are your values and goals to advance antiracism personally and professionally?
- What is your plan for developing a more comprehensive historical, sociopolitical, economic, racial and cultural context of the themes/topics/units you teach?
- What accountability structures do you have in place?

TEACHER LESSON IN SESSION

Anita B., Evanston Illinois

Anita B. is an award winning high school English teacher, an instructional coach and one of her school's induction professional development leaders.

WHAT DOES IT MEAN TO YOU TO BE AN ANTIRACIST EDUCATOR AND TO LEAD AN ANTIRACIST CLASSROOM?

The first thing I think is really important to say is to be an antiracist educator, for me, means that each and every year at the close of the school year I sit down and I reflect. I reflect on my weakest moments, my weakest places and it's often provoked by conversation, professional development or scholarship I've read that makes me see where I have a blind spot and an inability, and I need to do better. I set goals from these. For example, a few years ago, a professional development coordinator asked me a question that led me to think and change. I had shared something great I was doing. It was this research piece where students identified a group that they've never been taught about in school whose stories and histories are significant and of benefit. And the coordinator asked me, "Yeah, so you allow students to find that, but you don't bring that in and center it as something we all need to study as valid already." And she was right. I was giving students autonomy to go where they wanted versus bringing something in as an authority and saying this is important.

One of the goals for myself then was how am I centering the voices of Black men? What does that really mean? To really say that this has been left out, but it's really meaningful and important. And we're going to study the style and the elements of this in the same way that we do White literature. We're not going to look at this piece as written by a person of color or look at the contribution through the lens of a person of color, but a phenomenal person that contributed to this country, the brilliance and the beauty of this country. And that's a very different message, right?

HOW DOES THAT NOT BECOME A COLORBLIND APPROACH—SAYING WE'RE JUST GOING TO TEACH THE BRILLIANCE THAT IS THE THREAD OF AMERICA? DO YOU THINK THAT KIND OF WASHES OVER COLOR?

Honestly, there is discomfort that emerges when you talk about Black brilliance and joy in ways that are very clear because students haven't experienced it. And not just with Black folks, but with Indigenous folks and around gender and identity and the binary, there's a discomfort. I've found that it is important to give students access and probing questions versus telling them, and give them entryways the way we do as scholars. Asking what is the purpose of this. How does this impact your view of your world? And providing an organic space which is very scary for teachers because you don't know what's going to emerge, especially when it's around race, something that is so taboo and stigmatized in our society. There's a lot of fear that manifests particularly in teachers, as I need to control the conversation. I let go. I spend months grounding this classroom, in norms and building community so that there is safety and tolerance because there are going to be challenging conversations. It's going to put people in discomfort, and we spend a lot of time building that foundation. I taught gender studies this year, and this was my goal. As a heteronormative, cisgendered, Indian woman who has a very nuclear family, I was so afraid to mess up. This was the first class I've taught where every student picked the class. They were there for a purpose. They wanted to be there. I've never taught a class where every student chose to be in this space. I had a huge number of students of color, women of color, two transgender female students, and then LGBTQ-identifying and heteronormative women. To center race in that space and to see the way in which intersectionality was so important to recognizing the shortcomings of feminism. It was really humbling, and I was learning with them. And just to be courageous enough to bring the voice of Audrey Lorde and bell hooks and really read it with them and unpack it. To be vulnerable and name all my privileges and oppressions and ask them to do the same, and then ask the question, Who's not in this space?

I do get scared of screwing up and offending someone and hurting someone. That's my fear. And I premise that fear out loud in the space. I say, "I'm going to tell you I've been conditioned, and there's so many ways I've been conditioned to think this way. This is hard for me, and so I have anxiety around this." But I'm not afraid to put that out there.

WHAT DO YOU SEE AS A RESULT OF YOU LAYING THAT OUT FOR STUDENTS? YOU TALKED A LITTLE BIT ABOUT THE ENTRY POINTS AND NOT CONTROLLING THE CONVERSATION. WHAT IMPACT DO YOU SEE OF THOSE REALLY NOTED DECISIONS THAT YOU'RE MAKING AS AN EDUCATOR ON STUDENTS?

I see them showing up in their truth. I see them either through writing or verbally or in small groups—which I give them multiple ways to engage in expression—naming their lived experiences and how they have been limited. One of the most profound things I learned about a student this year, who is a writer not a talker and is very quiet, was that this student has a transgender brother. The student shared, "My mom kicked him out of our house. We're not allowed to talk about it, and I need to talk about it. I don't understand. I love him, but I don't know how to have this conversation. I want to read, and I want to know because I just can't talk about it at home." And that's why she picked this course, so you realize this is about students' lives, or it can be. It's a whole different thing.

I ask students how is education different from learning? I took this from Dr. David Stovall. Students said, "Education is forced. Learning happens outside of school." And I said, "How do we flip that? Name the ways." And in the class, that's what we strive to do. Yeah, it falls flat sometimes or it works for certain people and it doesn't for others. But as long as we center the voices of those most impacted by this institution and we name who is not being heard, we are working toward antiracism.

YOU TALKED ABOUT CREATING GOALS FOR YOURSELF EACH YEAR. HOW DO YOU MEASURE YOUR GOALS?

I do quarterly reflections, layers, to hear my students' voices and to try and get their honest feedback. That's not always easy because curricular violence has occurred. But this year, there was this STEAM course that sent a group of four students to my gender studies course. The model of the STEAM course was that they get a client, and the client is a consumer of my course. So these STEAM students polled students of color who were taking my course. They got raw data, qualitative data about their experience: the biggest victories and the biggest holes. Then they brought that data to me, and they did what consultants do. We blew up the course and rebuilt it based on the real-life data. The students depended on me, and they were depending on the authentic voice of my students. It was the first time I've ever experienced real student–teacher collaboration at an equal platform. I got really hard feedback to listen to. A student shared, "Yeah, I felt like you were overtalking me in this moment where I was really trying to share something." While in my mind, I was trying to connect with the student. I know that now looking back in the moment of that particular conversation that I needed to listen.

The other way I measure effectiveness is achievement. It is a really big indicator of buy-in. I call the students who have the lowest level of skill or the poorest disciplinary habits low fliers, and they're my temperature for how I'm doing. When I'm not getting work from them, when they're not reading, I'm like, "Okay, let me see what's the barrier here." I really try to facilitate conversations to help me understand.

WHAT DO YOU DO WHEN YOU GET NAYSAYERS AND PUSHBACK?

Something is changing here. I used to get a lot of that initially in my career. There were a lot of people who characterized me as idealistic or just one of those foofy teachers where all the kids do everything. No, I have high expectations. I'm a rigorous teacher. I am also creative and I incorporate artistic expression into my courses. I am adaptable, and I don't fear trying things so people said things. When I got my PhD, a lot of that subsided. Then, I got an instructional coaching position, and it gave people more courage to try things. This year, I got a teaching excellence award.

I also have privilege that works in my favor as an Indian woman, as a PhD, as somebody who has 17 years of service, as an instructional coach and as someone who's perceived to be a hard worker. We, women of color, have, many of us, this overcompensating thing that we've done in our careers because we're so afraid to look dumb or stupid, so we're overprepared. And it's very hard for us to say no, so I have this reputation and it leads people to see me in a certain light, even though they would see someone else very differently.

COMPREHENSION CHECK
◆ How does Anita demonstrate her intentionality around antiracism?
◆ Which one of Anita's accountability measures can you adopt?
◆ How does your privilege or lack thereof affect the pushback you receive?

Expect detours

As with all learning, gaining antiracist knowledge will not be a linear process. We will never know everything, and we will definitely make mistakes. Knowing this going in will ensure we are open to learning and growth and not afraid to admit when we are wrong. Like Anita, we have to be open to learning from and being guided by the perspectives of our students. **While sometimes all the new learning and changes based on reflection and**

feedback may seem like detours, they are opportunities for us to course correct. On this journey, it is easy to fall, while believing we are engaging in antiracism, into the traps of White saviorism or what Paolo Freire calls false generosity. White saviorism is the idea that White racialized people have the power, authority and responsibility to save racialized people of the global majority from their own plight. This can lead to condescending, patronizing and harmful behavior, as well as a perpetuation of the idea that White racialized people are superior. Similarly, false generosity is the notion that people in positions of power often think they know what's best for those they serve. Both of these traps lead us further away from antiracism than toward it. When we assume a stance of critical humility and learning, we can begin to challenge the idea of superiority that keeps White supremacy in place. Instead of making decisions for others, we can take a more collaborative approach. Students, families and communities must have agency and power over their own destinies. This shift in perspective can help disrupt the power structure that maintains White supremacy and keep us on the right path.

Forget the Joneses

If you're serious about being an antiracist, don't worry about what Keisha, Jessica or Holly are doing. Focus on yourself and remember that everyone's experience is unique. Yes, we are on this journey together and need one another because this work does not happen without a coalition of support. Remember, this is human-centered work and antiracism is not a one-size-fits-all endeavor; rather, it requires identifying and addressing the unique challenges in each context. Therefore, the actions of antiracism must be personal and contextual. What I do in Illinois isn't replicable in Florida, Tennessee or Texas—or other parts of my own city and state. Hence, there is no universal checklist or pretty protocol to follow; the success of our efforts depends on our ability to tailor our approaches to each school and community because learning is most effective when it is proximate.

COMPREHENSION CHECK

Here are some guiding questions for your journey:
◆ What does this work mean for me and for those who I serve every day?
◆ How is this work also larger than my everyday sphere?
◆ Am I embodying antiracism, or am I just on this journey for Instagram or Twitter or to look and sound good?
◆ How am I avoiding the trappings of White saviorism and false generosity?
◆ How can I sustain my antiracist praxis?

Change is a choice

Is your head spinning? Are you looking for the exit, thinking, *"I did not sign up for all of this?"* Are you feeling overwhelmed by the task of reimagining and reframing ELA instruction for antiracist liberation? The truth is that we've been comfortable teaching ELA the way it was taught to us. However, as high school English educator, Lisa T. reminds us, today's students and the world are different. Heck, I wish I had an antiracist ELA teacher 30 years ago, but now it is up to us first-generation antiracist educators— to blaze the trail. This will require some heavy lifting, but it is necessary for real change to happen. Saying the right words and understanding the theory is not enough—we must take action for societal change (use Figure 8.1 to create your own antiracist action plan).

While our antiracist journey will have its curves and roundabouts, it will also have forks in the road and you will have to choose the route you will follow. The choices made on this journey are up to you. This is a personal and collective journey of healing because racism creates wounds for us all. The work of antiracism is therefore, also, healing work. It is the work of truth and acknowledging the damage, emotional and bodily, of a system designed to deny and destroy people's humanity. So, yes, we

ANTIRACIST ACTION PLAN

GOALS

What specific antiracist goals do I want to achieve? Why are these goals important?

EVALUATION

SELF	STUDENTS	OTHERS
Goal specific questions	Questions you will ask students	Questions you will ask others

Reflection
Responses/thoughts/ideas garnered from each evaluation

NEXT STEPS

Actions/Changes	Accountability
Based on feedback and reflection, what are the appropriate next steps/changes I need to make. How will they advance racial equity, justice and challenge the status quo?	Who will hold me accountable to this actions/changes?

FIGURE 8.1 Personal antiracist action plan template.

may have to make sacrifices and take risks in order to fight for racial justice and equity. That is the heartset and mindset work. It is the work of learning, unlearning and relearning. It is the work of repairing relationships and building community. It is the work of understanding the systems of racism that have been created and continue to operate. It is the work of making choices that will create a more just and equitable world. It is the work of being an ally and an advocate. It is the work of being in relationship with others who have experienced racism and have their own experiences to share. It is the work of creating a world where everyone is valued and respected. It is the work of creating a world where we can all be our best selves.

Figure 8.1 features a personal antiracist action plan template to help guide our actions on this journey.

WAYPOINT

At the end of most of my interviews with educators, I asked: *If you were to ask other educators about being antiracist, if given the opportunity, what question would you ask them?*

Here are their questions for you:

What are you doing that I'm not? Or what can I steal? ~Shannon B.

What is the work that you're doing outside of the classroom space? ~Yolanda G.

What scares you the most? ~Mark L.

What are you afraid of What's going to happen if you aren't an antiracist educator? ~Jordan L.

What are you reading? ~Sarah R-W.

What topics do you study and what books have you picked? Karyn K.

What's the end game for the kids that you teach? What are you trying to do? And then if you haven't figured out what you're trying to do, how do you intend to have any impact? ~Heather D. pre K

What are you going to do next? And what's the first step? ~Nora F.

THINK–ACT–REIMAGINE

Think	Act	Reimagine
What antiracist goals are you setting for yourself?	Utilize the reflection questions.	Yourself on this journey next year, in five years, in ten years.
How are you evaluating your antiracist progress?	Engage in learning from the study guide.	Your students as second generation antiracist leaders
To whom are you accountable?		

FIGURE 8.2

DO NOW

◆ Pick a resource from the study and get to work
◆ Complete your antiracist action plan

Glossary Praxis and Resources

Barn Raising: Collaborative Groups https://drive.google.com/file/d/1N322LLgqjL2HTDKiY0uoqJ7hbEojwvK7/view?usp=share_link

Bring improvisation into the classroom *The Second City Guide to Improv in the Classroom: Using Improvisation to Teach Skills and Boost Learning* by Katherine S. McKnight

Classroom community meetings https://www.browardschools.com/cms/lib/FL01803656/Centricity/Domain/13726/Class%20Meetings%20Implementation%20Outline.pdf

Cogenerative dialogues https://www.weteachnyc.org/resources/collection/cogenerative-dialogues/

Community Study https://ohioleadership.org/storage/ocali-ims-sites/ocali-ims-olac/documents/Course-Two-Socio-Political-Awareness-Facilitators-Guide.pdf

Conduct an empathy interview https://learningforward.org/wp-content/uploads/2020/10/tool-empathy-interviews.pdf

Confronting White Nationalism in Schools https://www.pps.et/cms/lib/OR01913224/Centricity/Domain/4/ConfrontingWhiteNationalisminSchoolsToolkit.pdf

Culturally Relevant Intentional Literacy Communities https://www.kqed.org/mindshift/60112/learning-from-students-families-as-a-step-toward-equity-in-literacy-instruction#:~:text=Culturally%20Relevant%20Intentional%20Literacy%20Communities,imperative%20to%20being%20culturally%20relevant.

Disability Awareness https://hiehelpcenter.org/disability-awareness-class-lessons/

EdCafe https://whatisanedcafe.wordpress.com/

Faces of Power Activity https://iacp.berkeley.edu/change-analysis/power-analysis

Four Resources Model for reading and viewing   https://www.education.vic.gov.au/school/teachers/teachingresources/discipline/english/literacy/readingviewing/Pages/fourres.aspx

LGBTQIA+ Standards   https://www.glsen.org/activity/inclusive-curricular-standards

LGBTQIA+ Texts   https://www.learningforjustice.org/magazine/publications/best-practices-for-serving-lgbtq-students/appendix-a-lgbtq-books-characters

Liberatory Design Deck   https://www.liberatorydesign.com/

Mitigating Bias with Mindful reflection (teachers)   https://ggie.berkeley.edu/practice/mindful-reflection-process-for-developing-culturally-responsive-practices/#tab__2

Organize listening circles   https://www.wested.org/resources/short-term-impacts-of-student-listening-circles/#:~:text=A%20student%20listening%20circle%20engages,and%20implementing%20school%20improvement%20practices

Problem Posing   https://rethinkingschools.org/articles/planting-seeds-of-solidarity/

Racialized reader response   *Letting Go of Literary Whiteness: Antiracist Literary Instruction for White Students* by Carlin Borsheim-Black and Sophia Tatiana Sarigianides
http://www.drbickmoresyawednesday.com/weekly-posts/when-selecting-diverse-ya-texts-is-not-enough-racializing-reader-responses-of-yal-with-white-readers-by-sophia-tatiana-sarigianides-carlin-borsheim-black

Student-led learning   (Learning Studios)   https://www.pittsfieldnhschools.org/learning-studios/

Student Surveys   https://www.edutopia.org/video/student-surveys-using-student-voice-improve-teaching-and-learning

Student Voice   https://medium.com/@spencerideas/10-ways-to-incorporate-student-choice-in-your-classroom-e07baa449e55
https://library.belenetwork.org/resources/student-voice-learning-condition-guide/

WeeklyCircles https://www.edutopia.org/video/weekly-circles-students-and-faculty

Youth Participatory Action Research https://yparhub.berkeley.edu/

References

1 billion. EdBuild. (n.d.). Retrieved April 3, 2022, from https://edbuild.org/content/23-billion

Anderson, G. (2021, February 9). *Systemic racism has led to education disparities.* Temple Now | news.temple.edu. Retrieved March 25, 2022, from https://news.temple.edu/news/2020-06-25/systemic-racism-has-led-education-disparities

Baldwin, J., & Peck, R. (2017). *I am not your negro: A companion edition to the documentary film directed by Raoul Peck / by James Baldwin; compiled and introduced by Raoul Peck.* Vintage Books.

Behnke, D. (2022, April 13). *Living in Wisconsin: 'Hmong people are truly American, if not more American than most Americans'.* PBS Wisconsin. Retrieved May 11, 2022, from https://pbswisconsin.org/news-item/living-in-wisconsin-hmong-people-are-truly-american-if-not-more-american-than-most-americans/

Bell, D. A. (1992). *Faces at the bottom of the well.* New York: Basic Books.

Blackwell, D. M. (2010). Sidelines and separate spaces: Making education anti-racist for students of color. *Race Ethnicity and Education, 13*(4), 473–94. https://doi.org/10.1080/13613324.2010.492135

Blaisdell, B. (2020). Cupcakes, white rage, and the epistemology of antiblackness. *Taboo: The Journal of Culture and Education, 19*(1). Retrieved from https://digitalscholarship.unlv.edu/taboo/vol19/iss1/6

Blakemore, E. (2022, April 13). Thomas Edison didn't invent the lightbulb-but here's what he did do. *History.* Retrieved May 3, 2022, from https://www.nationalgeographic.com/history/article/thomas-edison-light-bulb-history?loggedin=true

Boggs, G. L., & Kurashige, S. (2012). *The next American Revolution Sustainable Activism for the twenty-first century.* University of California Press.

Brault Foisy, L.-M., Matejko, A. A., Ansari, D., & Masson, S. (2020). Teachers as orchestrators of neuronal plasticity: Effects of teaching practices on the brain. *Mind, Brain & Education, 14*(4), 415–28. https://doi.org/10.1111/mbe.12257

Brooks, L. (2021, September 24). *Social Justice in the class-room: How teachers inspire students to be heroes.* Working In The Schools. Retrieved October 30, 2022, from https://witschicago.org/social-justice-in-the-classroom

Brown McClain, J., Harmon, M., & Phillips Galloway, E. (2021). Eliminating prerequisites for personhood: A framework for enacting Antiracist language Instruction. *Language Arts, 99*(1), 25.

Bucio, A. (2015). *Student study.* Evanston, IL.

Christensen, L. (1992). Tales from an Untracked class. *Rethinking Schools, 2*(1), 14–6.

Darling-Hammond, L. (2016, July 28). *Unequal opportu-nity: Race and education.* Brookings. Retrieved April 4, 2022, from https://www.brookings.edu/articles/unequal-opportunity-race-and-education/

Darling-Hammond, L. (2017). Teaching for social jus-tice: Resources, relationships, and anti-racist practice. *Multicultural Perspectives, 19*(3), 133–38. https://doi.org/10.1080/15210960.2017.1335039

de los Ríos, C. V., Martinez, D. C., Musser, A. D., Canady, A., Camangian, P., & Quijada, P. D. (2019). Upending colo-nial practices: Toward repairing harm in English educa-tion. *Theory into Practice, 58*(4), 359–67. https://doi.org/10.1080/00405841.2019.1626615

Dei, G. (1993). The challenges of anti-racist education in Canada. *Canadian Ethnic Studies, 25*(2), 16–36.

Dei, G. (1996). Critical perspectives in antiracism: An introduc-tion. *Canadian Review of Sociology/Revue Canadienne de Sociologie, 33*(3), 247–67.

DeLeon, A. P. (2006). Beware of "black" the ripper! racism, representation, and building antiracist pedagogy. *The Social Studies, 97*(6), 263–67. https://doi.org/10.3200/tsss.97.6.263-267

DiAngelo, D. R. (2022, May 20). White Fragility: Why it's so hard to talk to white people about racism. *The Good Men Project.* Retrieved May 20, 2022, from https://goodmenproject.com/featured-content/white-fragility-why-its-so-hard-to-talk-to-white-people-about-racism-twlm/

Dimock, M. (2016, July 5). *Global Migration's rapid rise.* Pew Research. Retrieved September 25, 2022, from https://www.pewtrusts.org/en/trend/archive/summer-2016/global-migrations-rapid-rise

Dumas, M. J., & Ross, K. M. (2016). "Be Real Black for me": Imagining BlackCrit in education. *Urban Education, 51*(4), 415–42. https://doi.org/10.1177/0042085916628611

Dunn, A. H., Sondel, B., & Baggett, H. C. (2019). "I don't want to come off as pushing an agenda": How contexts shaped teachers' pedagogy in the days after the 2016 U.S. Presidential Election. *American Educational Research Journal, 56*(2), 444–76. https://doi.org/10.3102/0002831218794892

Eaker-Rich, D., & Van Galen, J. (1996). *Caring in an unjust world: Negotiating borders and barriers in Schools.* SUNY Press.

Expanding efforts to ensure the health and safety of Hispanic workers. United States Department of Labor. (n.d.). Retrieved April 3, 2022, from https://blog.dol.gov/2021/09/27/expanding-efforts-to-ensure-the-health-and-safety-of-hispanic-workers

Explore history. Blackwell School. (n.d.). Retrieved February 10, 2022, from https://www.theblackwellschool.org/explore-history

Ferlazzo, L. (2019, October 12). *We shouldn't "empower" students – instead we should create the conditions where they can take it.* Larry Ferlazzo's Websites of the Day… Retrieved August 10, 2022, from https://larryferlazzo.edublogs.org/2019/10/06/we-shouldnt-empower-students-instead-we-should-create-the-conditions-where-they-can-take-it/

FitzGibbon, C. (2020, October 30). *Racism: Historically-informed discussions in the classroom*. Facing History and Ourselves. Retrieved September 2, 2022, from https://www.facinghistory.org/ideas-week/racism-historically-informed-discussions-classroom

Forgiarini, M., Gallucci, M., & Maravita, A. (2011). Racism and the empathy for pain on our skin. *Frontiers in Psychology, 2*, 108. https://doi.org/10.3389/fpsyg.2011.00108. PMID: 21687466; PMCID: PMC3108582.

Freire, P. (1971). To the coordinator of a "Cultural Circle". *Convergence, 4*(1), 61–3.

Giroux, H. (1997). Rewriting the discourse of racial identity: Towards a pedagogy and politics of whiteness. *Harvard Educational Review, 67*(2), 285–321.

Glavin, C. (2014, February 6). *History of reading education in the U.S.* History of Reading Education in the U.S. | K12 Academics. Retrieved June 23, 2022, from https://www.k12academics.com/reading-education-united-states/history-reading-education-us

Gotlib, I. H., Miller, J. G., Borchers, L. R., Coury, S. M., Costello, L. A., Garcia, J. M., & Ho, T. C. (2022). Effects of the COVID-19 pandemic on mental health and brain maturation in adolescents: Implications for analyzing longitudinal data. *Biological Psychiatry Global Open Science*. https://doi.org/10.1016/j.bpsgos.2022.11.002

Greene, D. T. (2016). "We Need More 'US' in Schools!!": Centering black adolescent girls' literacy and language practices in online school spaces. *The Journal of Negro Education, 85*(3), 274–89. https://doi.org/10.7709/jnegroeducation.85.3.0274

Grossman, J. (2015, December 1). *Everything has a history: Perspectives on history: AHA*. Retrieved July 1, 2022, from https://www.historians.org/publications-and-directories/perspectives-on-history/december-2015/everything-has-a-history#:~:text=%E2%80%9CEverything%20has%20a%20history%E2%80%9D%20means,popular%20journals%2C%20print%20and%20digital

Guinier, L. (2004). From racial liberalism to racial literacy: Brown v. Board of Education and the interest-divergence dilemma. *Journal of American History*, *91*(1), 92–118. https://doi.org/10.2307/3659616

Hammond, Z. L. (2015). *Culturally responsive teaching and the brain*. Corwin Press.

Haney-Lopez, I. F. (1997). Race, ethnicity, and erasure: The salience of race to LatCrit theory. *La Raza Law Journal, 10*, 57–125.

Hansberry, L. (1997). *A raisin in the Sun*. Random House.

Harsma, E., Manderfeld, M., & Lewis Miller, C. (2021). *Maverick learning and educational applied research nexus*. Mankato: Minnesota State University.

Harvey-Torres, E., Johnson, K., Vakil, S., & Davis, B. (2021). Critical digital literacy, identity, and liberation: Developing culturally responsive pedagogies for marginalized youth. *Journal of Adolescent and Adult Literacy, 64*(4), 443–52.

Herbel-Eisenmann, B., Gau Bartell, T., Breyfogle, M. L., Bieda, K., Crespo, S., Dominguez, H., & Drake, C. (2013). Strong is the Silence: Challenging Interlocking Systems of Privilege and Oppression in Mathematics Teacher Education. *Journal of Urban Mathematics Education, 6*, 6–18.

Hill, J. (2022, April 29). *Practical Frameworks and Techniques for Promoting Anti-Racism in Student Learning Assessment* [Conference presentation]. *Tenth Annual AMCOA Assessment Conference*, Duke University. https://www.mass.edu/strategic/documents/Anti-racism%20in%20assessment%20practice.pdf

Hilty, E. (2011). *Thinking about schools: A foundations of education reader*. Routledge.

Hixon, J. G., & Swann, W. B. (1993). When does introspection bear fruit? Self-reflection, self-insight, and interpersonal choices. *Journal of Personality and Social Psychology, 64*(1), 35–43.

hooks, b. (1996). *Teaching to transgress: Education as the practice of freedom*. Routledge.

hooks, b. (1997). Representing whiteness in the black imagination. In R. Frankenberg (Ed.), *Displacing whiteness: Essays in social and cultural criticism* (pp. 165–79). Duke University Press.

Huber, L. P. (2009). Disrupting apartheid of knowledge: Testimonioas methodology in Latina/o critical race research ineducation. *International Journal of Qualitative Studies in Education*, 22(6), 639–54. https://doi.org/10.1080/09518390903333863

Huff, L. (2022, February 28). *Through a white colonial lens: A look into the US education system*. School of Marine and Environmental Affairs. Retrieved November 28, 2022, from https://smea.uw.edu/currents/through-a-white-colonial-lens-a-look-into-the-us-education-system/

Hughes, L., Rampersad, A., & Roessel, D. E. (1995). *The collected poems of Langston Hughes*. Knopf Doubleday Publishing Group.

Identifying gifted students: Addressing the lack of diversity in gifted education. School of Education Online. (n.d.). Retrieved April 3, 2022, from https://soeonline.american.edu/blog/lack-of-diversity-in-gifted-education

Integration and diversity. Integration and Diversity – The Civil Rights Project at UCLA. (n.d.). Retrieved April 4, 2022, from https://civilrightsproject.ucla.edu/research/k-12-education/integration-and-diversity

K-12 disparity facts and Statistics. UNCF. (2020, March 20). Retrieved April 4, 2022, from https://uncf.org/pages/k-12-disparity-facts-and-stats

Kemp, A. (2019). *Teaching global antiracism: Best practices for educators* (Critical Multiculturalism Series). SAGE Publications Ltd.

Key equity terms and concepts: A glossary for shared understanding. Center for the Study of Social Policy. (2019, October 1). Retrieved February 10, 2022, from https://cssp.org/resource/key-equity-terms-and-concepts-a-glossary-for-shared-understanding/

Kincheloe, J. L. (2007). Critical pedagogy in the twenty-first century: Evolution for survival. *English Teaching: Practice & Critique*, 17(3), 331–46. https://doi.org/10.1108/ETPC-05-2017-0074

King, J. E. (1991). Dysconscious racism: Ideology, identity, and the miseducation of teachers. *The Journal of Negro Education*, 60(2), 133. https://doi.org/10.2307/2295605

Kishimoto, K. (2016). Anti-racist pedagogy: From faculty's self-reflection to organizing within and beyond the classroom. *Race Ethnicity and Education, 21*(4), 540–54. https://doi.org/10.1080/13613324.2016.1248824

Kivel, P. (1996). *Uprooting racism: How white people can work for racial justice.* New Society Press.

Kosciw, J. G., Clark, C. M., & Menard, L. (2022). *The 2021 National School Climate Survey: The experiences of LGBTQ+ youth in our nation's schools.* GLSEN.

Kynard, C. (2010). From Candy Girls to Cyber SistaCipher: Narrating Black females' color-consciousness and counterstories in and out of school. *Harvard Educational Review, 80*(1), 30–53. https://doi.org/10.17763/haer.80.1.4611255014427701

Kynard, C. (2021). "Troubling the Boundaries" of anti-racism: The clarity of black radical visions amid racial erasure. *WPA: Writing Program Administration – Journal of the Council of Writing Program Administrators, 44*(3), 185–92.

Lamberson, N. (2021, March 31). *Zitkála-šá: On creativity, copyright, and cultural empowerment.* Copyright: Creativity at Work. Retrieved July 16, 2022, from https://blogs.loc.gov/copyright/2021/03/zitkla-on-creativity-copyright-and-cultural-empowerment/

Lee, J. (2022, May 18). *Confronting the invisibility of anti-Asian racism.* Brookings. Retrieved April 4, 2022, from https://www.brookings.edu/blog/how-we-rise/2022/05/18/confronting-the-invisibility-of-anti-asian-racism/

Levy, D. J., Heissel, J. A., Richeson, J. A., & Adam, E. K. (2016). Psychological and biological responses to race-based social stress as pathways to disparities in educational outcomes. *The American psychologist, 71*(6), 455–73. https://doi.org/10.1037/a0040322

Lorde, A. (1983). There is no hierarchy of oppressions. *Homophobia and Education, 14*(3–4), 9.

Lorde, A. (2015). *Sister outsider: Essays and speeches.* Crossing Press.

Lyiscott, J. (2020, April 28). Liberation Literacies: Teaching for Social Justice [web log]. Retrieved July 1, 2022, from https://blog.heinemann.com/liberation-literacies1.

Marrero, L. (2023, January 23). *Teaching tolerance amid contentious turbulence*. The Education Trust. Retrieved January 23, 2023, from https://edtrust.org/the-equity-line/teaching-tolerance-amid-contentious-turbulence/

Matias, C., & Zembylas, M. (2014). 'When saying you care is not really caring': Emotions of disgust, whiteness ideology, and teacher education. *Critical Studies in Education, 15*(3), 319–37. https://doi.org/10.1080/17508487.2014.922489

McDaniel, C. (2004). Critical literacy: A questioning stance and the possibility for change. *The Reading Teacher, 57*(5), 472–81.

McLaren, P. (1997). Unthinking whiteness, rethinking democracy: Or farewell to the blonde beast; Towards a revolutionary multiculturalism. *Educational Foundations, 1997*, 5–39.

McLaren, P., & Kincheloe, J. (2007) (Eds.). *Critical pedagogy: Where are we now?* Peter Lang.

McLaughlin, M., & DeVoogd, G. L. (2004). *Critical literacy: Enhancing students' comprehension of text*. Scholastic.

McNair, T. B., Bensimon, E. M., & Malcom-Piqueux, L. E. (2020). *From equity talk to equity walk: Expanding practitioner knowledge for racial justice in Higher Education*. Jossey-Bass.

Menakem, R. (2017). *My grandmother's hands: Racialized trauma and the pathway to mending our hearts and Bodies*. Central Recovery Press, LLC.

Menendian, S., Gambhir, S., & Gailes, A. (2021, June 21). *The Roots of Structural Racism Project*. Othering & Belonging Institute. Retrieved June 28, 2022, from https://belonging.berkeley.edu/roots-structural-racism

Mezirow, J. (1990). How critical reflection triggers transformative learning. In J. Mezirow (Ed.), *Fostering critical reflection in adulthood* (pp. 1–20). Jossey-Bass Publishers.

Mezirow, J. (2006). An overview of transformative learning. In P. Sutherland & J. Crowther (Eds.), *Lifelong learning: Concepts and contexts* (pp. 24–38). Routledge.

Michelle, M. J. (2006). Teaching for critical literacy: An ongoing necessity to look deeper and beyond. *English Journal, 96*(2), 41–6.

Miller, N. S. & About The Author Naseem S. Miller She joined The Journalist's Resource in 2021 after working as a health reporter in newspapers and medical trade publications. (2022, July 20). *Disparities persist in Native Americans' death rates, life expectancy: Study*. The Journalist's Resource. Retrieved April 3, 2022, from https://journalistsresource. org/home/american-indian-death-disparities/

Moeller, J., Brackett, M. A., Ivcevic, Z., & White, A. E. (2020). High school students' feelings: Discoveries from a large national survey and an experience sampling study. *Learning and Instruction, 66.* https://doi.org/10.1016/ j.learninstruc.2019.101301

Monaghan, E. J. (1998). *Reading for the enslaved, Writing for the Fee: Reflections on Liberty and Literacy*. James Russell Wiggins Lectures in the History of the Book in American Culture. Worcester, MA.

Moore, D. W., Monaghan, E. J., & Hartman, D. K. (1997). Values of literacy history. *Reading Research Quarterly, 32,* 90–102. https://doi.org/10.1598/RRQ.32.1.6

Mulcahy, C. (2018, March 2). *Critical literacy: A literature review.* CARR: Connecticut Association for Reading Research. Retrieved September 4, 2022, from https://ctreadingresearch. org/critical-literacy-a-literature-review/

National Center for Education Statistics. (2019). *NAEP report card: Reading.* The Nation's Report Card. Retrieved July 13, 2022, from https://www.nationsreportcard.gov/reading/ nation/scores/?grade=4

National Council for Teachers of English Standing Committee on Global Citizenship (2019). *Decolonizing the classroom: Step 1*. Retrieved June 12, 2022 from https://ncte.org/blog/ 2019/04/decolonizing-the-classroom/

Noblit, G. W. (1993). Power and caring. *American Educational Research Journal, 30*(1), 23–38. https://doi.org/10.2307/ 1163187

Noddings, N. (1984). *Caring: A feminine approach to ethics and moral education.* University of California Press.

Noddings, N. (1992). *The challenge to care in schools: An alternative approach to education.* Teachers College Press.

Obama, M. (2021). *Becoming*. Corwin.

Orfield, G., & Jarvie, D. (2020). (publication). *Black Segregation Matters: School Resegregation and Black Educational Opportunity*. UCLA Civil Rights Project. Retrieved February 10, 2022, from https://www.civilrightsproject.ucla.edu/research/k-12-education/integration-and-diversity/black-segregation-matters-school-resegregation-and-black-educational-opportunity/BLACK-SEGREGATION-MATTERS-final-121820.pdf.

Paul, S., & Brown, L. (2000). *Memoir of James Jackson, The attentive and obedient scholar, who died in Boston, October 31, 1833, aged six years and eleven months*. Harvard University Press.

Perry, P., & Shotwell, A. (2009). Relational understanding and white antiracist praxis. *Sociological Theory, 27*(1), 33–50. https://doi.org/10.1111/j.1467-9558.2009.00337.x

Phillips, J., Risdon, N., Lamsma, M., Hambrick, A., & Jun, A. (2019). Barriers and strategies by white faculty who incorporate anti-racist pedagogy. *The Journal of Teaching and Learning, 3*, 1.

Pimentel, O., Pimentel, C., & Dean, J. (2016). The myth of the colorblind writing classroom: White instructors confront White Privilege in their classrooms. *Performing Antiracist Pedagogy in Rhetoric, Writing, and Communication*, 109–22. https://doi.org/10.37514/atd-b.2016.0933.2.05

Pollock, M., & Nieto, S. (2008). *Everyday antiracism getting real about race in school*. New Press.

Prendergast, C. (2003). *Literacy and racial justice: The politics of learning after Brown v. Board of Education*. Southern Illinois University Press.

Preserving the complicated history at a segregated Texas School. National Parks Conservation Association. (n.d.). Retrieved March 2, 2022, from https://www.npca.org/advocacy/96-preserving-the-complicated-history-at-a-segregated-texas-school

Racial discrimination in Healthcare. How Structural Racism Affects Healthcare. (2021, June 15). Retrieved April 3, 2022, from https://www.stkate.edu/academics/healthcare-degrees/racism-in-healthcare

Ravilochan, T. (2021, June 23). *The Blackfoot wisdom that inspired Maslow's hierarchy*. Resilience. Retrieved April 29, 2022, from https://www.resilience.org/stories/2021-06-18/the-blackfoot-wisdom-that-inspired-maslows-hierarchy/

Rembert, K. (2021, March 5). *Classrooms are political*. Education Week. Retrieved October 31, 2022, from https://www.edweek.org/teaching-learning/opinion-classrooms-are-political/2020/10

Rembert, K., Cerna-Prado, V., Ojeda-Jimenez, E., Rabin, E., Washington, D., & Winchester, C. (2019). *Equity and Diversity by Design: Recommendations on Recruiting and Retaining Teachers of Color in Illinois* [White Paper]. Teach Plus. https://teachplus.org/wp-content/uploads/files/publication/pdf/teach_plus_diversity_and_equity_by_design_final.pdf

Richardson, J. (2017). Can we talk about race? An interview with Beverly Daniel Tatum. *Phi Delta Kappan, 99*(3), 30–6. https://doi.org/10.1177/0031721717739590

Roberts, M. (2010). Toward a theory of culturally relevant critical teacher care: African American teachers' definitions and perceptions of care for African American students. *Journal of Moral Education, 39*(4), 449–67. https://doi.org/10.1080/03057241003754922

Rolón-Dow, R. (2005). Critical care: A color(full) analysis of care narratives in the schooling experiences of Puerto Rican Girls. *American Educational Research Journal, 42*(1), 77–111. http://www.jstor.org/stable/3699456

Rolón-Dow, R., Flynn, J. E., & Mead, H. (2020). Racial literacy theory into practice: Teacher candidates' responses. *International Journal of Qualitative Studies in Education*. Advanced online publication. https://doi.org/10.1080/09518398.2020.1783013

Rovner, J. (2021, February 3). *Racial disparities in youth incarceration persist*. The Sentencing Project. Retrieved April 3, 2022, from https://www.sentencingproject.org/publications/racial-disparities-in-youth-incarceration-persist/

Schaeffer, K. (2021, November 12). *Among many U.S. children, reading for fun has become less common, federal data shows*. Pew

Research Center. Retrieved August 15, 2022, from https://www.pewresearch.org/fact-tank/2021/11/12/among-many-u-s-children-reading-for-fun-has-become-less-common-federal-data-shows/

Schieble, M., Vetter, A., & Martin, K. M. (2020). *Classroom talk for social change: Critical conversations in English language arts.* Teachers College Press.

Sealey-Ruiz, Y. (2021). *Racial literacy* (Policy research brief by the James R. Squire Office of the National Council of Teachers of English). Retrieved from https://ncte.org/resources/policy-briefs/

Sefa Dei, G. J. (2014). Personal reflections on anti-racism education for a global context. *Encounters on Education, 15,* 239–49. https://doi.org/10.15572/ENCO2014.13

Sleeter, C. E. (1994). A multicultural educator views white racism. *Education Digest, 59*(9), 33.

Smith, B., Smith, B., & Frazier, D. (2015). *The Combahee River Collective Statement.* United States. Retrieved from the Library of Congress, https://www.loc.gov/item/lcwa N0028151/

Solórzano, D. G., & Yosso, T. J. (2001). From racial stereotyping and deficit discourse toward a critical race theory in teacher education. *Multicultural Education, 9*(1), 2–8.

Stapleton, R. (2019). Teaching global antiracism in the classroom: Strategies and resources. *Harvard Education Review, 89*(4), 543–61. https://doi.org/10.17763/1943-5045-89.4.543

Statement on anti-racism to support teaching and learning. NCTE. (2018, August 3). Retrieved January 27, 2022, from https://ncte.org/statement/antiracisminteaching/

Stephens, L.-A. (2015, June 2). *The 'belief gap' prevents teachers from seeing the true potential of students of color.* Edpost. Retrieved August 30, 2022, from https://www.edpost.com/stories/the-belief-gap-prevents-teachers-from-seeing-the-true-potential-of-students-of-color

Stephens, G., Silbert, L., & Hasson, U. (2010). Speaker–listener neural coupling underlies successful communication. *Proceedings of the National Academy of Sciences, 107*(32), 14425–30. https://doi.org/10.1073/pnas.1008662107

Superville, D. R. (2021, September 15). *Principals need help building anti-racist schools*. Education Week. Retrieved October 14, 2022, from https://www.edweek.org/leadership/principals-need-help-building-anti-racist-schools/2020/09

Thomas, E. E., Bean-Folkes, J., & Coleman, J. J. (2020). Restorying critical literacies. In E. B. Moje, P. P. Afflerbach, P. Enciso, & N. K. Lesaux (Eds.), *Handbook of reading research*. Routledge.

Toliver, S. R., & Hadley, H. (2021). Ca(n)non fodder no more: Disrupting common arguments that support a canonical empire. *Journal of Language and Literacy Education, 17*(2), 1–28.

Toliver, S. R. (2021). Freedom dreaming in a Broken World: The black radical imagination in black girls' science fiction stories. *Research in the Teaching of English, 56*(1), 85–106.

Tuck, E., & Yang, K. W. (2012). Decolonization is not a metaphor. *Decolonization: Indigeneity, Education & Society, 1*(1), 1–40.

Ullucci, K., & Battey, D. (2011). Exposing color blindness/Grounding color consciousness: Challenges for teacher education. *Urban Education, 46*(6), 1195–225.

United Nations Educational, Scientific and Cultural Organization. (2022, June 24). *What you need to know about literacy*. UNESCO.org. Retrieved July 9, 2022, from https://www.unesco.org/en/education/literacy/need-know

USAFacts. (2020, September 23). *White people own 86% of wealth and make up 60% of the population*. USAFacts. Retrieved April 4, 2022, from https://usafacts.org/articles/white-people-own-86-wealth-despite-making-60-population/?utm_source=google&utm_medium=cpc&utm_campaign=ND-Race&gclid=CjwKCAjwkMeUBhBuEiwA4hpqEK29f9R26VV0-CPOukuZECwSY7aJtgYAmboxIZ_wbhCyfC5-Oa5Q1RoC_RYQAvD_BwE

Valenzuela, A. (1999). *Subtractive schooling: U.S. – Mexican Youth and the politics of caring*. SUNY Press.

Vetter, A., & Hungerford-Kressor, H. (2014). We gotta change first: Racial literacy in a high school English classroom. *Journal of Language and Literacy Education* [Online], *10*(1), 82–99. Retrieved from http://jolle.coe.uga.edu.

Ward, C., Ninomiya, M. E. M., & Firestone, M. (2021). Anti-indigenous racism training and culturally safe learning:

Theory, practice, and pedagogy. *International Journal of Indigenous Health, 16*(1), 304–13. https://doi.org/10.32799/ijih.v16i1.33204

Webb, S. (2017, January 23). *Yeah, but they're white*. Learning for Justice. Retrieved November 1, 2022, from https://www.learningforjustice.org/magazine/yeah-but-theyre-white

Wiesel, E. (1986, December 10). Acceptance speech. NobelPrize.org. Retrieved October 9, 2022, from https://www.nobelprize.org/prizes/peace/1986/wiesel/acceptance-speech/

Willis, A. (2008). *Reading comprehension research and testing in the US: Undercurrents of race, class, and power in the struggle for meaning*. Lawrence Erlbaum.

World Literacy Foundation. (2018). *The Economic & Social Costs of Illiteracy*. Retrieved from TheEconomicSocial CostofIlliteracy-2.pdf

Wray, Christopher. White supremacy and far-right extremism are among the greatest domestic security threats facing the United States. *Congressional Hearing,* September 2019.

Yosso, T. J. (2002). Toward a critical race curriculum. *Equity and Excellence in Education, 35,* 93–107.

Zitkála-šá. (1921). *American Indian stories*. Hayworth Publishing House.